D1010933

C.2

3 0050 01452 4275

DATE DUE

4 - 7	5:03 pm
4 - 7	7:49 pm
4/8	9:00 am
4/8	12:43 pm
4/0	2:08 pm

GAYLORD

PRINTED IN U.S.A.

KING

KING

PILGRIMAGE TO THE

MOUNTAINTOP

HARVARD SITKOFF

Hill and Wang

A division of Farrar, Straus and Giroux

New York

Hill and Wang
A division of Farrar, Straus and Giroux
18 West 18th Street, New York 10011

Copyright © 2008 by Harvard Sitkoff
All rights reserved
Distributed in Canada by Douglas & McIntyre Ltd.
Printed in the United States of America
First edition, 2008

Endpaper and frontispiece photographs © Bettmann/Corbis

Library of Congress Cataloging-in-Publication Data
Sitkoff, Harvard.
    King : pilgrimage to the mountaintop / by Harvard Sitkoff. — 1st ed.
      p. cm.
    ISBN-13: 978-0-8090-9516-2 (hardcover : alk. paper)
    ISBN-10: 0-8090-9516-5 (hardcover : alk. paper)
    1. King, Martin Luther, Jr., 1929–1968. 2. Arican Americans—Biography.
3. Civil rights workers—United States—Biography. 4. Baptists—United States—
Clergy—Biography. 5. African Americans—Civil rights—History—20th century.
I. Title.

E185.97.K5S535   2008
323.092—dc22
[B]

                                                  2007029276

Designed by Jonathan D. Lippincott

www.fsgbooks.com

1   3   5   7   9   10   8   6   4   2

Dedicated to Gloria,
my wife, my partner, my love

History says, *Don't hope*
On this side of the grave.
But then, once in a lifetime
The longed-for tidal wave
Of justice can rise up,
And hope and history rhyme.

— Seamus Heaney, *The Cure at Troy*

CONTENTS

PREFACE

Martin Luther King, Jr., is as relevant today as in the 1960s, perhaps more so. That is the reason for *King: Pilgrimage to the Mountaintop*. It brings to life the King who, in the face of great odds, altered American habits of thought and action more than any other figure of his century, and made the United States far more just, democratic, and egalitarian. *King: Pilgrimage to the Mountaintop* reminds us of why he moved the conscience of a generation, of how he changed hearts. Moreover, in a world of war, poverty, and murderous racial and religious hatreds, it emphasizes King's unfulfilled radical agenda. This portrayal of Martin Luther King is not the King generally celebrated today.

His radicalism, not just in the last year of his life but throughout much of his career, has been airbrushed out of the historical picture. As C. Vann Woodward famously wrote: "The twilight zone that lies between memory and written history is one of the favorite breeding places of mythology." Nowhere is this truer than in contemporary celebrations of King's birthday that portray him as a moderate, respectable ally of presidents and a facile spokesperson for the American Dream. The same government that once reviled him, viewing him as "dangerous" and a "pariah" for his alleged ties to Communists and his preaching radical liberation theology, now holds him up as a model of peaceful, incremental change. Because of his goodness, so the story goes, whites recognized the errors of their ways and made all the necessary changes in race relations to rectify the nation's shameful past. As such, King is the nice man who helped solve the problems of the past, rather than someone who challenges us to solve the problems of our present injustices and inequities. His canonization has turned him into a historical relic no longer relevant. Ignored is his lifelong commitment to social justice, his abhorrence of war and militarism, his insistence on ending every vestige of colonialism and imperialism, and his crusade to end poverty and privation. Ignored is his claim that the American civil rights movement was but one aspect of an international human rights revolution against "political domination and economic exploitation."

The endless replaying of his "I Have a Dream" speech has drowned out King's dream of a just society based on "a radical redistribution of economic and political power." It has drowned out what he reiterated in 1965: "I still have a dream that one day all of God's children will have food and clothing and material well-being for their bodies, culture and education for their minds, and freedom for their spirits." And it disregards the King who, as early as the 1950s, called for world disarmament, an end to apartheid in South Africa, a global war on poverty, and "special treatment" to assist African-Americans to overcome historic racism. Although politicians holding forth on King Day fail to recall this, or his strident condemnations of America's war in Vietnam and his unequivocal demands for "basic structural changes in the architecture of American society," *King: Pilgrimage to the Mountaintop* emphasizes them and sees them rooted in his long-held belief in religiously inspired democratic socialism and the Christian Social Gospel tradition.

Like Woodward, I hope to illuminate why, in sharp contrast to the funeral of Coretta Scott King in 2006, attended by the president of the United States and three ex-presidents, neither President Lyndon Johnson nor the two ex-presidents then alive bothered with the funeral rites for Martin Luther King, Jr. As many Americans hated King as loved him, and by 1968 most had turned their backs on him. They disapproved of his aims and tactics. A vast majority condemned his forceful criticism of America's role in the Vietnam War and of how that conflict caused domestic needs to be downplayed or dismissed. Even more decried his involvement in an unruly strike by garbage workers, and considered unnecessarily provocative and reckless his plan to bring an army of the dispossessed to Washington to wage a nonviolent campaign of civil disobedience against all those institutions that denied dignity and opportunity and hope to the downtrodden.

The King often shunned by those in power and despised by many in the population is the King I have depicted. *King: Pilgrimage to the Mountaintop* is based on the latest scholarship, and makes great use of the publication of *The Martin Luther King, Jr., Papers* by the University of California Press, as well as writings by and about others involved with King. One cannot write a synthesis such as this without relying heavily on the extraordinary work of scholars, journalists, and movement participants. Such works as *Martin Luther King, Jr.: The Making of a Mind* by John J. Ansbro, *Going Down Jericho Road* by Michael J. Honey, and David J. Garrow's *Bearing the Cross* have set the standard for scholarship on King. They remain unsurpassed in their depth of research and quality of analysis. But I have chosen to write neither another monograph by an academic for academics nor another biographical tome that too few have time enough to read. Instead, I have sought to craft a brief yet stirring narrative for a twenty-first-century readership that illustrates the historical forces that shaped King, and how he, in turn, changed American society. In addition to King's radicalism, *King: Pilgrimage to the Mountaintop* highlights both his awesome achievements and failures; it describes the American-style apartheid of the South that King was born into and would do so much to overturn; it explains his foibles, and why he sometimes acted more like a politician than a preacher; it examines the legendary black preaching tradition, the source of King's oratorical power, and the importance of it to the successful drive to end racial segregation and disenfranchisement; it dramatizes the interplay between King and the movement for racial justice, and how that dynamic changed both King and the movement; it documents FBI chief J. Edgar Hoover's effort to destroy King and the movement by harassment and persecution; and it depicts King both making history and being made by history.

Most of all, *King: Pilgrimage to the Mountaintop* emphasizes the centrality of King's faith to his political and social activism. At heart a clergyman and Baptist preacher, King experienced the movement as a sacred mission. His goals and strategies were rooted in the African-American Christian folk religion—the religion of his slave forebears. The black church sustained King's Social Gospel dream, and gave him the courage, the oratorical skills, and the spiritual vision to change the course of American and world history. Coupling his religious ideas with the nation's core civic values enabled him, at one and the same time, to inspire and energize black Americans to struggle for their rights, and to sway white Americans to understand and support that endeavor. However overwrought or sometimes paralyzed by fear he became, King's bibical faith enabled him to keep his eyes on the prize, to put righteousness before expediency, despite the beatings, jailings, inner turmoil, and constant threats of assassination.

At the same time, I also stress King's fallibility. This is not a sanitized biography. I have tried to acknowledge and to explain his flaws and weaknesses. Martin Luther King, Jr., was not a saint. He was an imperfect man with many of the failings of other mere mortals. Certainly he should have been a better husband and father, should have been a more honest scholar. Hardly infallible, frequently indecisive and irresolute, he compromised too much and at times acted timidly. And he failed as often as he succeeded.

Many, I fear, will find my account of the murder of King to be too abrupt. That more surely needs to be explained, I wholeheartedly agree. But far too much still remains unclear and unknown about the assassination. Its aftermath, moreover, requires a book at least as long as this one.

Finally, I have tried to place King in the context of the movement for freedom and for justice and for equality that he helped make and that made him. As Vincent Harding reminds us, King simultaneously nurtured and drew sustenance from, shaped and was shaped by that movement. The interplay between them changed both, so King never stood still for long. He moved with history, going from merely asking for more courteous trreatment of blacks on the Montgomery buses to struggling for the complete abolition of the Jim Crow system, to transforming American society on behalf of its poorest, most neglected peoples of all races. I think it important to underline that King and the movement were not synonymous, that many civil rights campaigns were neither initiated nor led by King, and that success in the black freedom struggle often depended far more on the extraordinary efforts of the ordinary people who walked the streets of Montgomery and filled the jails of Birmingham than it did on the charisma of those at the top. At the same time, I acknowledge that King was the movement's preeminent spokesperson, symbol, and leader. He was the right man, with the right talents, at the right time. The eloquent conscience of his generation, King, as stated in the citation for his posthumous Presidential Medal of Freedom, "made our nation stronger because he made it better." Yet his dreams of true brotherhood, of a world without war, of "a world in which men no longer take necessities from the masses to give luxuries to the classes," remain dreams. And the lessons of his life, that "injustice anywhere is a threat to justice everywhere," that "freedom is a constant struggle," remain to be learned.

KING

1

EDUCATING A

PREACHER KING,

1929–54

Of course I was religious. I grew up in the church. My father is a preacher, my grandfather was a preacher, my great-grandfather was a preacher, my only brother is a preacher, my daddy's brother is a preacher. So I didn't have much choice.

⌐⟶

On January 15, 1929, Alberta Williams King gave birth in the up-stairs bedroom of her parents' home. Michael King, the beam-ing father, and grandfather Alfred Daniel Williams joyously prayed that the infant, "Little Mike," might someday become a preacher like them. They did not prattle about the tubby baby becoming president of the United States or a Nobel Peace Prize winner or any such non-sense. For the squalling boy born at 501 Auburn Avenue that cold day was a Negro—the preferred designation, with a capital N, of those in the house—and this was Georgia, in the heart of Dixie.

In the American South of the first third of the twentieth century, where well over three quarters of African-Americans then lived, most just scraping by in agriculture or menial jobs, blacks possessed few rights and less power. In the immediate aftermath of the Civil War, Congress had passed constitutional amendments and civil rights laws to endow the freed slaves with their rights as citizens. The withdrawal of federal troops from the South in 1877, however, constituted both a symbolic and a substantive delay in the journey from slavery to equal civil and political rights.

Freed of interference from the national government, southern whites waged an aggressive assault on blacks, which caused their status to spiral downward rapidly. Beginning in the 1890s, all the former Confederate states changed their constitutions to disfranchise most black voters by means of literacy and/or property qualifications, poll taxes, and other clauses implicitly aimed at African-Americans. The disenfranchisement clauses were upheld by the Supreme Court in 1898 (*Williams v. Mississippi*) on the grounds that they did not discriminate "on their face" against Negroes, and most blacks lost the right to vote. The number of registered black voters in Louisiana dropped from 130,334 in 1896 to just 1,342 eight years later. The 181,000 African-Americans who voted in Alabama in 1890 plummeted to only 3,000 in 1900. The Republican Party virtually disappeared from the South, and state Democratic parties established primary elections—the only meaningful political contests in the region—in which only whites could vote. Ben "Pitchfork" Tillman of South Carolina could well boast on the floor of the Senate in 1900, "We have scratched our heads to find out how we could eliminate the last one of them. We stuffed ballot boxes. We shot them. We are not ashamed of it."

Political impotence left African-Americans at the mercy of an unfair and unforgiving criminal justice system, and unable to prevent southern states from enacting legislation to give segregation by custom the weight of law. Called Jim Crow laws—after a minstrel song of 1830 that depicted blacks as childlike and inferior—they mandated the separation of the races in hotels and restaurants, trains and streetcars, parks and playgrounds, post offices and dressing rooms, hospitals and prisons, libraries and theaters. Signs saying WHITE ONLY and COLORED appeared over toilets and water fountains. Blacks and whites even had to be buried in separate cemeteries.

The Supreme Court sanctioned this de jure (legal) segregation in *Plessy v. Ferguson* (1896) with the empty caveat that the separate facilities for African-Americans were to be equal to those for whites. In practice, they never were. A year later, the highest court in the land endorsed segregated public schools as a means to prevent "commingling of the two races upon terms unsatisfactory to either," and in 1899 allowed separate schools for whites and blacks even where facilities for black children did not exist. By then the South spent two and a half times as much on a white child in school as it did on a black child, and the gap in expenditures would increase markedly over the next three decades.

In the 1890s the viciousness of racist propaganda soared, and lynching rose to an all-time high, averaging 188 per year. About three quarters of the victims were southern blacks deemed too assertive, successful, or "uppity"—not showing the proper deference to whites. What laws accomplished too gradually, lynching did swiftly. It was the most potent way, wrote black journalist Ida B. Wells, to enforce white supremacy, to "keep the nigger down." To intimidate blacks further, and to amuse whites, southern newspapers reported in graphic detail how white lynch mobs gouged out the eyes and cut off the genitals of black victims before dousing them with gasoline and burning them alive. Not uncommonly, spectators traveled long distances to watch a lynching and vied to be photographed alongside mutilated corpses. Mobs also enforced white supremacy through pogroms or anti-Negro riots, such as those in Wilmington, North Carolina, in 1898 and in Atlanta in 1906.

African-Americans did not accept oppression without complaint or resistance. Many migrated to the freer North. Others joined the National Association for the Advancement of Colored People (NAACP) or gave financial support to its campaigns against disfranchisement and lynching. Still others joined boycotts, such as the one in Savannah in the 1890s, to thwart the effort to introduce segregation on streetcars. One Atlanta lawyer rode a bicycle to work to avoid sitting at the back of a segregated bus. As historian Robin D. G. Kelly reminds us, some African-Americans refused to step off a sidewalk so that a white might pass; or bought a copy of a Negro newspaper; or wore a flashy suit; or "accidentally" destroyed an employer's shirts while ironing. These acts of "everyday resistance" testified to the persistent freedom struggle waged by African-Americans, much as the diversity of black oppositional activity and spirit across the country and through the years indicated that the struggle was never a single movement with a single goal orchestrated by a single leader.

Although most southern black churches neither initiated nor supported militant protests, the African-American church often served as the institutional base for local protest movements. More often than not, the minister was the most educated black professional in town, and the church was usually the only place where a mass meeting could be held. Having heard the story of Genesis explained as an act of creation that gave each individual dignity and human rights, and the story of Exodus as one of escape from oppression, the congregants not infrequently took their preacher's words to heart and pressured him to be a protest leader.

These stories resonated differently from one part of the South to another, and from one decade to another. Atlanta was not Mississippi, and Atlanta at the time of King's birth was not the Atlanta of the 1906 race riot. The 1929 city of 270,500 had quadrupled in size since 1890, and it prided itself on being part of the "New South." Rather than re-fighting lost causes, many Atlantans sought racial peace so that both races could devote themselves to economic advancement. For blacks, this accommodationist stance meant enduring Jim Crow and political marginality while building up their own schools, businesses, and churches. Consequently, behind the veil of segregation, a cluster of middle-class African-American leaders emerged.

This is the world Little Mike, or M.L., as his family called him, grew up in. His granddaddy A. D. Williams, a slave preacher's son, had run away to Atlanta as a small boy, turned himself into a preacher, and built Ebenezer Baptist Church from an impoverished congregation of thirteen into one of Atlanta's largest and most bourgeois black churches. Reverend Williams also made himself into a community leader and member of the black social elite. He joined the Georgia Equal Rights League, railed against the exclusion of blacks from juries and voting booths, led voter registration drives, and served as the first president of the Atlanta chapter of the NAACP; he was also an officer of the Atlanta Baptist Ministers Union and the National Baptist Convention. Insisting that others refer to him as Dr. Williams, A.D. purported to have two degrees from Morehouse College, one of the six black institutions of higher education that constituted Atlanta University. Befitting his presumed status, Reverend Williams married Jennie C. Parks, a graduate of Spelman College, also a part of Atlanta University. With their daughter, Alberta, they moved in 1909 into a two-story Queen Anne–style house—featuring an imposing wraparound porch and an up-to-date coal furnace in the basement—on "Sweet" Auburn Avenue, Atlanta's grand black boulevard.

A decade or so later, Michael King appeared at that stately house and at the newly built redbrick Ebenezer Baptist Church, also on Sweet Auburn. Born in 1899, the second of ten children, Mike spent his childhood working the fields outside Stockbridge, Georgia. He lived in fear of his alcoholic sharecropper father, and at age fourteen, he dropped his hoe and left for Atlanta, "smelling like a mule" but determined to make something of himself. He found work in a tire plant and, using his memories of Sunday school, trained himself as a circuit preacher for the poor churches on Atlanta's remote fringes. He emulated the illiterate old-time preachers he'd heard as a kid, copying "the gestures, the cadences, the deeply emotive quality of their styles of ministry" and parroting the idiom, the drama, and the rhetorical fireworks of African-American folk preaching.

Knowing he needed an education to rise in the world, Michael King began the fifth grade at age twenty. By day he did manual labor, carrying freight in the railway yards. Then he washed, donned his one black suit, and attended evening classes, eventually earning a high school equivalency degree and becoming assistant pastor at Ebenezer. The burly preacher modeled himself on A.D. and, as Williams had done, sought a lettered, cultured wife. The reverend's daughter, Alberta Williams, a college graduate who had grown up in comparative comfort, fit the bill. After six years of chaperoned teas and church socials, they were married on Thanksgiving Day, 1926. Michael moved into Alberta's bedroom in the Williams home and, six years later, succeeded his deceased father-in-law as pastor of Ebenezer.

Daddy King, as the short preacher with a commanding demeanor liked to be called, followed A.D. in race leadership. He, too, headed Atlanta's NAACP chapter, as well as its Civic and Political League. As an officer of the Negro Voters League, he organized voter registration drives and supported the protest of African-American teachers who demanded the same salary given to white teachers. He used city hall elevators marked WHITES ONLY and refused to ride the segregated buses. Most vitally, with his practical, businesslike church leadership, he shrewdly guided Ebenezer through the worst of the Great Depression. In appreciation, his church made him the highest-paid Negro minister in Atlanta and in 1934 sent him on a summer-long tour of Europe and the Holy Land. It included a conference of Baptist ministers in Germany that so impressed Michael that he changed his, and his son's, name to Martin Luther King.

The significance of the name Martin Luther, however, played no role in the young King's boyhood: Family and friends continued to call him M.L. or Little Mike. Growing up in the gingerbread house on Sweet Auburn that looked down the hill at the black ghetto, he neither protested nor rebelled against his privileges. He relished the adulation given him as the firstborn son. Life, he would later write, "had been wrapped up for me in a Christmas package."

The Auburn Avenue elite of middle-class black educators, entrepreneurs, and especially ministers neither served whites nor had to compete with them. Few other blacks possessed as much independence from the white power structure. Neither regulated nor employed by whites, they provided products and services to the Negro population, nourished a sense of black community, and led the main organizations in which African-Americans governed themselves.

A child of that elite, M.L. grew up with a feeling that he would later call "somebodyness"—the knowledge that he had been created in the image of God, able to reject someone else's negative image of him. His mother, Alberta, "Mama" King, or "Bunch," as her husband affectionately called her, instilled self-respect in M.L. and in his older sister, Christine, and younger brother, Alfred (A.D.). She explained racial discrimination and segregation as a temporary social condition rather than the natural order, M.L. recalled, and said "that I must never allow it to make me feel inferior." He would long remember her repeating, "You are as good as anyone."

Daddy King, too, dwelled on that, teaching his children that they were likewise children of God and beings of infinite worth to Him. He taught them that a loving God cared about all His children, and that they needed to work with God to demand equal treatment and to struggle for their rights. Daddy forbade his children, to the extent possible, from patronizing segregated theaters and businesses, which he insisted violated God's will and moral order. "With this heritage,"

Martin Luther King, Jr., later wrote, "it is not surprising that I also learned to abhor segregation, considering it both rationally inexplicable and morally unjustifiable."

But he could not escape it. Despite being insulated from the worst of Jim Crow and growing up with a strong sense of himself as someone special, M.L. experienced frequent reminders of the degradations caused by racism. However much a prince of his community, he was just a "nigger" to most white Atlantans. He could not sit and drink a Coca-Cola in a downtown five-and-ten or use the "white" water fountain in the park. When he started school, the mother of his best (white) friend told him that they could no longer play together and he should "not come around here anymore." When he was eight, a white woman slapped him viciously, saying, "You are the nigger that stepped on my foot." M.L. saw the Ku Klux Klan riding through his black neighborhood intimidating residents, and he witnessed vicious police brutality against young black men who drove through red lights.

From Daddy King, M.L. learned not to be humiliated by such racism. Once, when a policeman stopped Daddy's car and addressed him with "Listen, boy," Daddy immediately cut him off. "That," he said, pointing to M.L., "is a boy. I am a man." On another occasion, when they went downtown to a shoe store, a clerk informed them they would have to sit in the Negro section in the rear. "There's nothing wrong with these seats," Daddy retorted. "Sorry," the clerk insisted, "you'll have to move." Daddy snapped, "We'll either buy shoes sitting here, or we won't buy shoes at all." Walking away, M.L. recalled his father muttering, "I don't care how long I have to live with this system, I will never accept it."

But acquiescence often could not be avoided. In April 1944, at age fifteen, M.L. traveled to Dublin, Georgia, to participate in a public speaking contest, "The Negro and the Constitution." In a manner that would become familiar to many Americans two decades later, M.L. dazzled his audience by blending biblical allusions, Lincolnian rhetoric, and pragmatic arguments, and by ending with a flourish, proclaiming that he looked forward to the day when his "brother of blackest hue" might stand beside whites "a Negro—and yet a man!" M.L. came in second. Worse, on the long bus ride home, the driver demanded that M.L. and his teacher obey the rules of segregation and give up their seats to newly boarded whites. M.L. would not move.

"Hey, I mean you. Get out of that seat and let those people sit down."

M.L. did not move.

"Move or I'll call the police, you black son of a bitch."

He still would not move. Only his teacher's pleading led him to stand in the back of the bus, hanging on to a strap all the ninety miles to Atlanta. "That night will never leave my memory," he wrote later. "It was the angriest I have ever been in my life."

That summer M.L. worked on a tobacco farm in Connecticut. He experienced sitting anywhere he chose to on buses and attending the same church with whites. Yet the owner of a diner in New Jersey refused to serve him and his friends, forcing them to leave at gunpoint. And when he returned to Atlanta, he had to move to the Jim Crow car at the nation's capital and eat behind a curtain in the dining car. "I felt as if the curtain had been dropped on my selfhood. I could never adjust to the separate waiting rooms, separate eating places, separate rest rooms, partly because the very idea of separation did something to my sense of dignity and self-respect." The image of the curtain stayed with him the rest of his life. King struggled, not very successfully, to obey his parents' admonition to hate segregation but love those who practiced it; he confessed to have come "perilously close to resenting all white people."

After attending a number of Atlanta's public schools for blacks and an experimental school attached to Atlanta University, M.L. skipped the ninth grade at Booker T. Washington High School and, at age fifteen, passed the entrance exam for Morehouse College, which had lost most of its students to the military and needed to fill seats. Beginning in September 1944, M.L. hardly distinguished himself. Nicknamed "Tweed" for his snazzy suits, M.L. was more interested in his finery than in his classes, preferred partying to studying, and behaved more like a social butterfly than a social activist. Preoccupied with sex and food, the vain clotheshorse only gradually raised his eighth-grade reading level and barely managed to graduate with a grade point average of 2.48 on a four-point scale. His professors judged him, at best, as promising, never as outstanding. His only A came in a course on theology taught by a proponent of a socially involved black modern ministry.

During college, M.L. struggled to assert himself against his overbearing father, a bull of a man as strong in will as in body. At fifteen, M.L. pleaded with his father, an old-fashioned disciplinarian, to stop "whupping" him for every infraction of his many rules; he then delighted in jitterbugging, smoking, and playing cards—sins against his Baptist teachings. Eager to add yet another light-skinned woman to his list of conquests, M.L. frequently bragged of "wrecking" coeds. He increasingly criticized Daddy's bourgeois pro-Republican and pro-capitalist politics, chafed under his autocratic rule of home and church, and mocked Daddy's emotional pyrotechnics at Sunday services.

Cringing as gruff Daddy boomed thunderbolts and threats of doom or used the patois of a field hand to encourage the lusty whooping and moaning characteristic of lower-class churches, M.L. dreamed of being a dignified man of culture and learning. He wanted no part of "the emotionalism of much Negro religion, the shouting and stomping. I didn't understand it, and it embarrassed me."

Siding with his Morehouse teachers' preference for the empirical method and for historical accuracy, M.L. disdained his father's reliance on received wisdom and dogmatism. He pictured himself as a lawyer or doctor or professor, engaged in the struggle for equal rights like Benjamin Mays, Morehouse's distinguished president, who told students, "I wouldn't go to a segregated theater to see Jesus Christ himself."

Hearing Mays decry Jim Crow and preach the Social Gospel at the weekly chapel service, M.L. made the college president his role model of a socially concerned African-American intellectual. Following his mentor's lead, he wrote a letter to *The Atlanta Constitution* protesting racial inequality:

We want and are entitled to the basic rights and opportunities of American citizens; the right to earn a living at work for which we are fitted by training and ability; equal opportunities in education, health, recreation, and similar public services; the right to vote; equality before the law; some of the same courtesy and good manners that we ourselves bring to all human relations.

In his junior year, M.L. elected to become a prelaw sociology major. He modeled himself on Thurgood Marshall, the NAACP attorney leading the courtroom battle for Negro rights. M.L. decided he would not fulfill Daddy's expectation that his son follow in his father's ministerial footsteps.

Still worse to Reverend King, M.L. no longer believed as did Daddy. To a man who neither challenged biblical authority nor tolerated a challenge to his own authority, M.L.'s preference for intellectual sophistication over faith seemed sheer blasphemy. M.L. had earlier shocked his Sunday school class by denying the bodily resurrection of Jesus. He scoffed at the doctrine of original sin and insisted the virgin birth was metaphorical, not literal. Now, in college, he "regretted going to church." Encouraged by his professors in his rebellion against the religious orthodoxy of his forebears, M.L. spent his years at Morehouse in a "state of skepticism," thankful that "the shackles of fundamentalism were removed from my body."

Nevertheless, in his senior year at Morehouse in 1947, the eighteen-year-old elected to enter the ministry. Well aware that ministers were men of importance and influence in the black community, he recalled his decision as "not a miraculous or supernatural something," but instead a growing realization that the ministry could be a force for intellect and racial protest, in addition to the best way to fulfill his "inner urge to serve humanity." M.L. aimed to preach the hopeful promise of delivery or redemption—in this world as well as the next—and to teach self-respect, "somebodyness." He determined to explain the Bible in a way that affirmed the equality and worth of all humanity in God's eyes. Unlike Daddy, with his literal belief in Scripture, M.L. imagined himself a "rational" minister dealing with "ideas, even social protest." He envisioned his pulpit as a forum for racial justice, much like that of his role model, Benjamin Mays. M.L.'s sermons would express the political and social aspirations of working-class blacks. They would blend the Social Gospel of the Negro church with the democratic socialism popular among left-liberals in the New Deal era. His church would not be characterized by emotionalism and otherworldly escapism. His parishioners would think quietly rather than shout "Hosanna." And he would not avoid polysyllabic words.

He certainly did not in his trial sermon at Ebenezer. Standing proudly in front of the striking stained-glass window portraying Christ in the Garden of Gethsemane, the young King waxed eloquent on the varied dimensions of a complete life. Whether understood or not, his parade of quotations and references, allusions and illustrations, delivered in his rich baritone voice wowed the congregation. Daddy was so overjoyed with his son's choice of career—despite his insistence on leaving Atlanta for a liberal, freethinking seminary in the North— that he immediately ordained Martin as a full-fledged minister of Ebenezer. It did not matter that the sermon Martin delivered had been almost wholly borrowed from *Hope of the World* (1933), a collection of sermons by the white liberal preacher Harry Emerson Fosdick of the Riverside Church in New York. Daddy King himself often used the ideas and words of others verbatim. It was common practice among folk preachers.

Late in the summer of 1948, Martin Luther King, Jr., arrived in Chester, Pennsylvania, a small town outside Philadelphia, to begin his studies at Crozer Theological Seminary. No longer under Daddy's dominion, Martin proposed to use the word of God to fulfill his own "inescapable urge to serve society."

From his flare-brimmed fedora down to his glossy two-toned shoes, Martin appeared the model of sartorial snazziness. But in demeanor, he could not have been more reserved and solemn. Experiencing extended racial integration for the first time, in a student body about 10 percent African-American, King "was well aware of the typical white stereotype of the Negro, that he is always late, that he's loud and always laughing, that he's dirty and messy, and for a while I was terribly conscious of trying to avoid identification with it." He tried to be the very opposite of the coarse, slovenly African-American. He was never late, his shirts were freshly laundered, and his room was spotless. Martin admitted to being "morbidly conscious" of "the fact that he was a Negro in a mostly white world," of what he called "the burdens of the Negro race." He became "grimly serious," even berating another black student for having beer in his room. Desperate to validate himself and his race by excelling, he immersed himself in his schoolwork.

Once he'd earned his classmates' acceptance and teachers' approval, the buoyant Little Mike again emerged. He gradually allowed himself to join his classmates in games of pool and cards, in smoking and beer drinking. He became a popular, fun-loving, pipe-smoking gentleman elected president of the student body. Fancying himself a Don Juan, he also lured the willing ladies. Martin's letters to his mother dwelled on the many girls he dated, boasting that he had "met a fine chick in Philadelphia who has gone wild over the old boy" and bragging that "the girls are running me down."

His most serious affair came in his senior year. Martin fell passionately in love with Betty, the attractive daughter of a German immigrant woman working at Crozer. They longed to marry. Only the insistent warnings from friends and teachers that such an interracial marriage would ruin his chance of ever pastoring a major church, and that it would cause an irreconcilable breach with his parents, eventually forced the anguished King to end his six-month love affair. The price of a mixed marriage would cost more than he was willing to pay. Heartbroken, he went back to his books.

Martin learned enough at Crozer to impress his teachers and rank first in his class at graduation. Yet little of his learning changed him fundamentally. In the main, he drew from others to furbish the basic religious beliefs of his black heritage.

In his freshman year, he eagerly imbibed the Social Gospel of Walter Rauschenbusch, an outspoken critic of industrial capitalism who preached that Christianity needed to be as concerned with slums as with souls. Rauschenbusch's theological basis for social concerns reinforced Martin's quest for the "Kingdom of God" here on earth, much as Rauschenbusch's insistence on the unending improvability of the human condition resonated with the optimism that Martin attributed to his mostly happy childhood in a loving home. The Social Gospel gave him a vocabulary that resonated in the white liberal community of Crozer and beyond.

Martin also embraced the Social Gospel of Rauschenbusch for its validation of Benjamin Mays's "third way" between capitalism and communism. Profoundly influenced by his boyhood memories of those suffering from the Great Depression's pervasive poverty, Martin absorbed the vague distrust of capitalism felt by many postwar progressives who dreamed of abolishing colonialism, hunger, and racism. Imbued with what he called "anti-capitalistic feelings," he admired Karl Marx for his social theory but not his ethical relativism or materialistic interpretation of history. Martin thought the church should be in the forefront of those protesting against the hardships of the underprivileged, leading the way to a kind of Christian socialism.

In writing an essay on Jeremiah, King became preoccupied with the prophetic tradition. He thought the Prophets were the most important part of Scripture, and he pictured himself, like Jeremiah and Amos and Isaiah, preaching to society to right its wrongs. He would urge his followers to go into the lion's den, for "unearned suffering is redemptive." Religion, he insisted, "should never sanction the status quo." He envisioned himself railing against injustice, indicting oppressive institutions, and demanding moral reformation, rather than incremental changes in the status quo.

For a brief time, King evinced interest in Mohandas Gandhi and the notion of nonviolent resistance in the Indian freedom struggle. He also considered Hegel and the dialectic method of analysis, and Reinhold Niebuhr's "neo-orthodox" condemnation of pacifism and insistence on coercion in the battle against oppression. King flitted from one thinker to another at almost the same rate he "wrecked" young women.

Mostly, during his three years at Crozer, King elevated his preaching to an art form. He spent hours orating in front of his mirror, honing his homilies. He practiced closing his sermon folder ostentatiously so that everyone knew he preached without a prepared text. Echoing his father and the many guest preachers he had heard as a boy, King refined his call-and-response exchange and perfected his calm-to-storm delivery: Start slowly, deliberately, then gradually become louder and more rhythmical, and conclude with a rafter-shaking, thunderous crescendo. His fellow seminarians relished hearing him practice a sermon. Little wonder he took nine courses in pulpit oratory—the most possible—and received his highest grades in them.

He had learned well the "three Ps" of oratorical excellence: proving, painting, and persuasion, or winning over the mind, imagination, and heart. Steeped in the black sermonic tradition, King was well on his way to being a great preacher, though he was hardly a great theologian or scholar.

His student papers, like his sermons, borrowed large chunks of words and ideas from others without proper attribution. Many pastors, of course, learned to preach by using the phrases, stories, and mannerisms gleaned from other preachers. Religious speech was viewed as communal, not private, property. Language as a shared commodity had deep roots in black culture. The ability to absorb and articulate the great ideas of others, to join or merge one's voice with others', and then shape a call to stir the souls of a congregation was a community tradition, not verbal theft.

But writing down other people's words and ideas as if they are your own is plagiarism. Time and again in his course papers at Morehouse and Crozier, King used the sentences and concepts of others without attribution. Sometimes it appeared to be a matter of scholarly sloppiness, forgetting to use quotation marks or cite another's work in a footnote. At other times, cribbing a grandiose notion or phrase seemed his way of proving himself to others, of demonstrating the intellectual ability of Negroes. In part, his exceptional aural memory, his ability to quote extensively what he had once heard or read, worsened his plagiarism. Mostly, he borrowed eclectically to express his own viewpoints in the manner that gained him the plaudits of his peers and professors.

More interested in politics than in systematic theology, in social ethics than in scholarship, King also appropriated the liberalism of others and blended it into the religious Social Gospel he had learned as a boy. The result would be traditional black Christianity interlaced with enough Euro-American theology and philosophy to please his instructors and eventually enthrall and enrapture both black and white audiences. It eschewed the otherworldly escapism or quietism characteristic of many black churches of the day; it also nurtured resistance to racial inequality. At its heart was a theology of protest that stressed the common humanity and equality of all in God's eyes, and promised an exodus from oppression and injustice, a deliverance to freedom. Expressing the revolutionary potential of Christianity, King's religion harkened back to the religion that had nurtured insurgent slave ministers and inspired abolitionists.

Graduating from Crozer with a $1,200 scholarship for further studies, twenty-two-year-old King headed off in a new green Chevrolet, a present from Daddy, to begin a doctoral program at Boston University in the fall of 1951. Since Yale had turned him down, he had chosen BU's School of Theology for its advocates of social justice and proponents of the philosophy of Personalism.

While another Baptist preacher's son, Malcolm Little—later known as Malcolm X—pursued his education in nearby Charlestown State Prison, King plunged into the philosophical study of religion. He ranged widely through the BU curriculum and took additional courses in philosophy at Harvard. He loved intellectual inquiry. But rather than changing his belief system, or even seriously challenging it, his erudition amplified his storehouse of quotations. The sermons he gave at various Boston churches aimed to impress. They were a compendium of everything he was learning, of every philosopher and theologian he was reading.

More than any other philosophical system, Personalism provided the intellectual framework for King's prior conceptions of the worth of dignity of all humanity and of an objective moral order sustained by a fatherly, loving, and personal God. It offered a rational God to undergird his faith. Although he took seriously Niebuhr's emphasis on power and realism, he preferred the way Personalism blended Protestantism with ethical issues and social causes and judged the meaning of all matters by its effects on an individual life. It led one to judge a state or a law by its effect on a person: Any violation of the worth of an individual was evil. Thus, segregation, which debased personality, and caused people to be treated as things, was evil.

King claimed that Personalism gave him the "metaphysical and philosophical grounding" for his most basic convictions. It enabled him to graft a philosophical system onto the theology of protest he learned as a boy. The thinking man's personal God accentuated the enduring themes of his black religion: hopefulness, the expectation of future deliverance from earthly injustice, and man, acting in concert with God, casting out evil from the world.

For King, the doctorate meant prestige, a distinguished title, a cachet of privilege. Pursuing it was hardly a mind- or life-altering experience. His years at Boston University replicated patterns he had set at Morehouse and Crozer—broadening his intellectual base to impress listeners and gain their admiration; using the concepts of others without attribution in his writing assignments, including major portions of his doctoral dissertation; seeing the ministry as a social mission, not a divine inspiration; seeking a philosophical/theological foundation for his political beliefs; perfecting his oratory and pulpit showmanship; and, as a friend recalled, "gallivanting around Boston, the most eligible bachelor in town." King could no more resist the lure of the flesh than he could home-cooked soul food.

Despite a surfeit of dates, Martin met an old friend for lunch in January 1952 and complained to her that Boston women did not measure up to the southern women he had known. Sympathetic, she offered to introduce him to a fellow student studying voice at the New England Conservatory of Music. That night Martin telephoned Coretta Scott to ask for a date. "You know every Napoleon has his Waterloo. I'm like Napoleon," he oozed. "I'm at my Waterloo, and I'm on my knees."

"That's absurd. You haven't seen me yet," Coretta snapped.

Martin persisted: "Your reputation has preceded you."

"He had quite a line," Coretta remembered. "Smoothness. Jive. Some of it I had never heard of in my life. It was what I called intellectual jive." Not having any better prospects at the time, Coretta agreed to see him for lunch the next day.

"I have a green Chevy that usually takes ten minutes to make the trip from BU, but tomorrow I'll do it in seven," he boasted.

The first thing that struck Coretta on meeting the pudgy, five-feet-seven Martin was how unimpressive he seemed. But as he talked and talked about politics and philosophy, about economic and racial injustice, "he just radiated so much charm." He sounded so eloquent, so brainy, that "he became much better-looking."

Coretta tried responding in kind. "Oh, I see you know about some other things besides music," he blurted impudently. "You can think, too."

On the drive back to the conservatory, Martin announced that Coretta had all the qualities he wanted in a wife: character, intelligence, personality, and beauty. "You don't even know me," Coretta huffed. Nonplussed, Martin proposed a second date.

"You may call me later," Coretta replied, although she wanted nothing to interfere with her goal of becoming a concert singer. She had promised herself, after a failed love affair during her years at Antioch College, that she wouldn't become emotionally involved again. Raised in rural Alabama, she thought rich Atlantans were terrible snobs; and as a Methodist, she harbored a prejudiced view of Baptist preachers as "narrow-minded and not too well-trained." As a young girl, she had seen her home burned down under suspicious circumstances; then a white logger had burned her father's sawmill. "They will do anything," she said. Yet, inordinately proud, Coretta demanded equality as her God-given right. Blessed with a beautiful singing voice, piercing eyes, and silky dark skin, she believed she belonged at center stage.

Against the odds, the second date led to a third and then many more. However much Coretta shrank from the prospect of being a preacher's wife, Martin's ardor gradually melted her reserve and led her to adore him.

Although Daddy kept the pressure on his son to marry the right woman from the black Atlanta elite and return to Ebenezer, Martin wanted no part of it. Back home during the summer of 1952, he persuaded Coretta—or Corrie, as he called her—to travel south and meet his family. Atlanta turned icy that August as a chillingly aloof Daddy and his coldly proper wife paid Coretta little mind. They thought her a willful, sassy girl determined to have a career and think for herself. The tensions continued when Martin's parents came to Boston in November, determined to end the love affair. Daddy bluntly informed Coretta that many girls from Atlanta's finest families sought to marry Martin. She came from a fine family as well, Coretta retorted, insisting that she had much to offer. Unable to persuade Martin, the patriarch relented. The young couple would marry in June.

Despite the intention to wed, Martin secretly saw other women. Confessions of his cheating and intense arguments ensued. Nevertheless, on June 18, 1953, Daddy King married Coretta and Martin in the garden of her parents, Obie and Bernice Scott, in rural Perry County, Alabama. Since no local hotel accepted African-Americans, the couple spent their wedding night at the home of a family friend, an undertaker. They would later joke of having honeymooned in a funeral parlor.

After spending the rest of the summer working in Atlanta, the couple returned to Boston to finish their studies. As Corrie completed her courses at the conservatory, Martin prepared for his comprehensive exams and began reading for his dissertation. The time had also come to decide what church job offer Martin would accept. Daddy, naturally, insisted that his son share the Ebenezer pulpit with him. Martin refused.

Coretta, too, had views. She had already accepted Martin's decision to be a minister, despite her disdain for most of them. She had acceded to Martin's traditional views of married women as homemakers and mothers, giving up her dream of being a concert performer and allowing him to thwart even her modest ambition to teach music. But she drew the line at leaving the North to return to the rigidly segregated, backward Deep South. Corrie pleaded. Martin was adamant. Corrie relented.

King's best offer would come from the Dexter Avenue Baptist Church in Montgomery, Alabama. Despite Daddy's warning, "That's a big nigger's church," with too many big-shot professionals who would make their preacher miserable, Martin visited the city in January. He was warmly welcomed by the young pastor at First Baptist Church, Ralph D. Abernathy, who joked that at his church, you preached about Jesus, but at Dexter, they preferred you talk about Plato or Socrates.

King did just that, giving a highly intellectual sermon, "The Three Dimensions of a Complete Life," chock-full of quotations and lessons drawn from just about every philosopher and theologian he had ever read. He had perfected his delivery of it on numerous previous occasions, and the sermon worked wonders. Two months later, Dexter offered its pastorship to King at a salary of $4,200 a year. It would make the graduate student the highest-paid Negro minister in Montgomery.

Martin accepted. He would begin in September. "I'm going back South," he insisted, "because that's where I'm needed." He relished being independent of his father. A church that appreciated an intelligent minister, an "upper-income congregation" made up of doctors, lawyers, and professors of Alabama State College, suited him fine. He did not want foot-stomping "Hallelujah!" parishioners. Unlike so many black ministers in the South, wholly concerned with the souls of their congregants rather than with their earthly condition,

King proposed to speak the word of God to fight the racist injustices of man.

Although WHITES ONLY and COLORED signs remained throughout the South, King sensed a turning of the racial tide. World War II had significantly changed the lives of many blacks. Many enlisted in the Double V campaign, fighting for victory over the Axis abroad and racial discrimination at home. Membership in the NAACP multiplied nearly ten times, reaching half a million in 1945. Negro labor leader A. Philip Randolph threatened nonviolent direct action to force President Franklin Roosevelt to issue Executive Order 8802, the first such order on race since Reconstruction. It prohibited discriminatory employment practices by federal agencies and all unions and companies engaged in war-related work. And a new organization, the Congress of Racial Equality (CORE), sought to desegregate public facilities in the North by the same forms of nonviolent direct action that Gandhi used in India.

Some two million African-Americans secured employment in industry and another two hundred thousand in the federal civil service. Black membership in labor unions doubled; the number of skilled and semi-skilled black workers tripled; and the average annual wage for African-Americans increased from $457 to $1,976, compared to a gain from $1,064 to $2,600 for whites.

More than seven hundred thousand southern blacks relocated to the North and West, turning a strictly southern matter into a national concern. Freed from the stifling constraints of caste, most found a better life. At the least, they could now vote, prompting politicians of both parties to pay more attention to civil rights issues. The powers in Washington did so as the United States increasingly found itself appealing to the nonwhite peoples of the world. White racism suddenly was seen as a peril to national security. Moreover, the pictures in the newspapers and the scenes in the postwar newsreels of the Holocaust made Americans sensitive, as never before, to the horrors of racism and the harm caused by its attitudes and practices.

Last but hardly least, about a million African-Americans served in the armed forces. Despite the indignities of segregation in the military, most returned to civilian life with heightened expectations for racial equality and with a new sense of self-esteem gained from participation in the war effort. They were determined to gain all the rights enjoyed by whites.

The reality of racism continued to prove an embarrassment in the Cold War as the United States sought to denounce the Soviet Union for ignoring human rights, and to court newly independent nations in Africa and Asia. In part to improve the American image in the non-white world, President Harry S. Truman established the first President's Committee on Civil Rights. Its 1947 report, *To Secure These Rights*, spelled out the many moral, economic, and international reasons for the enactment of legislation outlawing lynching and the poll tax; for establishing a permanent Fair Employment Practices Committee; and for desegregating the armed forces, housing, public schools, and interstate transportation. The following year Truman issued executive orders banning racial discrimination in the military and in federal hiring. The Supreme Court did its part by declaring segregation in interstate bus transportation unconstitutional; outlawing the "white primary" and restrictive housing covenants that forbade the sale or rental of property to minorities; and significantly narrowing the possibility of racially separate education being in fact equal education that was thus constitutional.

As the Kings prepared to leave Boston, Chief Justice Earl Warren announced the unanimous decision of the Supreme Court in *Brown v. Board of Education of Topeka* May 1954. A dagger in the heart of Jim Crow, *Brown* declared state-mandated segregation in public schools to be unconstitutional. It invalidated the "separate but equal" doctrine that had prevailed since *Plessy v. Ferguson*, knocking out the legal underpinning for racial separateness in all public facilities, not just schools. The government immediately had Warren's opinion translated into thirty-four languages for broadcasts abroad.

The decision thrilled King, as it did millions of African-Americans. He described it as a "world-shaking decree" and judged it a "noble and sublime decision." It validated the NAACP's litigation strategy, and like many others, King thought it heralded a speedy end to all the inequities and indignities of Jim Crow. What a wonderful time, he mused, to be coming home to the South.

King began his pastorship at Dexter on September 1, 1954. Typically, he would rise at five-thirty to work three hours on his dissertation, "A Comparison of the Conceptions of God in the Thinking of Paul Tillich and Henry Nelson Wieman." He would then minister to the needs of his congregants and closely manage the affairs of the church. He reminded his deacons that "leadership never ascends from the pew to the pulpit, but invariably descends from the pulpit to the pew," and he made sure that the elaborate system of committees he initiated ran smoothly, especially his prized Social and Political Action Committee. It practically functioned as an NAACP adjunct, and Dexter contributed more to the association than any other church in town. Having boasted to his new friend Ralph Abernathy that he would "bring to the Dexter Avenue congregation the greatest social gospel and action program it had ever experienced," King required that "every member of Dexter must be a registered voter" and must join the NAACP.

King devoted the rest of his day to writing and memorizing his upcoming sermons and speeches. He spoke frequently at Baptist associations and at churches in the North. While constantly honing his abilities to elicit just the audience response he sought, he whetted the classic Social Gospel tenet that Christianity demanded the active pursuit of social justice. In an early 1955 sermon broadcast on Montgomery's black-oriented radio station, WRMA, the young pastor urged his listeners to rid America "of every aspect of segregation."

"It scars the soul and degrades the personality," he proclaimed. "It inflicts the segregated with a false sense of inferiority, while confirming the segregator in a false estimate of his own superiority. It destroys community and makes brotherhood impossible. The underlying philosophy of Christianity is diametrically opposed to the underlying philosophy of racial segregation."

True to his own epistle, King served on the interracial Alabama Council on Human Relations, a state affiliate of the liberal Southern Regional Council, and on the executive committee of the local NAACP. The smartly dressed young preacher strongly supported the association's voter registration drives, educational programs, and courtroom challenges to racial inequality. Though Jim Crow might be on its deathbed, King insisted, "We must do everything to keep it down."

Yet the newly minted Ph.D., Dr. Martin Luther King, Jr., did not want to make waves. He had just completed his doctoral dissertation in April and was awaiting the birth of his first child in mid-November 1955. He declined the local NAACP's offer of its presidency. He would fight for right with the backing of others, but as the newest and youngest minister in town, he fretted about sticking his neck out conspicuously.

BAPTISM BY FIRE,

1955–56

*Returning violence for violence multiplies violence, adding
deeper darkness to a night already devoid of stars . . . Hate cannot drive out hate; only love can do that.*

────

On December 1, 1955, Rosa L. Parks, a trim and primly composed forty-two-year-old seamstress, boarded a city bus at Court
Square in Montgomery, the birthplace of the Confederacy and once
the site of slave auctions. Weary from having worked the day in the
tailor shop of the Montgomery Fair department store, and holding
a bag of Christmas gifts, the light-skinned, bespectacled African-
American found a seat on the crowded bus in the row just behind the
first ten seats reserved by law for whites only. Over the next three stops,
the bus filled.

Seeing a white man standing, the driver, J. F. Blake, yelled, "Niggers move back!" When none did, he ordered the four blacks sitting in
Parks's row to stand in the back. "Y'all better make it light on your-
selves and let me have those seats," he said. All but Parks complied.

"Look, woman, I told you I wanted the seat." Blake had forced
Parks off the bus twelve years before. "Are you going to stand up?"

"No," the soft-spoken Parks murmured, the purposeful act of a politically conscious woman.

Later, she recalled, "I had almost a life history of being rebellious against being mistreated because of my color. I felt that I was not being treated right and that I had a right to retain the seat that I had taken . . . I had been pushed as far as I could stand to be pushed."

A woman of dignity and impeccable reputation, Parks stayed in her seat until she was arrested. "I could not see how standing up was going to 'make it light' for me. The more we gave in and complied, the worse they treated us."

Long before that December day, Rosa Parks had protested the indignities of Jim Crow. She refused to use drinking fountains labeled COLORED, and she climbed stairs to shun segregated elevators. Having joined the Montgomery chapter of the NAACP in 1943 and served as the organization's secretary, Parks had participated in voter registration campaigns and had recently spent a week at the Highlander Folk School in Monteagle, Tennessee, an interracial training center for labor, socialist, and religiously oriented community organizers—an experience that furthered her "strength to persevere in my work for freedom." She knew the persistent history of racial indignities on Montgomery's buses, of African-American passengers routinely being referred to as "niggers" and "black apes." Of their having to stand beside empty seats reserved for whites. Of their having to buy tickets from the driver in the front, then get off the bus to reenter through the rear door only to watch in frustration when the driver drove off. A daily, tormenting reminder of second-class status, bus segregation affronted blacks. It infuriated them.

And since World War II, it had become a prime racial flash point as African-Americans increasingly refused to give up their seats to whites. African-American discontent with segregation had resulted in increasing racial jostling and shoving on buses and frequent arrests of blacks who would not stand so that a white passenger might sit. In 1955 the arrest of three African-American women who refused to give up their seats had already aroused and angered black Montgomery, leading some to propose a bus boycott much like the one in Baton Rouge in 1953 that had led to a modified first-come, first-seated policy on its buses.

Moreover, the Supreme Court's *Brown* decision a year earlier had caused both a sense of hopefulness in the African-American community and impatience with the entire Jim Crow system in Montgomery, where fifty thousand blacks lived under the arbitrary power of seventy thousand whites. Increasing numbers of African-Americans would no longer countenance patently inferior educational and recreational facilities, disrespectful and often brutal police behavior, and income barely half that of whites. The injustice of disfranchisement—just two thousand blacks in all of Montgomery County could vote—rankled more than ever. They particularly resented a bus system that profited primarily from their dimes and functioned largely to enable blacks to serve whites.

Some sensed change in the air. "We got it," the combative E. D. Nixon shouted as soon as word of Parks's arrest reached him. "We got our case!"

Edgar Daniel Nixon, a burly railroad porter, had been at the forefront of black protest in Montgomery for well over a decade. The former president of the local NAACP and the head of the Montgomery chapter of the Brotherhood of Sleeping Car Porters, Nixon immediately grasped that Parks—a respected and respectable churchgoing community activist of the right class and color—was just the kind of woman around whom the politically minded black community could mobilize to protest racial discrimination on the city's buses.

"This is what we've been waiting for," Nixon told Parks. Was she willing to be the "symbolic case" in a legal challenge to the arrest? Despite her husband's fears—"Rosa, the white folks will kill you"— Mrs. Parks agreed.

That same day Parks's attorney, Fred Gray, telephoned news of the arrest to Mrs. Jo Ann Robinson, an English professor at the all-black Alabama State College and president of the black Women's Political Council (WPC), adding, "If you ever planned to do anything with the council, now is the time." Robinson herself had been mistreated by a bus driver for unwittingly sitting in the whites-only section shortly after she had moved to Montgomery. Just four days after the *Brown* decision in May 1954, she had written to the mayor, calling for an end to black riders "being insulted and humiliated by bus drivers" and hinting at a "city-wide boycott of buses."

Having already mapped plans for an eventual boycott of the Montgomery bus line, Robinson responded to Gray's query by convincing

Nixon to call for a one-day boycott of the buses on Monday, December 5, the day of Parks's trial. Robinson then drove to the college campus and stayed up all night printing thousands of handbills warning, "This must be stopped . . . Until we do something to stop these arrests, they will continue. The next time it may be you, or your daughter, or mother." The flyers called for "every Negro to stay off the buses Monday in protest," urged African-Americans who needed to get to work or to school to "take a cab, or share a ride, or walk," and invited all to attend a mass meeting on Monday night "at the Holt Street Baptist Church for further instruction." By the next afternoon, Robinson and two student volunteers had delivered her circulars to virtually every black business, barbershop, beer hall, and school.

Meanwhile, Nixon pressed Montgomery's black ministers to endorse the bus boycott and attend an emergency meeting to prepare for the event. "Brother Nixon," a hesitant Martin Luther King, Jr., replied, "let me think on it awhile. Call me back." He was the newest and youngest black pastor in the city, not quite twenty-seven. He knew that most of his fellow black men of the cloth shied from politics and protest and accommodated to the racial mores of Montgomery. Indeed, Martin's predecessor, Vernon Johns, had been fired by the Dexter elders when white authorities labeled him a racial firebrand. King understood that he had been hired to be a less confrontational pastor, one who would take care of church business and stay out of trouble. Moreover, he shared with his fellow ministers a wariness of Nixon's fiery reputation. Still thinking like a graduate student, he saw each side of an issue. He rationalized: Would not a boycott by blacks be just like the White Citizens' Council boycott of businesses owned by African-Americans supporting school desegregation? And would not the prudent course be to continue along the proved path of litigation rather than the uncertain road of direct action?

Although still wary of being perceived as a troublemaker, Martin agreed to attend the next day's meeting at the urging of Ralph Abernathy. Martin valued the advice of the deliberate yet combative preacher from the heart of Alabama's Black Belt. Abernathy knew and understood the common people of Montgomery, and Martin took to heart his friend's conviction that the Parks arrest represented a special opportunity. He would go along if he did not have to take a leading role.

"I'm glad you agreed," Nixon said to King when he called back, "because I already set the meeting at your church."

Huddled in the basement meeting room of silk-stocking Dexter, some seventy contentious black leaders could agree on little more than to support the one-day boycott and to reconvene on Monday to assess the situation. The divisions in the cliquish black leadership—the Citizens' Steering Committee quarreling with the Progressive Democrats, the civic spokesmen at odds with the men of the cloth, the NAACP squabbling with the WPC—merely strengthened the cagey King's desire not to stand out.

But watching the buses on the South Jackson line at dawn on Monday, December 5, changed King. First one, then another, and another bus, usually filled with African-American domestic workers and laborers, passed by empty. King ran to his car and rapidly drove from one bus line to another. Hardly a black could be seen on a bus. Instead, he saw African-Americans trudging to work, riding mules, farm tractors, and horse-drawn wagons, thumbing rides, carpooling, and sharing taxicabs.

"A miracle had taken place. The once dormant and quiescent Negro community was now fully awake," King would later write. "I knew that there is nothing more majestic than the determined courage of individuals willing to suffer and sacrifice for their freedom and dignity."

That same morning a judge fined Rosa Parks ten dollars "and four dollars' cost of court" for violating a state segregation ordinance. She appealed the decision so that Nixon might be able to expand the boycott beyond the single day. The empty buses forced the decision of Montgomery's reluctant black church and civic leaders. Meeting that afternoon at Mount Zion, Parks's church, they agreed to continue the campaign until the bus company met certain limited demands for more equal and humane—although still segregated—seating. They asked for nothing more than what was already in place in other Deep South cities and had already been proposed by the WPC—"the right, under segregation, to seat ourselves from the rear forward on a first come, first served basis." None envisioned the immediate dismantling of segregation.

The assembled leaders also accepted Ralph Abernathy's proposal for a new organization to direct the boycott as well as his suggestion that it be named the Montgomery Improvement Association (MIA). To surmount jealous factionalism, it would be an umbrella organization composed of many civic groups and churches. To avoid stirring white hostility, its name omitted any such words as "protest" or "civil rights" or "boycott." And by emphasizing its local origins, it hoped to avoid the repression then being experienced by the NAACP—the organization that white southerners considered the greatest threat to white supremacy.

Still seeking the safe, consensual path, those at the meeting unanimously agreed to select Martin Luther King, Jr., as the MIA president. They had timidly "passed the buck" to the newcomer, who would later claim, "It happened so quickly I did not even have time to think it through. If I had, I would have declined the nomination."

The "scholarly" Dr. King had been chosen to prevent the election of the "reckless" Nixon or some of the others identified with a particular faction or church. He had not yet made enemies or chosen sides in the long-running quarrels and long-standing rivalries among his peers. He had impressed the others with his academic credentials and the way he had taken command of his Dexter congregation. The fact that he was a Baptist preacher made him acceptable to the more conservative among them. His position as head of the prestigious Dexter Avenue Baptist Church, with its many influential congregants, provided him with vital community resources, and it gave him a platform from which to communicate to African-Americans in a city that had just gotten its first black newspaper and black radio station. Most of all, contemplating the very strong possibility of the boycott's failure and subsequent white retaliation, the others feared being cast as the leader. King, however, was expendable: As well connected as he was, they assumed, he could always get a pulpit in another city. His genius for inspirational oratory and leadership was a consequence of, not a reason for, his selection to head the boycott.

With under a half hour to prepare to address the first evening mass meeting, the new president of the MIA felt "possessed by fear" and "obsessed by a feeling of inadequacy." How could he rise to the occasion? How could he excel and distinguish himself? "I prayed to God. I wanted a speech that would combine militancy and moderation, that would stir them to courageous action but not to hate or resentment."

He quickly sketched an outline and then drove to the Holt Street Church, nestled in a black working-class neighborhood.

The local activists with deep roots in the black protest tradition and the preexisting networks and structures of support—the civic associations, the educational and professional groups, the women's clubs and church organizations—had brought out a huge crowd. Several hundred blacks crammed the sanctuary and the basement auditorium, while several thousand more lined the sidewalks surrounding the church, listening on loudspeakers to rousing renditions of "Onward, Christian Soldiers" and "Leaning on the Everlasting Arms," to somber Scripture readings, and to pleas for financial support by numerous ministers.

Then an unassuming Martin King mounted the podium. Few in attendance had ever heard him speak, and the short, chubby preacher was hardly a commanding presence in the pulpit.

"We are here this evening for serious business," he intoned slowly, *"and we are determined to apply our citizenship to the fullness of its means."* In his rich, deep voice, he calmly recalled the history of bus segregation and asked the black community to protest the arrest of Rosa Parks—*"not one of the finest Negro citizens, but one of the finest citizens in Montgomery."* [THAT'S RIGHT.] [YESSIR.]*

Having captured his listeners with his deliberate enunciation, King quickened his cadence and wagged an admonishing finger. *"You know, my friends, there comes a time, there comes a time when people get tired—tired of being segregated and humiliated, tired of being trampled over by the iron feet of oppression."* Loud applause and shouts forced King to pause, then to pause further as the throng outside added a rising, clamorous approval.

The volume and pitch of the preacher's words rose. *"There comes a time, my friends, when people get tired of being thrown across the abyss of humiliation, where they experience the bleakness of nagging despair.* [YES!] *There comes a time when people get tired of being pushed out of the glittering sunlight of life's July and left standing amidst the piercing chill of an alpine November."* A wave of clapping hands and stomping feet shook the church and again made King wait.

*Brackets indicate audience responses taken from transcripts.

⌈*"We had no alternative but to protest."*⌉ King pointed again for emphasis. *"For many years, we have shown amazing patience.* [THAT'S RIGHT!] *We have sometimes given our white brothers the feeling that we liked the way we were being treated. But we come here tonight to be saved from that patience that makes us patient with anything less than freedom and justice."* [SPEAK! SPEAK!] King's baritone resounded: *"The great glory of American democracy is the right to protest for right."* Looking down at his hands on the sides of the lectern, he contrasted that right with those *"incarcerated behind the iron curtain of a communistic nation,"* and with the violence and lawlessness of white supremacists who defied the Constitution, stirring more shouts of "Keep talking" that momentarily drowned him out.

"If we are wrong," King contended, *"the Supreme Court of this nation is wrong.* [YESSIR.] *If we are wrong, God Almighty is wrong!"* [THAT'S RIGHT.] Straining to be heard above the din, he thundered, *"If we are wrong, Jesus of Nazareth was merely a utopian dreamer and never came down to earth! If we are wrong, justice is a lie."* [YEAH.] [IT'S TIME. YES!] The preacher waited. ⌈*"And we are determined here in Montgomery to work and fight, until justice runs down like water and righteousness as a mighty stream!"*⌉ The rafters shook.

To still the crescendo of cheers, King held both palms aloft and bowed his head. *"If you will protest courageously and yet with dignity and Christian love"*—his voice lowered—*"when the history books are written in future generations, the historians will have to pause and say: 'There lived a race of people, black people, fleecy locks and black complexion, of people who had the moral courage to stand up for their rights. And thereby they injected new meaning and dignity into the veins of civilization.'* [THAT'S RIGHT!] [YESSIR.] [SPEAK. SPEAK!] *This is our challenge,"* he concluded with his head aloft, *"and our overwhelming responsibility."*

The rhythm of the words, the power of the rising and falling voice, the bold vision of triumphing over wrong stunned the crowd into sudden silence as King abruptly stepped away from the pulpit, trembling from his effort. Then, rising as one, the congregation shouted its resolve to continue the boycott.

Spurred by the prophetic zeal of the Old Testament and reminders of the Sermon on the Mount, hundreds of hands reached out to touch the young pastor as he self-assuredly strode up the aisle to leave. As though he had been preparing for this speech since he was a boy, King had utilized all the pulpit tradecraft he had learned at Crozer, all the careful study of the mannerisms and organizational styles of the black folk preachers he had witnessed at Ebenezer, and all the hours he had spent weekly perfecting his showmanship to give the crowd a first glimpse of his true oratorical potential.

He had expressed his people's deepest feelings, their heartfelt beliefs. He had legitimated their protest in the words of the Founding Fathers and Jesus. He had aroused their righteous anger and tempered it by insisting that they protest without threat or intimidation in the spirit of Christian love. Affirming the inherent dignity of all people, King had bolstered their self-esteem and self-confidence and imparted to them a mission and destiny.

In retrospect, Montgomery—the Cradle of the Confederacy—had just experienced the symbolic birth of a renewed, revitalized movement for freedom and justice. Building on the protests that had gone before, the Montgomery bus boycott would go beyond its predecessors and have far greater impact. It would, in King's words, "astound the oppressor, and bring new hope to the oppressed." Another chapter in history had begun. It would shape America's future. The youthful minister had assumed the leading role in the theater of the real.

But only in retrospect. King's words did not appear in *The New York Times* or on the evening news. He proceeded irresolutely. "We are not asking for an end to segregation," he murmured when explaining to his followers the MIA's hardly historic demands. Indeed, Roy Wilkins of the NAACP refused the MIA's request for help because it was "asking merely for more polite segregation." But even that proved too much for Montgomery's white authorities to accept. Officials of the bus company, claiming adherence to the law, refused at first even to discuss any modifications. Only grudgingly did they agree to the plea by the Alabama Council on Human Relations that they meet with the MIA and the city commissioners on Thursday, December 8, to consider the matter.

King began the meeting with a summary of the MIA's three demands: greater courtesy from bus drivers; employment of African-American drivers on the four routes serving mostly blacks; and the seating of African-Americans from the back toward the front, and of whites from the front toward the back, without any section being permanently reserved for one race. Segregation would be maintained, but African-Americans would neither have to surrender their seats to whites nor have to stand while seats reserved for whites remained empty.

The attorney for the bus company, Jack Crenshaw, responded with defiance. He postponed indefinitely the matter of "hiring nigra" drivers on the bus lines that carried predominantly black passengers, and he rejected outright any change in the existing seating arrangements. To comply with the MIA's demands would lead African-Americans "to go about boasting of a victory they had won over white people," chided Crenshaw. "This we will not stand for." The intractable resistance from the bus company met the MIA's equally adamant refusal to compromise. Each thought the other would capitulate quickly.

The MIA's optimism rested on its assumptions that the bus company could not afford to lose three quarters of its riders and that a majority of white Montgomery would accept a "first come, first served" seating system that retained segregation. It was, after all, no more than what already existed in Atlanta, Macon, Mobile, Nashville, and other southern cities. And had not Montgomery's leading newspaper noted that the MIA demands might easily be met? King and Montgomery's black leaders expected their moderate proposal to be "granted with little question" in a few days. A week, Jo Ann Robinson recalled, "that was the longest, we thought."

Their optimism had been buoyed by the steady trend of Supreme Court decisions, culminating in *Brown*; by the growth of black political influence in the North and in parts of the South; by successful decolonization movements abroad, like that in Ghana; by the increasing prosperity of the United States and the proliferation of television and a consumer culture; and by the desegregation of such parts of American life as professional sports and popular entertainment. The arc of history appeared to be bending in the right direction.

At the same time, the intransigence of the bus officials, backed by Montgomery's city fathers, to consider a more equitable seating plan reflected the strident mood of "massive resistance" against desegregation by white southerners following *Brown*. An uncompromising defense of segregation now dominated politics in the South. The time had come, white spokesmen maintained, to draw the line against further changes in the racial status quo. They would even oppose the "law of the land" to keep blacks "in their place." Encouraged by McCarthyism, some whites insisted that demands to erode segregation had to be coming from Communist agitators or New York liberals, because "our niggers are not that smart." "We intend to make it difficult, if not impossible, for a Negro who advocates desegregation to find and hold a job, get credit, or renew a mortgage," announced the head of the Alabama White Citizens' Council.

Putting an end to talk of compromise, Montgomery mayor William A. Gayle announced, "The white people are firm in their convictions that they do not care whether the Negroes ever ride a city bus again, if it means that the social fabric of our community is to be destroyed." What might have been a short-lived local dispute now escalated.

The adamant white "never" meant that Montgomery's blacks would have to refuse to ride the buses for much longer than any anticipated at the outset. To assist them in their resolve, the MIA enlisted the black-owned taxicabs to accept African-American passengers for ten cents, the price of bus fare. The city responded by threatening the arrest of any cabdriver not charging the full forty-five-cent taxi fare required by city ordinance.

Uncertain how to proceed, King contacted Reverend Theodore Jemison, the organizer of the ten-day bus boycott in Baton Rouge in 1953, Operation Free Lift. Jemison counseled the young pastor to establish a voluntary, private carpooling operation, since no law prohibited driving people for free. King did so, and at its peak, more than two hundred volunteer drivers picked up some twenty thousand rides a day at forty-two morning and forty-eight evening locations. Blacks of all classes crammed into station wagons, called "rolling churches" because many had the names of churches painted on their sides. Even some upper-class African-Americans who previously did not associate with black laborers volunteered to chauffeur cooks and janitors to work.

In retaliation, city police harassed black drivers with lengthy checks of taillights and windshield wipers, ticketing them for every trivial, even imaginary, traffic violation. Jo Ann Robinson, though a cautious driver, received seventeen traffic tickets in under two months. In spite, the bus company slashed its service in all the major black neighborhoods. Some blacks were evicted from their homes; others were fired from work. Among them, Rosa Parks and her husband lost their jobs.

But such acts merely solidified the resolve, and blacks stayed loyal to the boycott. They shared rides, stayed home, and walked to work, keeping the boycott about 90 percent effective as the days turned into weeks, then into a new year. In mid-January the MIA executive board decided "it is now a test as to which side can hold out the longer time, or wear the other down." King increased the number of mass meetings from two to six a week. The hymns and sermons, harnessing the spirit of black religion, boosted morale like nothing else. They gave the boycott both legitimacy and religious fervor. Some adherents sang, "Ain't gonna ride them buses no more, / Ain't gonna ride no more. / Why don't all the white folks know / That I ain't gonna ride no more."

Others circulated tales of the disabled African-American who said, "I'm not walking for myself, I'm walking for my children and grandchildren," and of the seventy-two-year-old woman known to all as Mother Pollard, who, declining the offer of a ride, proudly exclaimed to the car-pool driver, "My soul has been tired for a long time, now my feets is tired, but my soul is rested."

At the same time, the unity and determination of Montgomery's whites frayed. Housewives who wanted their black maids to continue cooking and cleaning took to picking them up and, after a day's work, driving them home. Storeowners, complaining to city hall that the boycott was hurting sales, demanded that the matter be settled quickly. So, too, did the bus company, as it realized it could not long afford the loss of $2,500 per day. Even a white Lutheran minister, Reverend Robert Graetz, joined the boycott.

In a letter to *The Montgomery Advertiser*, the city's major newspaper, a white librarian favorably compared the boycott to Gandhi's nonviolent campaign against the British: "It is hard to imagine a soul so dead, a vision so blinded and provincial as not to be moved with admiration at the quiet dignity, discipline, and dedication with which the Negroes have conducted their boycott. Their cause and their conduct have filled me with great sympathy, pride, humility and envy. I envy their unity, their good humor, their fortitude, and their willingness to suffer for great Christian and democratic principles."

Determined to crush the protest, Mayor Gayle went on television in early 1956 to stress that he and the city commissioners had joined the militantly segregationist White Citizens' Council. "We have pussy-footed around on this boycott long enough." They embarked on a new "get tough" policy, having police step up the harassment of car-pool drivers and the arrest of blacks awaiting rides at car-pool locations. They also sought to spread internal discord in the African-American community by persuading several ministers to announce that the issues had been resolved and the boycott concluded, and by initiating a smear campaign against King.

Rumors circulated that King had his hand in the till, using donations to the MIA to buy a station wagon for his wife and a Cadillac for himself; that he was a Communist outsider (from Georgia); and that the newcomer had shouldered aside the respected black leadership in Montgomery in order to have the limelight to himself. Shaken by the whisper campaign against him, King offered to step down as the MIA president. Increasing the pressure, city police arrested him on January 26 for doing thirty miles per hour in a twenty-five-mile-per-hour zone. Handcuffed and whisked off to the desolate city jail, King feared for his life, "sure now that I was going to meet my fateful hour on the other side."

Word of his arrest spread quickly through black Montgomery, and a crowd of King's supporters milled outside the jail. "Dey trying to be smart," threatened a black woman, "but if they beat dat boy dere is going to be hell to pay." A nervous warden hustled King out on his own recognizance.

Despite having acquired a pistol and surrounded himself with armed bodyguards, King lived in terror. "Almost every day," he pointed out, "someone warned me that he had overheard white men making plans to get rid of me." The threats took their toll, and with no end to the boycott in sight, he doubted he could endure the daily hate mail, the persistent obscene phone calls, the danger to his wife and child much longer. He admitted being "scared to death," worn down by the "paralyzing effect" of fear.

On January 27, the night after he was jailed, a telephone call awakened him late at night: "Listen, nigger, we tired of you and your mess. If you aren't out of this town in three days, we gonna blow your brains out and blow up your house." Click.

Wracked with fear, King could not sleep. His apprehension became unbearable. "I got to the point that I couldn't take it any longer. I was weak." He wondered how, without appearing a coward, he could give up his leadership role and leave Montgomery.

Sitting alone at his kitchen table, his knuckles pressed to his temples, King experienced the dark night of his soul. Bowed down over a cup of coffee, he began to pray, confessing his weakening, his faltering, his loss of courage. Suddenly, he felt something stirring within; he heard an inner voice. He believed it was Jesus telling him to fight on: "Stand up for righteousness. Stand up for justice. Stand up for truth. And lo, I will be with you, even until the end of the world." The voice "promised never to leave me, never to leave me alone. No, never alone. No, never alone. He promised never to leave me, never to leave me alone."

The revelation immediately assuaged King's uncertainty. His fright and despair vanished. For the first time, God became profoundly real and personal to him. King now knew "I can stand up without fear. I can face anything."

The test of that conviction came four nights later. On January 30 King left his two-month-old daughter Yolanda ("Yoki") sleeping in her crib, and Coretta and a family friend watching television in the parsonage, to deliver a boycott pep talk at the First Baptist Church. Humbly, he told the congregation that *"if M. L. King had never been born, this movement would have taken place. I just happened to be here."* [ALL RIGHT.] [YESSIR!] His voice boomed: *"There comes a time when time itself is ready for change. That time has come in Montgomery, and I had nothing to do with it."* When he finished, a church member approached to say, "Your house has been bombed."

Racing home, King found the parsonage surrounded by several hundred angry blacks, with more arriving every minute. The police struggled to restrain the angry throng, jeering the mayor and police chief. Pushing his way to the bombed-out porch, King saw people brandishing knives and baseball bats, bottles broken at the neck, handguns and hunting rifles. Once assured that his wife and child had not been harmed, the pastor sought to calm the furor.

Standing on his mangled porch, King called out to those who had, as Coretta Scott King said, "come to do battle." Everything is all right, he reassured them amid the rubble. "He who lives by the sword shall perish by the sword. I want you to love our enemies. Be good to them. Love them and let them know you love them."

King contended that no matter what happened to him, the movement "will not stop. For what we are doing is right. What we are doing is just. And God is with us. Go home with this glowing faith and this radiant assurance. With love in our hearts, with faith and with God in front, we cannot lose." Coretta saw tears shining on many faces: "They were moved, as by a holy exaltation." While some shouted "Amen," others began to sing "America" and then "Amazing Grace." "This could well have been the darkest night in Montgomery's history," King surmised. But "the spirit of God was in our hearts." "If it hadn't been for that nigger preacher," a white policeman said later, "we'd all be dead."

This moment, according to black historian Lerone Bennett, Jr., "changed the course of the protest and made King a living symbol." He had spoken of love and forgiveness before. "But now, seeing the idea in action . . . millions were touched, if not converted." Many others, including Coretta, would conclude that Martin's response to the bombing injected "the nonviolent philosophy into the struggle." In truth, the bombing led him to place armed guards around his house. His adoption of a Gandhian nonviolent creed as an integral part of the struggle would develop gradually, not as the consequence of any single act. It would take the tutelage of two pacifist outsiders to ensure King's grafting of Gandhism onto black Christianity.

More immediately, King chose to make clear that neither the arrest nor the bombing had dented his resolve. He argued until dawn with Daddy King, who had driven from Atlanta upon hearing of the bombing. His father demanded that Martin quit the boycott and become his co-pastor in Atlanta's Ebenezer: "Better to be a live dog than a dead lion!" Daddy pushed harder and harder, but the son stood firm: He would stay the course in Montgomery. Without sleep, Martin left in the morning to preach at Dexter.

There, he related his dark night of the soul to the congregation. "I heard a voice that morning saying to me, 'Preach the gospel, stand up for truth, stand up for righteousness.' Since that morning I can stand up without fear. So I'm not afraid of anybody this morning. Tell Montgomery they can keep shooting and I'm going to stand up to them. Tell Montgomery they can keep bombing and I'm going to stand up to them. If I have to die tomorrow morning I would die happy because I've been to the mountaintop and I've seen the promised land and it's going to be here in Montgomery."

The next day, February 1, with the legal and financial assistance of the NAACP, the MIA attorney filed suit in federal court on behalf of five Montgomery black women, requesting that bus segregation in Alabama be declared a violation of the Equal Protection Clause of the Fourteenth Amendment. *Browder v. Gayle* cited *Brown* to directly challenge the constitutionality of segregation.

In response, whites detonated a series of bombs at the homes and churches of MIA leaders, and the city fathers urged a local grand jury to indict King and eighty-nine others for violating an almost forgotten 1921 anti–labor union law that made it a misdemeanor to conspire "without a just cause or legal excuse" to hinder any company in its conduct of business. The grand jury complied on February 21. "We are committed to segregation by custom and by law," it stated, and "we intend to maintain it." The largest mass indictment in Alabama history charged all ninety, including twenty-four ministers and all the drivers in the car pool, with engaging in an anti-business conspiracy. City officials expected the indictment to break the movement's spirit and end the boycott.

However, the indictment united and emboldened Montgomery's African-Americans still further. Several thousand attended a mass meeting and vowed to continue the boycott, unequivocally turning down a compromise bus seating plan offered by Montgomery's premier white businessmen that promised blacks would be treated with courtesy and could board buses through the front door. As scores of black onlookers clapped and roared support, eighty-nine MIA members, led by E. D. Nixon, assembled at the city courthouse to be booked together, their smiles and haughty laughter showing they no longer feared the white man's jail. The city's effort to crush the boycott had backfired. It had only raised the morale of the rank and file.

On his way back to Montgomery after a series of lectures in Atlanta that day, King again had to deflect intense pressure brought by
his father that he remain safely in Georgia. To bolster his case, Daddy
King had assembled the elite black leadership of Atlanta. The leading
lights of African-American religion, education, and business initially
supported Daddy's tearful contention that Martin's life was in danger
if he returned to Montgomery, that "they gon' bury you over there."

But Martin was unrelenting. "I must go back to Montgomery," he
said; "I would rather go back and spend ten years in jail than desert
my people now." Given the struggle being waged by his followers,
"you can't decide whether to stay in it or get out of it—you must stay
in it." He vowed to fight on, to never give up: "I have begun the struggle, and I can't turn back. I have reached the point of no return."
Daddy King and the others gave up the fight, and the next day Daddy
accompanied his son to the Montgomery courthouse, where Martin
was photographed, fingerprinted, and released on bail.

That evening the spirit poured out of the five thousand boycott
supporters packed in and around the mammoth First Baptist Church.
They stood in ovation to greet the arrested MIA leaders, now symbols
of courage. Women held up their babies to be touched by them. As
the television cameras whirred, Martin Luther King, Jr., in what had
become his trademark singsong cadence, began: "*We are not struggling merely for the right of Negroes but for all the people of Montgomery, black and white. We are determined to make America a better
place for all people.*" [DOCTOR. DOCTOR.] [TELL IT NOW!] Elo-
quently, he repeated his rationale for "*the right to protest for right.*"
[TELL IT, DOCTOR!] [WE CAN'T STOP NOW.] He reiterated that this
"*is not a war between the white and the Negro but a conflict between
justice and injustice . . . We are not just trying to improve the Negro of
Montgomery but the whole of Montgomery.*"

His followers clapped and swayed to the rich religious oratory,
which reached deep into the southern black psyche and the black folk
pulpit. Then King concluded, as he had often before, almost singing:
"*If we are arrested every day, if we are exploited every day, if we are
trampled over every day, don't ever let anyone pull you so low as to hate
them. We must use the weapon of love. [SPEAK!] [YES, YES.] We must
have compassion and understanding for those who hate us.*"

For the first time, network television covered a mass meeting, and major newspapers gave it front-page coverage. The bombings and indictments had brought a national, even international, spotlight to the boycott, and especially on Martin Luther King, Jr. He was now the primary symbol of dignified black protest. The new medium of television, growing ever more influential, depicted the boycott as a drama of black victims and white villains, embedding that in the public consciousness and conscience. It impressed upon millions of Americans the oppression inherent in "separate but equal," providing the publicity essential to the success of peaceful resistance. Similarly, it fixed the image of King as a singular saint beseeching his flock to love their oppressors into redemption. Knowing that the winter cold made walking to work increasingly difficult, and that the three-month-old boycott showed no signs of soon ending in a settlement, King skillfully used the gust of media attention to remind his followers that people across the nation wanted them to continue, and that the eyes of the world were upon them.

The flurry of news stories also brought two apostles of nonviolence to Montgomery. Bayard Rustin arrived first. It would be hard to imagine a more unlikely character to impress and win over the circumspect young pastor. An illegitimate child raised by his grandparents in a Quaker community, the forty-five-year-old Greenwich Village activist and folksinger with a debonair British accent had been an organizer for the Young Communist League in the 1930s. He was also an aide to A. Philip Randolph (the "American Gandhi"), whose World War II March on Washington Movement sought advances for African-Americans by combining Gandhian nonviolence with mass direct-action techniques borrowed from the labor-union movement of the 1930s. After joining the Fellowship of Reconciliation (FOR), an international pacifist organization, Rustin helped establish the Congress of Racial Equality (CORE), a small, mostly white and middle-class offshoot of FOR begun in 1942 to desegregate public facilities in northern cities through Gandhian tactics of nonviolent direct action. As a conscientious objector, Rustin went to prison for twenty-eight months for resisting the draft.

Resuming his protest activities after the war, the bony, six-feet-three Rustin, with high cheekbones and a mane of prematurely gray hair, co-organized the Journey of Reconciliation, an effort to apply nonviolent resistance to the cause of desegregating interstate transportation. The 1947 bus ride in the Upper South landed Rustin on a chain gang. The following year, Rustin, again assisting Randolph, threatened mass draft resistance by blacks to try to force President Truman to desegregate the military. By the time he met King, the vagabond Rustin had also worked with Gandhi's Congress Party in India, with disarmament activists in England, with West African anti-colonialists such as Kwame Nkrumah, and had been arrested twenty-eight times for his protest activities.

Capping his status as an outsider in 1950s America—an illegitimate Negro, an ex-Communist, and a pacifist with a prison record—Rustin was homosexual. His arrest in 1953 for "lewd and lascivious behavior" with two men in a parked car in Pasadena, California, had led to a thirty-day jail term and his resignation from the FOR staff. When initially told this story, King sought to dismiss it as of no consequence. The spreading of nasty sexual rumors about African-Americans was hardly novel. Indeed, tales of King's own extracurricular sexual activities had begun circulating. Others in the MIA, however, as well as A. Philip Randolph, A. J. Muste of FOR, and James Farmer of CORE—who had financed and dispatched Rustin to Montgomery—knew that no popular movement in 1956 could afford the taint of either communism or homosexuality, much less both. Rustin had to go.

That did not end King's eagerness to continue conversing with Rustin about morality, movement strategy, and Gandhi. At their first get-together, they had hit it off immediately and talked far into the night about the meaning and theory of nonviolence. Rustin found that King knew very little about Gandhi and did not consider himself a pacifist, yet his commitment to peaceful protest gave Rustin heart. By telephone and correspondence, and in secret meetings in Montgomery and New York City, the two developed a deep philosophical and personal bond. Rustin gradually became a trusted adviser, eroding the preacher's hesitancy about identifying with Gandhian nonviolence. He also helped King see the broader philosophical meaning of the boycott, as part of a worldwide movement for human rights.

King was no easy sell. He had no wish to become a cloth-spinning ascetic, a vegetarian, or celibate, which Gandhi advocated for a true

follower of the nonviolent resistance that he called *satyagraha*. Although King had been mildly interested in Gandhi as a student, he
agreed with Reinhold Niebuhr's critique of Gandhi's unconditional
pacifism, and with the contention that justice required coercion as
well as suasion. King found it easier to discuss the bus boycott in the
tradition of Thoreau: "that what we were really doing was withdrawing
our cooperation from an evil system."

King had no problem with his followers and bodyguards being
armed for self-defense at the beginning of the boycott. He understood
that most Americans esteemed power, considered gun ownership a
constitutional right, and looked down upon what they deemed weakness, especially below "the Smith and Wesson line." Even among
religious blacks in the South, the great majority believed armed
self-defense was justifiable, and many made frank use of rifles to protect their property and families. In addition to his concern that Gandhism might lead to his being demeaned as unmanly by his critics,
the pastor realized that African-Americans, unlike Gandhi's Indians,
were not the majority facing a numerically small and foreign occupy-
ing regime. What had worked in India might not in the United States.

On February 27, as Rustin prepared to leave Montgomery or be exposed as a "pinko queer" by a hostile black newspaper editor, Glenn
E. Smiley arrived with a stack of books on nonviolence. A soft-spoken
forty-five-year-old white Methodist minister from Texas who had
joined the FOR staff in 1942 and, like Rustin, had been imprisoned as
a draft resister during the war, Smiley immediately recognized something special in King. "I believe that God has called Martin Luther
King to lead a great movement," he noted after their first meeting.
"King can be a Negro Gandhi." But he was not one yet, Smiley reported to the FOR. "King accepts, as an example, a body guard, and
asks for permits for them to carry guns. This was denied by the police,
but nevertheless, the place is an arsenal. King sees the inconsistency,
but not enough. He believes and yet he doesn't believe . . . If he can
really be won to a faith in non-violence there is no end to what he
can do."

Receptive to outside help, King listened to Smiley, learned from
Rustin, and had the self-confidence and intellectual background to
change, to grow, to become a believer. He did so in part because of his

awareness of earlier nonviolent protests by African-Americans and
their allies—in antebellum abolitionism; in campaigns against racial
discrimination in northern boycotts before the Civil War; in protests
against streetcar segregation during Reconstruction and at the turn of
the century; and in disobedience of Jim Crow laws and customs. King
recognized in Rustin's and Smiley's arguments the more militant
forms of nonviolent protest practiced in the 1930s: the "don't buy
where you can't work" boycotts, the mass marches on behalf of the
unemployed and the Scottsboro Boys, the sit-ins at relief offices. He
recalled A. Philip Randolph's wartime effort to link Gandhian noncooperation and civil disobedience with the confrontational tactics used
by labor in struggles with management, and CORE's 1947 nonviolent
Journey of Reconciliation.

King had followed with interest press accounts of Albert Lutuli in
South Africa, trying to make Gandhian nonviolence the keynote of
the African National Congress struggle against apartheid. Teachers
and family friends—Howard Thurman, Mordecai Johnson, and Benjamin Mays—whom King admired and emulated had visited India in
the 1930s and 1940s and returned to teach Gandhism in ways that
were consonant with the emphasis on love and redemptive suffering
in black church teachings. That King could understand and preach
Gandhian passive resistance and nonviolence as the gospel of Jesus
counted heavily in its favor, and he would often claim, "I went to
Gandhi through Jesus." That large numbers of black southerners
could recognize it as consistent with their traditional and folk Christianity also figured significantly in King's calculation.

In addition, Gandhian nonviolence fit the Personalist philosophical beliefs King had heard from his white professors. Given the divine
presence, the sacred, within each person, one should never violate the
dignity of one's opponent. One had to act in a manner that made future reconciliation possible. Choosing conversion over coercion dis-
armed the oppressor and made possible the Beloved Community, in
which the hatred and prejudice that underlay racial discrimination no
longer existed.

Gandhi's message fit much that King had previously proclaimed
about the nonviolent means and ends of the boycott. "We will meet
your physical force with soul force," he had informed white Mont-

gomery. "We will not hate you, but we will not obey your evil laws. We will soon wear you down by our capacity to suffer. And in winning our freedom, we will so appeal to your heart and conscience that we will win you in the process." It fit King's exhortations that blacks must protest in a manner that sought reconciliation, that won the hearts and minds of whites, that paved the way for interracial amity and harmony. It placed blame on the system of segregation, not on individual segregationists. It played on white feelings of guilt. Mohandas Gandhi hardly would have objected to King's maxims: "The end is reconciliation, the end is redemption, the end is the creation of the Beloved Community" and "While abhorring segregation, we shall love the segregationist. This is the only way to create the Beloved Community."

Nonviolent resistance made sense pragmatically. How better to undo unjust laws in the mid-1950s Deep South? King understood how thin and tenuous was the line between self-defense and aggressive violence, and how the latter could be suicidal as practiced by a largely powerless minority. Nonviolence gave Montgomery blacks a way to exhibit a morality that was superior to that of violent white racists; it distinguished their protest from the coercion that the White Citizens' Council directed against African-Americans who attempted to vote or boycott segregated buses. Further, it weakened the white community's unity and resolve. It stressed reconciliation and, in curbing inflammatory language and actions by African-Americans, calmed white fears of black retribution, thus reducing the likelihood of white violence. It also made great copy. News accounts of "the American Gandhi" and his band of nonviolent black protesters enhanced the media's good-guy-versus-bad-guy plot. Like nothing before, the aura of heroic black nonviolence won northern white sympathy and support as well as financial contributions to the MIA.

In addition to helping win King to the cause, Smiley, within weeks of his arrival in Montgomery, had begun to emphasize the relevance of nonviolence to the freedom struggle at the weekly mass meetings, to organize workshops on direct action and passive resistance, and to strengthen the bond between the MIA and such movement leaders in the North as A. Philip Randolph and James Farmer. At the same time, King's first published article, ghostwritten by Rustin for the April 1956 issue of *Liberation*, claimed that "the only way to press on is by adopting the philosophy and practice of non-violent resistance," and such terms as "passive resistance" and "soul force" increasingly appeared in King's speeches. King now frequently referred to the "little brown man in India—Mohandas Gandhi," who had "brought the British Empire to its knees," and he implored his audience: "Let us now use this method in the United States." The pastor meant active nonviolent protest. "To accept passively an unjust system is to cooperate with that system . . . Noncooperation with evil is as much a moral obligation as is cooperation with good."

As the bus boycott dragged on and on, from winter into spring and then summer, King, with the aid of Rustin and Smiley, refashioned Gandhian nonviolence into a uniquely African-American concept of mass direct action. Together they incorporated Jesus' injunction to love one's enemies, Henry David Thoreau's concept of civil disobedience, and A. Philip Randolph's techniques for massive protest demonstrations into King's own African-American spiritual creed. Rooted primarily in the values and themes of the black church, it synthesized moral passion and compassion, justice and love.

Opposition to segregation now became African-American Christianity in action. The church culture bequeathed to King by his father and grandfather defined the character of the Montgomery movement. What came out of the black church would go back in, as articulated by King, and by the other preachers associated with the boycott: Nonviolent direct action transformed the people and the communities who engaged in it, endowing them with never before felt resources of strength and courage; it converted those whose policy was protested; it dramatized injustice in America far better than anything else had and, because it was couched in the language of Christianity, led to financial and vocal support by others; it was the path to peaceable conflict resolution, to the Beloved Community; and it involved God as an agent of personal and social change—"God is with the movement."

King's couching Gandhism in the rhythms, cadences, and colloquialisms of the black church made all the difference. "Christ furnished the spirit and motivation," he contended, "while Gandhi furnished the method." Because he presented nonviolence as their Christian faith in action, his followers, most of whom would neither accept nonviolence as a way of life nor believe it would convert the oppressor, could nevertheless adopt nonviolent direct action as a method, a tactic or technique, to undo unjust laws. Moreover, by utilizing the emotional strength of black Christianity, King endowed pragmatic nonviolence with religious idealism and evangelical fervor. More than a political struggle, the boycott became a holy crusade to defy injustice while seeking reconciliation. And the African-American church, the fulcrum of spiritual and social life in the black community, became the center—the essence—of the movement. So rooted, the MIA could communicate to most Montgomery blacks; and, church-based, it mobilized the community as no association ever had.

The MIA needed this and all the other assistance it could get as southern whites hardened their resolve to resist changes in the racial status quo. Early in March the Alabama state legislature introduced its program of massive resistance to desegregation, including a measure to reinforce bus segregation. A week later, Alabama's congressional delegation, and nearly all of the South's representatives, approved a Southern Manifesto denouncing *Brown*. In Montgomery the boycott made whites unceasingly vigilant against African-American advances. Their city fathers would not relent. The trial of the indicted MIA leaders would commence on March 19, 1956.

Although King's lawyers fully expected him to be found guilty of violating the state anti-boycott statute, they mounted a defense aimed at the national media. More than a score of witnesses testified to the mistreatment suffered by black riders, to the humiliation and infamy they had endured. One woman's husband had been shot and killed for requesting the return of his dime on a bus too crowded to accommodate him. Another woman's blind husband had been dragged for blocks because the driver had prematurely closed the door on his leg. Such accounts exposed the human tragedy of racial discrimination and segregation. Opening the window on the obscenity of racism, they showed "just cause."

Yet four days later, the jury found King guilty of conspiracy. Sentenced to a year in jail or a five-hundred-dollar fine plus four hundred for court costs, he informed a bank of reporters and TV cameras outside the courtroom: "We will continue to protest in the same spirit of nonviolence and passive resistance, using the weapon of love." As news correspondents reported the protesters' determination and ethical vision, another intransigent white effort to destroy the boycott boomeranged. The city won a legal battle, but the black community claimed the moral victory.

That evening, at a mass meeting in Holt Street Baptist, King remained confident that "the forces of light will blot out the forces of dark. You don't get to the promised land"— he rocked back and forth on the balls of his feet—"without going through the wilderness." Jabbing his fingers to emphasize the point, he asserted, "There can never be growth without growing pains. There is no birth without birth pains." As on many a previous occasion, he concluded, "I believe that God is using Montgomery as His proving ground."

His opponents disagreed. When the bus company sought to capitulate, Montgomery's mayor and police chief promised to prosecute any bus driver who failed to enforce segregation, and the local circuit court ordered the company to retain segregation. In yet another move to stifle the boycott, the City Commission filed a request in state court for an injunction against the MIA's car pool, without which the boycott could not continue.

As the MIA awaited a decision on *Browder v. Gayle*—its challenge to the constitutionality of Alabama's bus segregation law—King, out on bail, traveled without pause to raise funds that would sustain the boycott and to spread the gospel of nonviolent militancy. The stress of the road and the strain of constant anonymous threats took their toll. He turned for help to In Friendship, a new relief organization to raise money for those fighting segregation in the South. Begun in early 1956 and chaired by A. Philip Randolph, In Friendship was the brainchild of Rustin and two other left-wingers who had come of age in the radical ferment of 1930s New York: Ella Baker, a national field secretary and later director of branches for the NAACP, who became an outspoken critic of the association's preoccupation with a legalistic approach to civil rights; and Stanley Levison, a wealthy attorney and professional fund-raiser for rumored Communist and Communist-front groups. Working in concert, the three activists encouraged the young pastor to expand the Montgomery protest into a broader nonviolent direct-action insurgency against Jim Crow.

Both Rustin and Levison worked covertly as King's ghostwriters, since he, as Rustin commented, "cannot find time at present to write articles, speeches, etc., himself." They also counseled him on tactics and strategy and advised him on handling the news media. More passionate and exciting than the legalistic NAACP yet deemed a reasonable and responsible leader of blacks, King became a sudden celebrity, a recognizable voice on news programs, a recognized face in newspapers and magazines.

His public ascent reflected, in part, the tremendous desire of African-Americans for a liberator. The dynamic young preacher—dramatizing the movement's aspirations and its willingness to sacrifice and suffer to achieve them—filled the void in an African-American leadership ravaged by the Red Scare's crusade against radicalism. King's fame in part resulted from his determination to express black needs in ways acceptable to many whites. He reworked the themes of the black struggle in the familiar and nonthreatening language of a Sunday-morning church service or high school patriotic assembly. He created a persona that meshed with the measured liberalization of white racial attitudes outside the South.

Despite King having won the battle for public opinion, the campaign against bus segregation would be decided by a handful of judges. On June 5 a federal appeals court outlawed segregation on Alabama's buses. On the basis of the precedent set in *Brown*, the judges voted two to one that the bus segregation statutes violated the Fourteenth Amendment. Although now ruled unconstitutional, the statutes remained in effect pending an appeal to the Supreme Court. The boycott went on, and with it the walking, now in the heat of an Alabama summer. As the temperature rose, so, too, did the harassment. The police constantly ticketed, even brutalized, car-pool drivers. Insurance companies canceled the liability insurance on the car pool's station wagons. The City Commission stepped up its pressure for a state injunction against the car pool as an unlicensed municipal transportation system. The Ku Klux Klan reestablished a klavern in Montgomery. A bomb wrecked Reverend Robert Graetz's home. Alabama's attorney general secured a court order shutting down the state NAACP.

Efforts to besmirch King's reputation continued as well. Recently demoted as the MIA's recording secretary, a bitter Reverend U. J. Fields accused King and his fellow officers of "misusing money sent

from all over the nation." King persuaded Fields to retract his allega-
tions and apologize publicly, leading many black Montgomerians to
want to see Fields fired as pastor of his church, even roughed up.
Conversely, King urged his followers to forgive the repentant pastor.
Recalling the parable of the prodigal son who returned, he asked,
"Will we be like the unforgiving elder brother, or will we, in the spirit
of Christ, follow the example of the loving and forgiving father?" The
MIA followers burst into applause, which added to their leader's
Christly aura. The crisis passed, though King had said nothing specific about the cavalier manner in which the MIA spent and accounted for its funds. In the years ahead, accusations of financial
impropriety, however fanciful, would continue to threaten King's
image.

While awaiting the Supreme Court's *Browder* decision, King redoubled his speaking engagements. In city after city, he told the story
of the bus boycott, explained his philosophy of nonviolent resistance,
and highlighted the emergence of the "new Negro," decisively acting
to end the scourge of segregation. When in Montgomery, he began
nonviolent training sessions "to prepare the people to go back to integrated buses with a sense of dignity and discipline." The sessions
proved necessary; however much MIA supporters—most of whom
were barely educated churchgoing women—nodded approval at
King's eloquent statements about the power of love and the creation
of the Beloved Community, few fully understood or could practice the
nonviolent "goodwill that will transform the deep gloom of the old
age into the exuberant gladness of the new age."

On November 13 the Alabama circuit court approved the city's request that the MIA's system of carpooling "cease and desist." It meant
black Montgomery would have to walk or go back to the segregated
buses. "The light of hope," King despaired, "was about to fade away
and the lamp of faith about to flicker." Suddenly, a reporter handed
him a Teletype story saying that the Supreme Court had unanimously
affirmed the appeals court's *Browder v. Gayle* decision that bus segregation was unconstitutional. "God Almighty has spoken from Washington, D.C.," a joyful MIA partisan exclaimed. The "darkest hour of
our struggle," King agreed, "had indeed proved to be the first hour of
victory."

That night, to intimidate the city's blacks, forty cars filled with hooded Klansmen drove through the African-American neighborhoods. They expected blacks to cower in fear, as had happened in the past. Instead, the porch lights stayed on and the doors remained open. "The Negroes behaved as though they were watching a circus parade," reported King. The paralyzing fear of white persecution had been lifted. The shaken Klan slinked into the night. "We got our heads up now," a black janitor insisted to a white reporter, "and we won't ever bow down again—no, sir—except before God."

The formal order ending bus segregation did not come until December 20, so blacks stayed off the buses. The training sessions to prepare Montgomery's African-Americans to ride on desegregated buses went on. A nonviolent code of conduct, "Integrated Bus Suggestions," drafted by FOR field secretary Glenn Smiley, listed eight general and nine specific recommendations, including: "If cursed, do not curse back. If struck, do not strike back, but evidence love and goodwill at all times. If another person is being molested, do not arise to go to his defense, but pray for the oppressor."

Volunteers at nightly church sessions demonstrated the techniques of nonviolence. Skits dramatized the necessity of insulted or assaulted black passengers never responding in kind. Repeatedly, King urged his followers to treat "even those who despise you as a sacred personality" and to "go back to the buses in a way that will astound those who would oppress us."

In early December the MIA hosted a weeklong Institute on Nonviolence and Social Change. It brought together a generation of young black educators and lawyers, especially clergymen-activists, to reflect on the lessons of the boycott and to discuss the future of nonviolence in the struggle for racial justice and equality. In his keynote address, "Facing the Challenge of a New Age," King dwelled on the motto adopted by the institute—"Freedom and Justice Through Love"—and stressed the power of nonviolence, the willingness to suffer, and the refusal to hit back. "The end is reconciliation; the end is redemption; the end is the creation of the beloved community."

Looking beyond bus segregation, King outlined an agenda for the movement that included seeking the ballot, pressing for civil rights legislation, and building black economic power. "We must have the moral courage to stand up and protest against injustice wherever we find it . . . This will mean suffering and sacrifices. It might even mean going to jail . . . We must be willing to fill up the jailhouses of the South. It might even mean physical death. But if physical death is the price that some must pay to free their children from a permanent life of psychological death, then nothing could be more honorable." The goal, he concluded, was that day when all Americans could live together in brotherhood; and "when this day finally comes, 'The morning stars will sing together and the sons of God will shout for Joy.' "

At long last, on December 20, signaling the end of the 382-day boycott, King exhorted the overflow crowd at St. John AME that the time had come to "move from protest to reconciliation." Wishing for "an integration based on mutual respect," King called upon his supporters to "be loving enough to turn an enemy into a friend." The next morning the MIA head paid his fare and took a seat next to the white Texan Glenn Smiley at the front of a bus. "It was a great ride," he declared. King relished the historic victory won by black Montgomery's massive collective struggle, yet he would not gloat. "We seek integration based on mutual respect."

But "not a single white group would take the responsibility of preparing the white community," noted King. "I would rather die and go to hell than sit behind a nigger," said an elderly white man who stood in the front despite empty seats in the rear of the bus. The seemingly innocuous act of a Negro seating himself in the front of a bus unleashed white venom.

Two days after bus desegregation began, gunshots shattered King's front door. The next night five whites assaulted a teenage African-American girl at a bus stop, and sniper fire several evenings later wounded an eight-months-pregnant black woman. Early in January a coordinated bombing campaign hit several African-American churches and the homes of Ralph Abernathy and Robert Graetz. African-Americans did not retaliate. The MIA issued a statement extolling nonviolence.

Whatever the future of reconciliation in Montgomery, the bus boycott proved the power of organized nonviolent collective action as an effective agent of social change. It demonstrated an ordinary people's ability to do the extraordinary. For the first time, an entire African-

American community had mounted a sustained direct-action protest in the heart of the Deep South and demonstrated that it could nonviolently overcome segregation. Blacks had rocked the Cradle of the Confederacy by uniting across class, education, and gender lines; by uniting the Ph.D.'s and "no D's," the classes and the masses; by uniting in faith to achieve an unprecedented mass church-based protest.

As King correctly noted in his memoir of the boycott, "While the nature of this account causes me to make frequent use of the pronoun 'I,' in every important part of the story it should be 'we.' " He depicted the boycott as "fifty thousand Negroes who took to heart the principles of nonviolence, who learned to fight for their rights with the weapon of love, and who, in the process, acquired a new estimate of their own human worth." At bottom, the meaning of what had happened in Montgomery, he contended, was that "there is a new Negro in the South, with a new sense of dignity and destiny." Montgomery's African-Americans had stood tall in the face of economic, legal, and physical intimidation, and in so doing, they had "replaced self-pity with self-respect and self-depreciation with dignity." King closed his account, "In Montgomery we walk in a new way. We hold our heads in a new way."

The determination and unity of Montgomery blacks in their yearlong boycott cracked the southern white myths that African-Americans were in favor of segregation and that only outside agitators sought to topple Jim Crow. It quickly, quietly led to other cities in the South ending their bus segregation. The MIA's victory also had a significant effect on the consciousness of African-Americans nationally. Blacks across the country followed the story of the "walking city" and witnessed the power of nonviolent protest.

Montgomery provided a model of the courageous "new Negro," King emphasized. "He had thrust off his stagnant passivity and deadening complacency, and emerged with a new sense of somebodyness and self-respect, and had a new determination to achieve freedom and human dignity no matter what the cost." The Montgomery bus boycott became "God's proving ground." It forged new tactics and strategies, demonstrated the strength of black alliances and networks, and provided a language and vision that would generate and sustain a decade of nonviolent resistance, of peaceful refusal to obey unjust laws. Combined with the bus boycotts that had taken place in Baton Rouge and Tallahassee, it brought men of the cloth into the vanguard of African-American protest in the South—simultaneously mobilizing the black community and legitimizing the movement.

A new generation of African-American preachers, taking dead aim at segregation, had wrested command of the growing ranks of southern blacks rejecting the racial mores of the day. The black church had proved it could mobilize mass support for protest activism more effectively than secular organizations could. More than just providing a physical base for mass meetings and a place to disseminate information, added King, the church had demonstrated that it "can be a great transforming power if it will be true to its mission." It had made the movement stronger, Bayard Rustin concurred, "because it is religious as well as political." This movement "has been built upon the most stable institution of the southern Negro community—the Church."

Equally vital, the Montgomery bus boycott changed Martin Luther King, Jr. He was shaped by it as much as he shaped the protest. The inexperienced leader's ability to appeal to, and impress, a range of black and white audiences had gradually emerged. Like no other black spokesman, he came to express the quest for desegregation as a grand and glorious mission. Like no other, he convinced black Montgomery of its proud destiny, raised its morale, and inspired self-sacrifice. He made oratory a handmaiden of social revolution.

And he donned Gandhi's mantle, offering himself for martyrdom as he helped fashion a nonviolent resistance both relevant to the African-American struggle in the South and acceptable to northern whites. King and the bus boycott became synonymous. He found his calling, the movement its leader. The "Negro Gandhi" became the "Moses of the Movement."

"I am really disturbed how fast all this has happened to me," King confided to a friend. "A man who hits the peak at twenty-seven has a tough job ahead. People will be expecting me to pull rabbits out of the hat for the rest of my life."

THESE HUMBLE

CHILDREN OF GOD,

1957–62

Most of these people will never make the headlines and their names will not appear in Who's Who. Yet when years have rolled past and when the blazing light of truth is focused on this marvelous age in which we live—men and women will know and children will be taught that we have a finer land, a better people, a more noble civilization—because these humble children of God were willing to suffer for righteousness' sake.

⟶

What rabbits could he pull out of his hat next? King's ceaseless travel and public speaking had exhausted him, the racial violence in Montgomery had depressed him, and he was obsessed with his martyrdom. Leading a mass meeting on January 15, 1956, King broke down: "Lord, I hope no one will have to die as a result of our struggle for freedom in Montgomery. Certainly, I don't want to die. But if anyone has to die, let it be me!" Days later, after unexploded sticks of dynamite had been found outside his home, King dwelled on his death with his congregation yet again; premonitions of his assassination became a recurring theme. He was sure that his life would end in murder, just as he was haunted by the thought that he would not fulfill his promise. He feared that the failure of similar bus boycotts in Tallahassee, Birmingham, and Rock Hill, South Carolina, proved that the Montgomery model, in Smiley's words, was "not exportable."

A bewildered King confided to associates, "I have no idea where this movement is going." He felt, as Gandhi purportedly said, "There goes my people, I must catch up with them, for I am their leader." But, unable to live up to his own, and the movement's, expectations, King floundered for almost half a dozen years, ceding the agenda of the civil rights movement to others.

King allowed Bayard Rustin, Stanley Levison, and Ella Baker to plan and promote a new civil rights council that would coordinate local black struggles in Dixie. The trio of New York radicals, having seen the Cold War and McCarthyism fatally erode the appeal of communism and kill off such radical organizations as the Southern Negro Youth Congress and the Civil Rights Congress, needed a new crusade — and a new crusader.

Some sixty southern black ministers and one white minister — Reverend Will Campbell of Mississippi — responded to their "emergency conference call," sent out under the name Martin Luther King, Jr. Gathering to meet at his father's church in Atlanta on January 10–11, their ranks included T. J. Jemison of Baton Rouge, Joseph Lowery from Mobile, Birmingham's Fred L. Shuttlesworth, and C. K. Steele of Tallahassee. King invited no one from the NAACP. Rustin thought the association's emphasis on litigation was too unimaginative and ineffective; instead, he envisioned the SCLC as more like the March on Washington Movement (MOWM) of 1941. The conferees adopted the name Southern Leadership Conference on Transportation and Nonviolent Integration. They then voted to petition President Eisenhower to demand compliance with the U.S. Supreme Court's anti-segregation rulings; to invite Vice President Richard M. Nixon to make a civil rights address in the South; and to ask the attorney general to urge southern authorities to obey the law of the land.

The delegates agreed to reconvene in New Orleans, chose King as the temporary chairman, and concluded with a "Statement to the South and Nation," appealing to the Christian ideals of love and reconciliation. "We advocate nonviolence in words, thought and deed, we believe this spirit and this spirit alone can overcome the decades of mutual fear and suspicion that have infested and poisoned our southern culture."

On February 14 about a hundred black activists met in New Orleans, formally elected King their president, and created the Southern Christian Leadership Conference (SCLC). The group's new name and motto, "To Redeem the Soul of America," highlighted its Christian orientation, distinguished it from the NAACP, and, its leaders hoped, provided protection against charges that it was a leftist "un-American" group. It would be an all-black, top-down coordinating conference of local affiliates, mostly churches, rather than a mass-membership association like the NAACP. Rustin had fought hard for this structure. He wanted to exclude whites in order to insulate the SCLC from Communist designs—much as A. Philip Randolph's MOWM had done—and to prevent SCLC affiliates from being awed by all-knowing whites.

Rustin understood the great pride that Montgomery's African-Americans took in having organized and led their own boycott movement. He wanted the SCLC to follow suit. It would be southern in origin, composition, and leadership. It would fill the void left by the repression of the NAACP in the South. Unlike the NAACP, headquartered in New York City, it couldn't be accused of being an outsider. Although well aware of de facto racial discrimination in the North, Rustin also knew that by focusing on de jure segregation in the South, African-Americans had the force of law on their side and could anticipate the financial support of liberal northern whites.

Most vitally, the SCLC—although not representative of the majority of black ministers, who steered clear of political activism—would be centered in the African-American church. The church helped facilitate mass participation and imparted to the SCLC a crusading and unifying quality: "the movement spirit." It made the SCLC seem less threatening to whites than a political organization; it also made the movement more respectable to, and respected by, African-Americans. The church was the most black-owned, black-controlled institution, and the one least vulnerable to state regulation and persecution. To appear still less controversial, the SCLC opted initially to emphasize voting rights education and voter registration rather than boycotts and other direct action against segregation.

The SCLC's hope that this might lessen the jealousy, even hostility, of other civil rights groups and their leaders came to naught. "I had labored a decade and a half in the vineyards of nonviolence," griped James Farmer of the Congress of Racial Equality, "now, out of nowhere, someone comes and harvests the grapes and drinks the wine." More worrisome to SCLC, Roy Wilkins, who had just assumed leadership of the NAACP, did whatever he could to keep the new organization from competing with the association for publicity and financial support. King's criticism of the NAACP's "needless fights in lower courts" angered Wilkins, much as what the SCLC might mean for the NAACP's own southern branches troubled him. Chagrined by King's ascendancy, the fifty-five-year-old executive secretary of the NAACP—who had been laboring for civil rights as many years as King had lived—refused to accept the young preacher as an equal. The decidedly uncharismatic Wilkins seethed at the press attention given to the SCLC and the popularity of the upstart who led it. His dismissal of demonstrations as "blowing off steam" merely earned him the retort from Levison that "steam propels a piston which drives the train forward."

Only at Randolph's urging did the jealous Wilkins agree to cosponsor with King a Prayer Pilgrimage for Freedom on the third anniversary of the *Brown* decision. At the Lincoln Memorial, after a long procession of African-American leaders and celebrities had spoken and sung to the audience of some twenty-five thousand—the largest civil rights demonstration in the United States to date—King ascended the podium to deliver the keynote address.

In the symbolic shadow of the Great Emancipator, King proclaimed that they had come to wrest their rights from a Congress and presidency who *"have betrayed the cause of justice,"* and from a *"quasi-liberalism"* so *"bent on seeing all sides that it fails to become committed to either side."* [THAT'S RIGHT.] [YES, YES.] Freedom was never freely given, King said, pointing at the throng. Because *"privileged classes never give up their privileges without strong resistance,"* he said, blacks must now do far, far more than they ever had done. His arms waved, his squat body swayed. *"Give us the ballot and we will no longer have to worry the federal government about our basic rights.* [ALL RIGHT, YESSIR!] *Give us the ballot and we will fill our legislative halls with men of good will, and send to the sacred halls of Congress men who will not sign a Southern Manifesto, because of their devotion to the manifesto of justice."* [AMEN! AMEN! AMEN!]

King's voice took flight: *"Give us the ballot and we will quietly and nonviolently, without rancor or bitterness, implement the Supreme Court's decision of 17 May 1954."* The huge assemblage echoed his refrain: *"Give us the ballot! Give us the ballot! Give us the ballot!"* *"Give us the ballot,"* the young minister chanted to the cheering crowd in front of the chiseled Lincoln's gaze. *"Give us the ballot, and we will transform the salient misdeeds of the bloodthirsty mobs into the calculated good deeds of orderly citizens."* [SPEAK!] [IT'S TIME, YESSIR!] Civil rights, he intoned to lusty cheers, were *"an eternal moral issue which may well determine the destiny of our nation in the ideological struggle with Communism. The hour is late. The clock of destiny is ticking out. We must act now, before it is too late."* [AMEN! AMEN!]

King had demonstrated his remarkable oratory once again. New York's black weekly, the *Amsterdam News*, wrote that King had "emerged from the Prayer Pilgrimage to Washington as the number one leader of sixteen million Negroes in the United States." *Look* magazine highlighted King, not the movement, in its coverage; *The New York Times* magazine made him the focus of an account of the Montgomery bus boycott; a *Time* cover story lauded "the scholarly Negro Baptist minister" for his Christian meekness; and NBC's *Meet the Press* featured him as a guest, only the second time in its history that the program had interviewed an African-American. King appeared alongside such show-business stars as Sammy Davis, Jr., and Frank Sinatra at fund-raising rallies and benefits. Howard University, Morehouse College, and the Chicago Theological Seminary awarded him honorary degrees. An overnight ambassador to the Washington establishment, he testified to congressional committees, conferred privately with Vice President Nixon, and met with President Eisenhower in the Oval Office. Even the NAACP, ever wary of competition, awarded King its Spingarn Medal for his contributions to the cause of racial justice.

King's rising fame, and growing ego, did not impede the SCLC's declining relevance. SCLC's much heralded Crusade for Citizenship, announced in August 1957, had set an ambitious goal of doubling the number of black voters in the South by the 1960 election. Yet by the year's end, bare handfuls of African-Americans had been added to the registration rolls. To generate enthusiasm, SCLC arranged for twenty-one southern cities to hold mass meetings for voter registration on Lincoln's birthday, February 12, 1958. King stirred his audiences, as usual: *"We must and we will be free. We want freedom now.* [NOW! NOW!] *We want the right to vote now.* [NOW!] *We do not want freedom fed to us in teaspoons over another hundred and fifty years."* But local fervor for direct action could not be roused. Most southern black preachers continued to play it safe. King contended that *"any religion that professes to be concerned with the souls of men and is not concerned with the slums that damn them, the economic conditions that strangle them, and the social conditions that cripple them is a dry-as-dust religion."* But an opiate was what most African-American churches in the 1950s gave their flocks. The crusade floundered.

SCLC's failures in part reflected the unfertile ground in the South of the late 1950s in which to plant the seeds of racial revolution. The movement faced a resurgent KKK, the mushrooming of White Citizens' Councils, and the coming to power of increasingly militant white segregationist politicians. Intimidation and repression all but silenced African-Americans and the dwindling band of white moderates. At the same time, black hopes rose that the federal government would ensure their rights. King counted on the United States' need to lead the "free world" to the abolition of segregation. Ending Jim Crow was the way to win the decolonized Third World, defeat communism, and shore up America's world dominance. Also, the Supreme Court's *Brown* decision, President Eisenhower's sending troops to Little Rock to enforce desegregation, and Congress's enactment of civil rights bills in 1957 and 1960—the first since Reconstruction—encouraged cautious optimism. It was a time to watch and wait, not to rock the boat.

SCLC's failures stemmed from its internal confusions. Why did it exist? To empower the grass roots in autonomous affiliates? To serve as King's personal vehicle for civil rights leadership? To mount coordinated southwide assaults on Jim Crow? Beset by rivalries from outside and contradictions within, SCLC vacillated between one-man centralized authority and dispersed local decision-making.

Some resented the "Great Leader" hogging the spotlight and thought him bedazzled by the bright lights. Others promoted a personality cult, hitching their wagon to the charismatic young preacher's ascent and happily rubber-stamping whatever King said or did. The resentment of NAACP officials, who derided Gandhian nonviolent resistance, and of African-American politicians such as Harlem congressman Adam Clayton Powell, Jr.—who, envious of King's prominence, even preferred the racial status quo to victories for the black preacher—added to the SCLC's woes.

Failure also resulted from the SCLC ministers' fear of having the too controversial Rustin as their director, then their refusal to allow Ella Baker, who had been reluctantly drafted to manage SCLC affairs in January 1958, to administer the organization in a professional manner. Like most other Americans in the 1950s, King and the movement leadership rarely challenged traditional gender roles and, sharing the patriarchal assumptions of most men of their time, thought nothing of pursuing racial injustice while ignoring gender equity. Accustomed to congregations where women predominated but remained subordinate, the thoroughly male-controlled SCLC would not accept Baker as an equal.

However much Baker dreamed of creating a mass movement, she could not do so given the conditions in which she toiled. SCLC had no regular office. It forced its director to use the pay phone at her hotel to make SCLC business calls. It required that she use the mimeograph machine at Ebenezer Baptist Church only after five P.M. Despite his having little time or inclination to do it himself, King would not cede control of everyday operations to a woman. He expected the deference due "the movement leader," but Baker would not defer to him or any of the other ministers, whom she thought arrogant and pompous. Baker resented King's star status and would not accept his contention that a pastor's authority was "divinely sanctioned." She rebuked him for retarding the emergence of the kind of democratic, collective organization she envisioned.

The Cold War abroad, moreover, hampered activist efforts to mount a liberal crusade at home. Countenancing only the most moderate, nonradical modifications in the system, most Americans deplored "extremism." Neither President Eisenhower nor the Democratic Congress risked standing up to bring down Jim Crow, and the post-*Brown* Supreme Court showed little predilection for further controversy.

With no clear goal in mind, King tried to attach the SCLC to the

National Baptist Convention, African-America's largest and often most conservative religious organization. That failing, he toyed with establishing an Institute for Nonviolent Resistance to Segregation, which would train a "nonviolent army" of volunteers to confront and vanquish Jim Crow. Nothing worked. Despondent, he sought refuge in dictating his account of the Montgomery boycott for Stanley Levison to transform into a book.

King's hectic yet irresolute pace took its toll: The rush to catch a train or plane, to meet a deadline, to deliver yet another and another and another speech, to little effect, drained him emotionally as well as physically. So did the frequent bomb threats and fiery crosses on his lawn, the tightrope of expectations and pressures. Yearning to do the right thing in the right way, to live up to his reputation, King verged on breaking down. His trepidation for his own life merged with his guilt for subjecting his family—grown larger with the birth of his son, Martin Luther King III, on October 23, 1957—to the apparent inevitability of his assassination.

To relieve the strain, King privately indulged an appetite for women and gluttony as grandiose as his ego. He consumed far more greasy pork, alcohol, and cigarettes than he should have; delighted in lewd, raunchy humor; and lost himself in frequent, boisterous extramarital sexual liaisons. "I'm away from home twenty-five to twenty-seven days a month," he rationalized; "fucking's a form of anxiety reduction."

The Pittsburgh Courier wrote that "a movement minister in the deep South, a man who has been making the headlines recently in his fight for civil rights, had better watch his step," since his opponents sought to catch "the preacher in a hotel room with a woman other than his wife." Privately, a Los Angeles friend warned King that the lure of women could be his downfall. He was a "marked man," the friend reminded him, and since women "too often delight in the satisfaction they get out of affairs with men of unusual prominence," he must "exercise more than care. You must be vigilant indeed." King could not.

In fact, the more he admired and aspired to Gandhi's "absolute self-discipline," the absence of "any gulf between the public and private," the more King succumbed to his reckless frailties. He prodded himself to do more for his people, yet jeopardized the movement for the solace of sex. He preached that the great burden of life is always to keep the higher self in command. "Don't let the lower self take over." But he could not.

In September 1958, King came to believe that God wanted to teach him a lesson, to remind him that redemption came through suffering. First, while attending the courthouse in Montgomery, King was suddenly, roughly manhandled by the police and arrested on a charge of loitering. Found guilty of disturbing the peace, he refused to pay the fine and accepted a two-week jail sentence. "America is in danger of losing her soul," King told the court. "Something must happen to awaken the dozing soul of America before it is too late." Not wanting any further negative publicity, Montgomery's police commissioner hurriedly paid King's fine to get him out of jail.

Later that month King went on tour to promote his account of the bus boycott, *Stride Toward Freedom*. He had provided ideas and materials from his earlier speeches and sermons, as well as the writings of others, and left the authorship of the memoir largely to Stanley Levison and editors his publisher had supplied.

Near the end of September, King's tour took him to Blumstein's department store in Harlem. As he sat autographing books, a well-dressed middle-aged black woman approached. "Are you Martin Luther King?" He felt something beating at his chest. He heard a woman's cry: "Luther King, I've been after you for five years." Dazed, he stared at the handle of the razor-sharp seven-inch Japanese letter opener she had plunged into his chest, close to his heart. While others waiting in line screamed and the store's security arrested the bespectacled woman, who made no attempt to escape, King slumped in a chair.

An ambulance rushed him to Harlem Hospital, where a team of surgeons removed ribs and part of King's breastbone in a three-hour operation to dislodge the blade touching the main artery from his heart. "If you had sneezed," his doctor observed, "your aorta would have been punctured and you would have drowned in your own blood."

As he recovered, King learned of the sad, failed life of his demented would-be killer, Mrs. Izola Ware Curry. "Coretta, this woman needs help," Martin urged his wife. "She is not responsible for the violence. Don't do anything to her; don't prosecute; get her healed." The authorities agreed; Curry was committed to Matteawan State Hospital for the Criminally Insane.

King chose to see the stabbing as a part of God's plan. God had singled him out for a special role; his unearned suffering would be redemptive. Thinking himself a martyr akin to Gandhi, who had been assassinated by one of his own people, King vowed that "however violent others are I will never inflict violence upon another." He would deliver his people from bondage through suffering.

He took strength from the triumph of a nonviolent movement that forced Britain to grant independence to Ghana, as well as from the poorer, nonwhite nations coming together to free themselves of white dominion by establishing an independent, nonaligned "third force" between the opposing American and Soviet alliances. "A new world is being born," he often remarked, "an old world is passing away." King equated the struggle to end racial oppression in the United States with the overthrow of white colonialism in Africa. "Both segregation in America and colonialism in Africa," he claimed, "were based on the same thing—white supremacy and contempt for life." In March 1957 he and Coretta traveled to Accra, Ghana's capital, for the independence ceremonies. He relished the fact that Nkrumah and those jailed with him did not wear the crowns of kings: "They walked in with prison caps." As the British flag came down, Martin and Coretta, for the first time in their lives, sat among blacks who ruled their own nation. He expected that the ultimate triumph of justice in Ghana would have "implications and repercussions" for "oppressed peoples all over the world as they struggled for freedom."

Two years later, in February 1959, King, Coretta, and Lawrence D. Reddick, a history professor at Alabama State College and King's first biographer, spent a month visiting India and meeting many of Gandhi's compatriots. "To other countries I may go as a tourist," King announced at the outset, "but to India I come as a pilgrim." He found its pervasive destitution far worse than he could have imagined, yet he came away impressed by the government's efforts to "atone for the immense injustices imposed upon the untouchables" by discriminating affirmatively. More than equality, India provided "special treatment"—via scholarships, financial assistance, and special admissions and employment opportunities—"to enable the victims of discrimination to leap the gap from backwardness to competence." King thought the spirit of Gandhi was still very much alive.

"I left India more convinced than ever before that nonviolent resistance was the most potent weapon available to oppressed people in their struggle for freedom." Violence, he affirmed, "leads to bitterness in the survivors and brutality in the destroyers. But the way of nonviolence leads to redemption and the creation of the beloved community."

In November 1959, King announced that he would leave Montgomery at the start of the new decade and copastor the redbrick Ebenezer Baptist Church on Auburn Avenue in Atlanta with his father. Cosmopolitan Atlanta suited Martin and Coretta more than provincial Montgomery, much as being a national civil rights leader appealed to him more than ministering to the Dexter Avenue Baptist Church. His ego craved the larger stage. The change would significantly reduce his pastoral duties, relieve him from having to preach every Sunday, and give him more time to devote to developing the SCLC. Being an important airline hub, Atlanta would make his traveling easier; and being "the city too busy to hate," it would make King and his family feel safer. Moreover, he hoped being close to the SCLC headquarters on Auburn Avenue might help him translate his rhetoric into action.

When justifying his decision to his Dexter congregation, King recalled the splendors of the Montgomery bus boycott and then dwelled upon the strain and weariness he had endured, upon his becoming a "physical and psychological wreck." But history, he said, had more in store for him. He had no choice but to go to Atlanta and battle racial injustice on a mammoth scale. "I cannot stop now." King wept as his congregation wept. "History," he concluded, "has thrust something upon me which I cannot turn away."

But turn him away was just what many Georgians wanted to do. He was not welcome, said the governor: "Wherever M. L. King, Jr., has been there has followed in his wake a wave of crimes including stabbings, bombings, and inciting of riots." Much of Atlanta's smug African-American elite agreed. The black Brahmans, living "on the hill" overlooking the black ghetto, deemed him a dangerous radical who might upset the cozy arrangement they had with the white power structure. They placed their faith in white "moderates," such as Mayor William B. Hartsfield, Ivan Allen, Jr., of the Chamber of Commerce, and Police Chief Herbert Jenkins, despite the fact that Atlanta African-Americans in 1960 remained mostly segregated and distinctly unequal.

Daddy King eagerly reassured the Atlanta establishment, black and white, that his son wasn't "coming to cause trouble." Instead, "he's chosen the pulpit." Martin made Atlanta his base and sanctuary but, despite his talk of what history intended, never launched an SCLC campaign there, remaining silent even when a local Episcopal school rejected his children on racial grounds.

It fell to younger African-Americans to refuse to accept and wait. The day after King delivered his farewell sermon at Dexter, four black students from North Carolina A&T College sat in at the Woolworth's segregated lunch counter in Greensboro and wouldn't leave until they were served. Within two weeks, hundreds of students in the South followed suit at more than a dozen lunch counters. The sit-in tactic had been used before—by labor unions in the 1930s, CORE in the 1940s, NAACP youth groups in the 1950s—but not until 1960 did those tentative, sporadic forerunners become a cohesive regionwide movement.

One sit-in ignited more. By the beginning of April, more than seventy cities had experienced sit-ins, and at year's end, some seventy thousand students had engaged in direct action, many of them claiming to have been inspired by Montgomery's bus boycott, to have read King's *Stride Toward Freedom*, and to have heard him at the April 1959 youth march to Washington, urging them to settle for nothing less than "total desegregation and total equality—now!"

Many students professed to be following the nonviolence of King. Hundreds wrote to him for encouragement and assistance, and he eagerly advised them on organizational and tactical matters. In a 1959 speech to the annual FOR convention, he had predicted that blacks throughout the South would employ "direct action against injustice." He went on, "We will not obey unjust laws or submit to unjust practices." Now, Levison wrote to him, the students had taken the struggle to a higher stage, "where the Montgomery bus boycott left off." It was regional in scope, involved a more direct confrontation with segregation, directly placed bodies on the line, and challenged the sanctity of private property. King welcomed students to the movement, termed their sit-ins "one of the most significant developments in the civil rights struggle," "a glowing example of disciplined, dignified non-violent action against the system of segregation," and assured them that they had "the full weight of the SCLC behind [them] in [their] struggle."

But it was Ella Baker, not King, who organized the students into the forefront of the movement. On her own, she invited more than two hundred student leaders to attend a Southwide Youth Leadership Conference at Shaw University, in Raleigh, North Carolina, on Easter weekend. They listened politely to King addressing them on the philosophy of nonviolence; to his suggestion of a nationwide boycott, "selective buying," to bring down Jim Crow; and to his advocacy of pressuring the federal government to compel intervention. They appreciated that King admitted his own uncertainty and that he thanked them for taking the initiative and saving the movement. They applauded King's call for protesters to go to jail rather than pay bail or fines—"a prison term for a freedom struggle is a badge of honor."

Their greatest acclaim, however, went to Jim Lawson, the head of the Nashville sit-ins, which would bring to the fore of the southern civil rights struggle such stalwarts as John Lewis, Diane Nash, and Marion Barry—who insisted that if he "was not a free man he was not a man at all." Lawson, who had recently been expelled from Vanderbilt University's Divinity School, was an articulate proponent of Gandhian philosophy and strategy. He had served a year in jail as a conscientious objector during the Korean War and three years as a Methodist missionary in India, and he dazzled the students with his rhetoric of social revolution, his depiction of nonviolence as "a way of life," and his vision of the Beloved Community. Lawson especially won their young hearts with his depiction of the sit-ins as a "judgment upon middle-class conventional, half-way efforts to deal with radical social evil," and his insistence that the movement could no longer abide those groups that relied on "fund-raising and court action."

In this spirit, Baker successfully pressed the students to form an independent, democratic organization with "group-centered leadership." Opposed to King's "cult of personality" and the "leader-centered" SCLC, Baker advocated "a mass movement with indigenous leadership." Insisting that "strong people don't need strong leaders," Baker left the SCLC to become an adviser for the independent Temporary Student Nonviolent Coordinating Committee, encouraging its group-centered decision-making process and its subsequent decision to become a permanent protest organization: the Student Nonviolent Coordinating Committee (SNCC), popularly called "Snick."

SNCC would become the movement's avant-garde, making direct and often militant action the key criterion for race leadership. With its cadre of organizers and full-time activists willing to put their bodies on the line for racial justice, SNCC would emerge as SCLC's chief rival and one of King's most severe critics. It would eventually renounce his ethic of love and reconciliation and drop all pretense of advocating nonviolence. But not in 1960. "We affirm," it announced in its founding statement, "the philosophical or religious ideal of nonviolence as the foundation of our purpose, the presupposition of our faith, and the manner of our actions." More than philosophically close, the headquarters of SNCC was "squeezed in one corner of the SCLC office" in Atlanta.

But King offered scant leadership to SCLC in 1960, much less to SNCC. In mid-February he was arrested on two criminal counts of perjury. Accused of falsely swearing to the accuracy of his 1956 and 1958 Alabama state tax returns, he faced imprisonment in Alabama and the savaging of his public reputation. Already rumors of a secret bank account, a lavish home, and a flashy car—however untrue—dogged him. King had thought the matter resolved when he earlier agreed to pay an additional $1,600 in back taxes, but Alabama authorities would not relent. Determined to harass King, see him behind bars, and ruin his public reputation, for the first time in the history of the state, they prosecuted an individual for perjury on a tax return. The need to raise money for a first-class team of lawyers and to prepare his defense preoccupied King, deeply pained by accusations of such petty venality. In late May an all-white jury heard the case for three days and quickly found the preacher not guilty, apparently accepting the argument of King's attorneys that the unreported sums were reimbursements for travel expenses rather than contributions taken by King for his own income.

He felt an immense burden lifted but rapidly found himself a marked man yet again. Although he had violated no traffic statute, Georgia police officers pulled King over when they observed him driving with a white woman in his car—the famous writer Lillian Smith. Consequently, the police noticed that King had not transferred his driver's license from Alabama to Georgia, as required after ninety days' residence in the state. In late September he appeared in DeKalb County court for the violation, receiving a twenty-five-dollar fine and a year's probation.

In mid-October he reluctantly agreed to join student activists at an Atlanta sit-in to demand service at the Magnolia Room restaurant in Atlanta's largest department store. Doing his utmost not to foul his father's nest, Martin had initially resisted when black students from Morehouse and Spelman colleges, having lost patience with Atlanta's purportedly progressive leadership, pressed him to join their sit-ins and go to jail with them. Shamed by students sniping that "his day" had passed, he eventually gave in, sat in, and went to jail with fifty others on October 19, 1960. As planned, all the protesters, including King, refused to seek bail or pay their fines. Mayor Hartsfield, however, struck a deal with the black "old guard," winning a temporary suspension of the protests in return for release of the detained on their own recognizance.

Except King. Unwittingly, he had violated the terms of the probation stemming from his guilty plea on a traffic violation. Accordingly, Atlanta authorities transferred him to DeKalb County, where he received a sentence of four months at hard labor. Late that night, a terrified King found himself in handcuffs and leg irons, in a police car hurtling over the dark clay roads of rural Georgia. "Where are you taking me?" he asked to stony silence. He expected that the car would soon stop and, like many other blacks, he would be summarily executed. Instead, he was deposited at Georgia's famously barbarous maximum-security Reidsville State Penitentiary, locked in a tiny cell with scurrying roaches.

Isolated for eight harrowing days, unable to bear his confinement, King broke down in tears and berated himself for weakness. "This is the cross that we must bear for the freedom of our people," he managed to write to Coretta. "I have the faith to believe that this excessive suffering that is now coming to our family will in some way serve to make Atlanta a better city, Georgia a better state, and America a better country. Just how I do not yet know, but I have faith to believe that it will."

Lacking that faith, a distraught Coretta King, with two toddlers to care for and a third child about to be born, phoned Harris Wofford, an old friend and John Kennedy's civil rights adviser, for help. "They are going to kill him," she pleaded. "I know they are going to kill him." Wofford called Kennedy's brother-in-law Sargent Shriver, who convinced the young senator from Massachusetts, currently running as the Democratic candidate for president, to convey his concern to Mrs. King and ask the Georgia governor to try to get Martin Luther King, Jr., out of jail. A brief flurry of phone calls and hints of deals and patronage from a future Kennedy administration resulted in King's release on bail by an arch-segregationist judge. King publicly expressed gratitude for Kennedy's help while adhering to his stated position of not endorsing political candidates, but an unrestrained Daddy King, despite his objection to Kennedy's religion, announced, "Now he can be my President, Catholic or whatever he is . . . I've got a suitcase of votes, and I'm going to take them to Mr. Kennedy and dump them in his lap." For its part, the Kennedy campaign flooded black communities with more than a million pamphlets urging African-Americans to cast their ballots for "the candidate with a heart" rather than " 'no-comment' Nixon."

The so-called Negro vote went 70 percent to Kennedy, a significant increase from 1956. Kennedy's razor-thin margin of victory and loss of Democratic seats in Congress, however, mattered more to him than the African-American votes. Determined to win back the votes of white southerners who had gone for Nixon, and to retain the support of white southerners in Congress, the newly elected president would do whatever he could to duck civil rights matters. To avoid offending the sensibilities of white segregationists, he had no words of thanks for Daddy King and would neither meet with Martin Luther King, Jr., during the transition nor invite him to his inauguration.

The cautious president and his protective brother, Attorney General Robert Kennedy, viewed King as a self-serving nuisance, certainly not an ally. Dreading whatever threatened a good working relationship with the southerners who controlled Congress, John Kennedy would not sacrifice the possibility of federal aid to education or medical reform legislation by introducing a civil rights bill or by supporting the proposal to reduce the votes needed to end a Senate filibuster from two thirds to three fifths.

Just after the birth of his second son, Dexter Scott, on January 30, 1961, King demanded in *The Nation* that the new president undertake "a radically new approach to the question of civil rights" by issuing executive orders and sponsoring legislation to wipe out racial discrimination. Kennedy refused to act. Accordingly, King denounced him for "critical indecisiveness." He thought the president had "the understanding and political skill" to achieve civil rights for African-Americans but lacked "the moral passion." He tried prodding the administration with such jibes as "The New Frontier is unfortunately not new enough" and "The President has proposed a ten-year plan to put a man on the moon. We do not yet have a plan to put a Negro in the state legislature of Alabama." But Kennedy did not budge, and King did not venture beyond taunts.

Others acted. King belatedly, timidly tried to catch up. On May 4, 1961, six white and seven black Freedom Riders boarded two buses in Washington, D.C., to test a recent Supreme Court decision prohibiting segregation in interstate transportation facilities. The plan came from the Congress of Racial Equality, hoping to establish itself as a major organization in the nonviolent campaign for racial justice, as well as to move the struggle from the local to the national level and impel the Kennedy administration to intervene. The Freedom Riders would challenge segregation by demanding unrestricted access to terminal restrooms, restaurants, and waiting rooms in the Deep South, where custom and law forbade it. "Our philosophy was simple," stated CORE's James Farmer. "We put on pressure and create a crisis so that they [federal government authorities] react."

After a couple of relatively uneventful days marred only by local toughs scuffling with the Freedom Riders in Rock Hill, South Carolina, for attempting to integrate the whites-only waiting room, King greeted them in Atlanta. He praised their courage and celebrated the fact that they had traveled some seven hundred miles in the South without major clashes. The Riders then crossed the state line into Alabama and along Route 78 toward Anniston. Outside the town, a white mob blocked the road. Armed with clubs, iron bars, and chains, the hoodlums smashed the windows and punctured the tires of the first bus before setting it ablaze and beating the fleeing passengers. An even more savage mob mercilessly attacked the Freedom Riders in the second bus, which bypassed Anniston for Birmingham.

The next day newspapers around the world carried prominent photographs of the burning bus and the bloodied Riders. The violent reaction to the Freedom Rides that Farmer had counted on had come to pass. The attorney general hurriedly sought protection for the Riders from state and local authorities. But Alabama governor John Patterson, elected in 1958 on a stridently white-supremacist platform, proclaimed that he wouldn't protect "this bunch of rabble rousers," and the bus drivers refused to transport them to their next destination, Montgomery. Scared and stymied, the battered CORE contingent decided to conclude their Freedom Ride and instead fly to New Orleans to celebrate the seventh anniversary of *Brown*.

While Governor Patterson and the Kennedys breathed sighs of relief that the Freedom Ride had ended, SNCC students from Nashville interjected themselves into the fray. They needed to prove that the movement could not be stopped by violence. "The impression would have been that whenever a movement starts," said Diane Nash, one of the Nashville students, "all you have to do is to attack it with massive violence and the blacks will stop . . . So, under those circumstances, it was really important that the ride continue." A group of twenty-one SNCC Freedom Riders left Birmingham on May 19 for Montgomery.

A bloodthirsty KKK mob attacked as soon as the new Riders arrived at the Montgomery bus terminal. "People came out of nowhere—men, women, children, with baseball bats, clubs, chains—and there was no police official around," Nashville student John Lewis observed. "They just started beating people." A woman screamed, "Kill the nigger-loving son of a bitch," and the Klansmen smashed James Zwerg, a white student from Wisconsin, in the face with his suitcase. One man then held the dazed Zwerg's head between his knees; a woman clawed his face with her nails; a man kicked his front teeth out. They then stomped William Barbee, a black rider. As women kept screaming for more blood, one Klansman held Barbee down while another bashed his skull with a baseball bat, inflicting brain damage that shortened his life. A horrified John Doar of the Justice Department described the beatings by telephone to Assistant Attorney General for Civil Rights Burke Marshall: "It's terrible! It's terrible! There's not a cop in sight. People are yelling, 'There those niggers are! Get 'em, get 'em.' It's awful."

To protect the Freedom Riders in Montgomery, Robert Kennedy dispatched four hundred federal marshals under the command of the deputy attorney general and future Supreme Court justice Byron White. King, on a speaking tour in Chicago, immediately announced that he would be in Montgomery "in the morning" and would preside over a mass rally in support of the Riders that Sunday night.

As the sun set on May 21, a white mob gathered outside Abernathy's First Baptist Church, and King prepared to lambaste Alabama officials for not protecting the Freedom Riders. More than a thousand blacks endured the taunts and threats of the crowd to listen to King. Once darkness came, the mob of several thousand segregationists laid siege to the large downtown church, blocking anyone from leaving the building. Some outside could hear King. *"The ultimate responsibility for the hideous action in Alabama,"* he thundered, *"must be placed at the doorstep of the governor of the state. We hear the familiar cry that morals cannot be legislated. This may be true, but behavior can be regulated.* [DOCTOR, DOCTOR.] [YEAH!] *The law may not be able to make a man love me, but it can keep him from lynching me."* [YESSIR!] Not mincing words, King asserted, *"Alabama has sunk to a level of barbarity comparable to the tragic days of Hitler's Germany."* As if on signal, whites hurled bricks and bottles, crashing through stained-glass windows. As the blacks in the church sang hymns and "Ain't Gonna Let Nobody Turn Me 'Round," federal marshals with tear gas and truncheons barely contained the attackers.

Unless reinforcements arrived quickly, King told Robert Kennedy by telephone, more than a thousand African-Americans might be killed. The attorney general, furious that the preacher had interfered unnecessarily in this matter, shot back, "You know just as well as I do that if it hadn't been for the United States marshals, you'd be as dead

as Kelsey's nuts right now!" Kennedy rebuked the Riders for furnish-
ing "good propaganda for America's enemies" and declared that further Washington involvement would create southern white fears
of federal encroachment and fuel the fires of massive resistance.
Kennedy stressed that he would not do anything more to help the
African-Americans tonight. However, Governor Patterson, bowing to
federal pressure, declared martial law minutes later. He dispatched Alabama National Guardsmen and state troopers to disperse the mob
and escort the besieged African-Americans home.

The Nashville contingent of Freedom Riders informed King later
that day that they would continue the protest and ride into Mississippi.
They rejected Robert Kennedy's call for a "cooling off period" as simply an effort to stop the Freedom Rides. So did CORE. "We had been
cooling off for a hundred years," retorted James Farmer. "If we got any
cooler, we'd be in a deep freeze. The Freedom Ride will go on." Reluctantly, King concurred and announced that the Rides would continue, somberly adding that the "Freedom Riders must develop the
quiet courage of dying for a cause."

Encouraged by Ella Baker, some students insisted that King had
a moral obligation to accompany them. Caught by surprise, he
squirmed. He claimed he needed time to think. This outraged the
Riders, sowing seeds of disappointment and disillusionment with his
leadership.

To try to assuage SNCC, Ralph Abernathy contended that King
had already put his body on the line many times. Wyatt Walker, who
had assumed the post of executive director of SCLC, insisted that it
made no sense for the movement's chief fund-raiser and most respected statesman to be put at risk. Neither argument persuaded the
SNCC contingent. Then King claimed that, being on probation, he
could not risk an additional arrest. This only further irritated the Riders, many of whom were about to violate their own probation terms
from the sit-ins. Responding to their taunts—"Where is your body?"—
an exasperated King proclaimed, "I think I should choose the time
and place of my Golgotha." His pompous likening himself to Christ
led some in SNCC, from then on, to refer derisively to King as "De
Lawd." For them, his moral authority had vanished.

Immediately informed by a SNCC volunteer of what had occurred, Robert Williams, then the most militant black proponent of armed self-defense and retribution, sent a telegram to King demanding that the preacher ride. "No sincere leader asks his followers to make sacrifices that he himself will not endure. You are a phony. Gandhi was always in the forefront, suffering with his people. If you are a leader of this nonviolent movement, lead the way by example."

It hit home. Overcome by remorse for not accompanying the brave students to Mississippi, for not matching their willingness to accept arrest and imprisonment, even court martyrdom, King searched in vain for a way to assert his leadership. He threw himself into assisting the Freedom Rides. He headed a Freedom Ride Coordinating Committee and raised funds to cover the legal expenses and provide scholarships for the Riders jailed in Mississippi. He knew it was not enough.

In a testy telephone exchange with Robert Kennedy, who continued to demand an end to the Rides and particularly the "jail, not bail" policy, King repeatedly justified the Rides and the students' acceptance of imprisonment. African-Americans, King pointed out, "must use their lives and bodies to right a wrong. Our conscience tells us that the law is wrong and we must resist, but we have a moral obligation to accept the penalty." This struck the attorney general as blackmail. "The fact that they stay in jail," Kennedy snapped, "is not going to have the slightest effect on me," and he demanded that King cease making "statements that sound like a threat."

"It's difficult," King responded, "to understand the position of an oppressed people." He hoped Kennedy understood that nonviolent protest was the best way to prevent communism or black supremacy. "It can save the soul of America. You must understand that we've made no gains without pressure and I hope that pressure will always be moral, legal, and peaceful." Making clear that African-Americans— especially he—had changed, King concluded, "I am different from my father. I feel the need of being free now!"

Undeterred, Robert Kennedy swayed some of the nation's major newspapers to denounce the continuation of the Freedom Rides; by June public opinion polls indicated that two thirds of Americans disapproved of them. In vain, King authored an article in *The New York Times Magazine* explaining the Rides, and the Riders' "extraordinary willingness to fill the jails as if they were honors classes." In closing, he wrote, "It was time for all America" to join the students in a campaign to "end Jim Crow now."

King himself would do so in mid-December 1961, when he received an urgent call from Dr. William G. Anderson, a young osteopath, to "come and join the Albany Movement." The Albany campaign had begun earlier that year when two SNCC field-workers, Cordell Reagon and Charles Sherrod, arrived in Albany, Georgia, to establish a voter registration drive. The movement then coalesced into an amalgam of African-American groups struggling to desegregate the city's interstate transportation facilities and end police brutality, as well as to integrate its libraries, medical facilities, and parks, and end the exclusion of African-Americans from juries and voting booths. The protest campaign surpassed the Montgomery bus boycott, the sit-ins, and the Freedom Rides in both the range and scale of participation. Risking arrest, Albany blacks engaged in massive, audacious demonstrations. But nothing worked. The protest faltered.

Hundreds of African-Americans languished in jail, in deplorable conditions. Fifty-four young black women were crammed into a cell built for six; others foundered in animal holding pens. Against the strenuous objections of the SNCC volunteers, who were leery of King turning it from a local people's movement into a leader's event, Anderson pleaded for whatever aid he could offer—even if only to come and "just speak for us one night." King agreed to do so.

The following night, December 15, King, Abernathy, and Walker flew into Albany, the state's fifth largest city. Once the heart of Georgia's cotton kingdom and now the center of its peanut industry, the former slave-trading city's lunch counters, hospitals, libraries, parks, and bus and railway stations remained rigidly segregated. "In the year 1961," reported Howard Zinn for the Southern Regional Council, "a Negro arrived in Albany on the colored part of the bus, entered a colored waiting room, drank from a colored water fountain, used a colored restroom, walked eight blocks to find a restaurant which would feed him, and traveled six miles to find a good Negro motel." Albany's entire justice system was white, and there was not a single black official in the over 40 percent African-American city.

As the nearly thirty-three-year-old Martin King prepared to speak, the fervor of the call-and-response singing of "Oh Freedom" from the wide-gabled Shiloh Baptist Church, and Mount Zion across Whitney Avenue, mesmerized him; the passionate clapping and singing of people packed to the rafters engulfed him. "Integration is on its way / Singing glory hallelujah / I'm so glad." Making his way through the sanctuary, the preacher found himself transfixed by the ever louder shouts: "Free-DOM, Free-DOM." "Everybody say freedom. Everybody say freedom. FREEDOM!" "Martin King says FREE-DOM! FREE-DOM FREE-DOM!"

He felt their yearning as the women in the pews responded to their children singing "Ain't Gonna Let Nobody Turn Me 'Round," then "Woke Up This Morning with My Mind Set on Freedom," then "Over My Head I See Freedom in the Air." "Hallelu, hallelu" rang out as King stepped to the pulpit, and then it abruptly stopped. "The sudden quiet," observed an enraptured reporter, "as full of meaning as the great cry of the song."

The fifteen hundred crammed into the two churches strained to hear King begin in his usual sonorous manner, linking the civil rights movement to the decolonization struggles in Africa. Gradually, his pace quickened. *"They can put you in a dungeon and transform you to glory. If they try to kill you, develop a willingness to die."* [ALL RIGHT.] His voice rose: *"Say to whites, 'We will win you with the power of our capacity to endure.'"* [NOW!] [FREEDOM!]

As an old man shouting "God Almighty!" punctuated his remarks, King ratcheted up the fervor of the congregation. *"How long will we have to suffer injustice?* [GOD ALMIGHTY!] *Not long, because the moral arc of the universe bends toward justice. How long? Not long! Because . . .* [GOD ALMIGHTY!] *How long will justice be crucified and truth buried?"* [GOD ALMIGHTY!] The stomping feet forced King to pause. *"Before the victory is won, some must face physical death to free their children from a life of psychological handicaps. But we shall overcome."*

"Shall overcome," both churches resounded, "shall overcome, shall overcome, shall overcome." One with his audience, King waved his arm. *"Don't stop now. Keep moving.* [IT'S TIME.] *Walk together, children.* [NOW.] *Don't you get weary?* [YES, YES.] *There's a great camp meeting coming . . ."* He looked down and stopped abruptly. The first words of "We Shall Overcome" rose from the pews. Soon the church itself seemed to sway.

The soul force of his people awed him as it never had. Anderson quickly called for a mass march the next day. "Be back in the morning at nine o'clock and bring your marching shoes, and Dr. King is going to march with us. Dr. King will lead us, won't you, Dr. King?" King nodded assent. He had vowed not to get involved, yet, so moved by the emotion in the church, so swept by the passion of Albany's blacks, he would walk with them.

The next day he told the waiting folk at Shiloh Baptist Church, "Hundreds of our brothers and sisters, sons and daughters, are in jail. We will not rest until they are released." King then led nearly 250 Albany blacks to the bus station, where police and paddy wagons blocked their path. "Do you have a written permit to parade or demonstrate?" Police Chief Laurie Pritchett challenged the marchers. Just going to city hall to pray, King responded; surely that did not require a permit. The genial-looking Pritchett had all the marchers arrested and herded off to jail.

"I have refused to post bond," King announced. "If I am convicted of this charge, I will refuse to pay the fine. I expect to spend Christmas in jail, and I hope that thousands will join me." Abernathy made bail in order to go back to Atlanta to raise money for a major protest effort, and Walker announced that the SCLC would commit its "total resources" to the Albany campaign. But as King discovered, the Albany movement had little of the cohesion and united community support he had enjoyed in Montgomery. Many of the black professionals and preachers in Albany preferred their bourgeois comforts and happiness in the hereafter to struggling now for desegregation. Others fretted that bail requirements would bankrupt them and resented "outsiders" coming in to settle their affairs. Some even agreed to be informants for Chief Pritchett. Still others, fearing that protest would worsen the racial situation, favored the NAACP's litigation approach. Yet the local NAACP would do nothing to help unless it ran the show. Similarly, SNCC fumed at the prospect of King reaping the harvest of the seeds it had planted. "We were working here long before De Lawd showed up to pull miracles," SNCC's Charles Jones commented. It would not play John the Baptist to King the Messiah.

Two days after the mass jailing, some Albany blacks met independently with Pritchett and agreed to suspend the protests in return for the release on bond of the jailed protesters, the desegregation of the bus and train terminals, and the creation of a biracial committee to work out further desegregation arrangements. A somewhat befuddled King allowed himself to be bailed out, lamely saying, "I would not want to stand in the way of any meaningful negotiations." The City Commission, however, immediately denied any agreement, claimed victory over the "outside agitators," and refused to discuss so-called Negro demands.

The movement had not made a single gain. The national press reported it as "a devastating loss of face" for King, "a stunning defeat." "I'm sorry I was bailed out," he later maintained. "I didn't understand at the time what was happening. We thought the victory had been won. When we got out, we discovered it was all a hoax. We had lost an initiative that we never regained." A disconsolate King returned to Atlanta.

After months of delay, in early July 1962 an Albany court ordered King to pay a fine of $178 or spend forty-five days in jail. Still embarrassed by having been bailed out, King chose to go to jail, terming his act a moral protest. He hoped it would restore his reputation, revitalize the fading Albany movement, and spur federal intervention. Within a week, however, an "unidentified, well-dressed Negro man" paid his fine. Pritchett had outfoxed him again. The police chief would not allow King to stay in jail and gain national sympathy and support.

But an evolving King resolved to stay in Albany and fight. The sit-ins and Freedom Rides had changed him. Using all the lessons he had learned since the Montgomery bus boycott, King tried to match the militancy that SNCC and CORE had injected into the struggle. More than his reputation was at stake; the very idea of nonviolent resistance was on the line. Seeking across-the-board desegregation of all public facilities, King vowed to "fill up the jails" and "turn Albany upside down."

Exhorting his followers with missionary zeal, King sent daily forays into white Albany, demanding service at lunch counters, libraries, parks, and movie theaters. But the canny Pritchett had done his homework. Having read King's *Stride Toward Freedom* and Gandhi's essays, he understood the dynamics of political theater. The police chief overcame Gandhian nonviolent protest with nonviolent law enforcement. He recognized that nonviolent civil disobedience worked when protesters incited white racist violence, creating local crises that forced federal intervention. So Pritchett repeatedly lectured his police and showed them films on how to handle the protesters. There would be no public use of clubs, police dogs, or fire hoses to break up demonstrations. Instead, each wave of protesters was quickly arrested and dispatched to jails in surrounding counties. The movement ran out of recruits before Pritchett ran out of jails. His public restraint—"killin' 'em with kindness"—denied the movement the outrage necessary to attract sympathetic publicity.

Adding to King's woes, on July 20 an ardent segregationist judge appointed by Kennedy to the United States District Court handed down a temporary injunction banning protest marches in Albany. It specifically enjoined King and his aides not to lead any demonstrations "designed to provoke breaches of the peace." What to do? Robert Kennedy cautioned King that if he disobeyed a federal court order, he would be the same as the white supremacists who disobeyed federal desegregation rulings, and that he would undercut the movement's ability to appeal to federal authority.

King could not disagree, although he considered the injunction both unjust and unconstitutional. He needed the national government as an ally in the struggle against intransigent white segregationist local officials. "The federal courts have given us our greatest victories," he noted, "and I cannot, in good conscience, declare war on them." He would work to get the injunction dissolved by a higher court. But, infuriating SNCC, he added that he would not defy a federal court order. SNCC responded that if King allowed the order to stop the movement, other racist judges would employ the same tactic and rob the movement of its principal resource: the right to protest. Although apologetic, King stood firm, which led SNCC's young militants to blast him as a bourgeois coward, accuse him of preoccupation with his own fame, and belittle him as a Bible-thumping anachronism.

On July 24 the Fifth Circuit Court of Appeals overruled the injunction, and King promised to lead a mass march the next day. That night some two thousand angry Albany blacks took to the streets, throwing stones and bottles at the police. When Pritchett said to reporters, laughing, "You see them nonviolent rocks?," an embarrassed King suspended demonstrations for a "day of penance." Just as Gandhi had done after the Punjab melee in 1919, King would postpone civil disobedience until nonviolent discipline could be restored.

He visited the bars and pool halls in Albany's toughest slum, urging the sullen men not to be violent: "I know if you do this, we are destined to win."

But not many, especially SNCC's field-workers, agreed. Believing that King had no right to imply African-Americans had committed a wrong, SNCC considered a day of penance demeaning. Some wanted no further part in the campaign of nonviolent resistance.

"It took Gandhi forty years to achieve independence," King noted ruefully. "We can't expect miracles here in Albany." Yet many African-Americans, expecting him to bring freedom to Albany "here and now," stopped attending the mass meetings, much less volunteering to go to jail. Making a last-ditch effort to keep the movement together and renew its fervor, King led a small demonstration in front of Albany's city hall on July 27, deliberately getting himself imprisoned for the third time. Also for the third time, the city suspended his sentence and threw him out of jail.

The Albany movement had been crushed. Looking for a way out, King rationalized that he was leaving Albany to remove any impediments to good-faith negotiations that would not otherwise occur. As in the past, city authorities had no intention of desegregating Albany's public facilities. They remained as closed to African-Americans in late 1962 as they had been in 1960. "Albany," crowed Police Chief Pritchett, "is just as segregated as ever."

King and the SCLC tried to put the best public face on their despair. They claimed Albany had been the most massive protest movement to date, proving that large numbers of African-Americans in the Deep South could be mobilized to engage in nonviolent civil disobedience and that ordinary folks, not just students, would go to jail by the thousands to overturn segregation. The most important thing, said King, "is what has happened to the Negro . . . He has gained a new respect for himself. He believes in himself." The experience of confronting the evil that had for so long oppressed them, King alleged, had liberated Albany's blacks psychologically. "Negroes have straightened their backs in Albany, and once a man straightens his back you can't ride him anymore." King heralded "the new Negro" with "a new sense of dignity and destiny" and "a determination to struggle and sacrifice until the walls of injustice crumble."

Nevertheless, the national press took King to task for failing to end "a single racial barrier" in Albany. *Time* stated that King's efforts in the past five years had "drained him of the captivating fervor that made him famous." Albany, an NAACP official stressed, "was successful only if the goal was to go to jail." The SNCC field-workers who remained in Albany grumbled about King's grandstanding and then his retreat from town when the movement lagged. Others declared nonviolence dead. "Albany, by any standard," wrote Lerone Bennett, Jr., "was a staggering defeat for King and the Freedom Movement." Even Wyatt Walker admitted that in Albany "one of the largest of the desegregation struggles was effectively broken and the entire desegregation movement faltered." At best, it provided valuable instructions for the future.

The lessons learned by the SCLC echoed a *New York Times* analysis in August 1962 that identified four major reasons for the failure in Albany. Pritchett's skillful opposition came first. He had shrewdly outmaneuvered King in the public relations battle. "A cunning man," as John Lewis of SNCC accurately described him, "as deceitful as he had to be," Pritchett had restrained his forces, had not allowed King to stay in jail, and had denied the press the brutality that had made headlines and created sympathy for the movement. Next came the unity of white segregationists. Albany's white establishment—convinced that if it surrendered an inch, blacks would demand a foot and then a yard— had arranged bail for King, concocted bogus truces, provided suspended sentences when they suited its purposes, and made oral agreements that could be easily broken. Each stratagem destroyed the momentum of the movement. The white establishment used the wealthier African-Americans who belonged to the Criterion Club and those middle-class blacks who owned the gas stations and small farms—eager not to lose their favored status and their connections with prominent whites—to question King's tactics and besmirch his reputation.

"There are Negroes who will never fight for freedom," King sadly surmised. "There are even some Negroes who will cooperate with their oppressors. The hammer blows of discrimination, poverty and segregation must warp and corrupt some. No one can pretend that because a people may be oppressed, every individual member is virtuous and worthy."

Whites also received untold assistance from the NAACP and

SNCC, both eager to tear King down to build themselves up. Determined to maintain its preeminence, the NAACP had instructed its Albany local to ignore SCLC's efforts to maintain a united front. Equally concerned with its own identity, SNCC had fumed at its exclusion from strategy sessions and press conferences. "I don't think that anybody appreciates going to jail, getting their balls busted day in and day out, and then you don't even get to speak on it," complained eighteen-year-old Cordell Reagon. SNCC field-workers encouraged local leaders to get rid of the SCLC, asserting that the Albany movement needed no "outside help." They had slammed King for being too conciliatory, for not staying in jail, for camera hogging.

SNCC's Julian Bond dismissed King as "a very simple man" who somehow "sold the concept that one man will come to your town and save you." King, according to Bond, "has been losing since he left Montgomery. He lost when he didn't go on the Freedom Rides when the students begged him to . . . He has been losing for a long time. And I think eventually that more Negroes and more white Americans will become disillusioned with him, and find that he after all is only another preacher who can talk well." Some in "Snick" took to calling King "Slick."

Miscalculations and mistakes by both SCLC and local black leaders also weighed heavily. Albany African-Americans wrongly escalated their demands in December 1961, expecting city authorities to give up when King arrived, and then, panicked over reports of jail conditions, sought an agreement at any cost. SCLC's Andrew Young recalled, "There wasn't any real strategy." He blamed the failure on a lack of readiness. "It was totally unplanned and we were totally unprepared. It was a miscalculation on the part of a number of people that a spontaneous appearance by Martin Luther King could bring change." Coretta Scott King thought her husband's acceptance of the injunction against demonstrating was "the factor that broke the backbone of the movement."

King pointed to the overly broad list of grievances and demands: ending black disfranchisement and police brutality; desegregating all transportation facilities and other public accommodations; and instituting a system of fair employment in Albany. The ultimatum demanding total white capitulation had backfired. "I think it would have been better to concentrate on one area," he said. It had been a mistake to protest against "segregation generally rather than a single and distinct facet of it." Direct action worked better when concentrated on a single aspect of racism, and one specific objective would have allowed the national media more effective communication of the plight of Albany blacks. "Our protest was so vague," King admitted, "that we got nothing, and the people were left very depressed and in despair." For the first time in the movement, victory had depended on large numbers of adult blacks willing to confront police and court arrest over an extended period of time. Moreover, King presumed, "We made a mistake in attacking the political power structure instead of the economic power structure. You don't win against a political power structure where you don't have the votes. But you can win against an economic structure when you have the economic power to make the difference between profit and loss."

In no small part, all the other causes of failure related to the unwillingness of the Kennedy administration to get involved. Still annoyed by the Freedom Rides, the Kennedy brothers adopted a hands-off policy throughout the Albany campaign. They maintained that a resolution would have to come from an agreement worked out by local black and white leaders.

The administration's preference for public order over racial justice incensed King. He was especially enraged that Robert Kennedy had telephoned Albany's mayor in December 1961 to congratulate him on how the "orderly manner" of arrests had maintained "peace." Although only federal intervention could have tipped the scales in the movement's favor, the Kennedys refused to become entangled in Albany as long as only a minimum amount of savagery occurred. The moral for King accentuated the lessons of the Freedom Rides: Only barbarity and disorder forced a federal response. Next time he would create a clash that would provoke blatant white violence and compel the Kennedy administration to act.

King also believed the Justice Department had acquiesced when the FBI sided with Albany segregationists. While quick to investigate African-Americans for possible wrongdoing, FBI agents in Albany looked the other way at violence by white law officers. They repeatedly ignored complaints by blacks about violations of their civil rights. "One of the greatest problems we face with the FBI in the South,"

King charged publicly, "is that the agents are white southerners who have been influenced by the mores of their community. To maintain their status, they have to be friendly with the local police and people who are promoting segregation. Every time I saw FBI men in Albany, they were with the local police force."

When J. Edgar Hoover read King's criticisms—particularly his accusation that "if the FBI were integrated, many persons who now defy federal law might come under restraints from which they are presently free"—the FBI director redoubled his effort to expose and destroy the "subversive" African-American preacher whom he personally detested and referred to as the "burrhead." Determined to discredit the civil rights movement by proving it Communist-dominated, Hoover had already begun to send memos warning Robert Kennedy that a top "known" Communist, Stanley Levison, was the number one adviser to King. Implying that King was either a Communist himself or a dupe being manipulated by Levison at the behest of the Soviet Union, Hoover persuaded the attorney general to authorize an FBI wiretap on Levison's phone. Robert Kennedy also urged members of the Justice Department who were personally acquainted with King to warn the civil rights leader to end his relationships with Levison and Jack O'Dell, the man Levison had recommended to run SCLC's New York office.

King turned a deaf ear to vague allegations about his associates, much as he had refused earlier to countenance the whisperings against Bayard Rustin. This intensified Hoover's obsession, and King's name was added to Section A of the Reserve Index, a list of dangerous people to be rounded up in a national emergency.

Unaware of Hoover's machinations, King and his aides met at a retreat in Dorchester, Georgia, in early January 1963. The defeat in Albany weighed heavily upon King. It had brought into the open criticism of his leadership and disillusionment with nonviolent protest. He ached to prove "you can struggle without hating, you can fight without violence." Beset by adversaries and rivals, Martin Luther King, Jr., craved a momentous victory in the freedom struggle now—in 1963, the year of the hundredth anniversary of the Emancipation Proclamation.

4

CONFRONTING THE

CONSCIENCE OF AMERICA,

1963

Tokenism is a palliative which relieves emotional distress, but leaves the disease and its ravages unaffected. It tends to demobilize and relax the militant spirit which alone drives us forward to real change.

To achieve a daring, dramatic victory in the anniversary year of the Emancipation Proclamation, King and his SCLC associates planned a protest campaign in Birmingham, Alabama, "the largest city of a police state," and "the most thoroughly segregated city in America." Its hotels, parks, playgrounds, restaurants, swimming pools, theaters, even elevators were separated by race. It had neither black policemen nor black firemen and nary a black clerk in a white-owned shop. Even laundry trucks with signs WE WASH FOR WHITE PEOPLE ONLY plied the city streets. "If we could crack that city," SCLC executive director Wyatt Walker claimed, "then we could crack any city." As Birmingham went, "so would go the South."

SCLC counted on the Birmingham protest to be different from the one in Albany. For one thing, King would be fully in charge. There would be no jockeying with SNCC or local organizations for control; there would be no divided leadership. Having been little more than a man of oratory for nearly half a decade, King would boldly act, not just react.

A newly reconstituted inner circle would bolster his resolve and augment Wyatt Walker's knack for organizing and direct action. It included C. T. Vivian, a spirited protégé of James Lawson, who had come from jail in Mississippi to be the director of SCLC affiliates; Washington bureau director Walter Fauntroy; the brawling "hatchet man" Hosea Williams, a grassroots organizer committed to direct action, nonviolent or not; the impulsive "Prophet," James Bevel, a true believer in Gandhian nonviolence who advocated mass civil disobedience; and from New Orleans, the suave Andrew Young as chief negotiator. Although King ultimately "called the shots," Andy Young recalled, SCLC was like "a jazz combo" in which each aide had "a chance to solo." They were backed by a well-orchestrated SCLC staff that had grown from five in 1960 to sixty in 1963.

King depended in Birmingham on the indomitable, uncompromising Reverend Fred L. Shuttlesworth, who had been beaten, bombed, dynamited, stabbed, and jailed, yet continued to fight. The wiry evangelist's Alabama Christian Movement for Human Rights— founded in 1956 in response to a state injunction outlawing the NAACP and the strongest of the eighty-five SCLC local affiliates— epitomized the activist infrastructure already in place in Birmingham. Though Walker admitted that "we bit off more than we could chew" in Albany, SCLC would not scatter its efforts in Birmingham. It would focus on desegregating the downtown department stores. King did not want another overambitious assault against all of the city's racism. He chose not to make demands on city officials, who depended on the overwhelmingly white electorate, but rather on downtown businessmen, whose profits rested on the buying power of the 40 percent of Birmingham's population of 340,000 that was African-American.

To gain its coveted victory, SCLC intended to provoke. "To take a moderate approach hoping to get white help doesn't help," Walker explained. "They nail you to the cross, and it saps the enthusiasm of the followers. You've got to have a crisis." That, and only that, "forces a resolution of the dilemma."

The U.S. Commission on Civil Rights had predicted that Birmingham's racial situation could "be expected to unleash acts of violence." A reporter for The New York Times had described the city as a racist tyranny, the paralyzing fear of African-Americans reinforced daily "by the whip, the razor, the gun, the bomb, the torch, the club, the knife, the mob, the police and many branches of the state's apparatus." The "Pittsburgh of the South" had no antebellum past, no tradition of civility, and lacked even the pretense of paternalism. The city banned the Metropolitan Opera from visiting Birmingham for performing only before unsegregated audiences; it confined most African-Americans to menial jobs; and it allowed only an insignificant number of blacks to vote.

As Birmingham was home to some of the most violent Klan and Citizens' Council groups in the country, civil rights activists considered it their most dangerous city. They dubbed it "Bombingham" and "Old Burninghell" for the eighteen racial bombings and more than fifty cross burnings that occurred between 1957 and 1963. None had been prosecuted, largely because Eugene "Bull" Connor, the police commissioner who personified the injustice and intransigence of racism, prided himself on "keeping the niggers in their place." SCLC counted on Connor to respond viciously to any effort to end segregation. "We presumed that Bull would do something to help us," recalled Walker. We expected to "turn Bull into a steer." That would, in turn, force President Kennedy's hand—the key to fundamental change throughout Dixie.

Kennedy's first two years in the White House had brought the movement little but delay and tokenism. According to King, the president had reneged on his promise of a comprehensive civil rights bill and instead sought to appease the white South. He had appointed known segregationists to lifetime judgeships on the federal bench. He had refused to aid liberals in their effort to eliminate the filibuster— the chief tactic southern legislators counted on to doom civil rights legislation. He had delayed issuing his promised executive order to end racial discrimination in federally assisted housing for nearly two years, then he had issued a ruling without teeth. And when called upon by the Commission on Civil Rights to cut off federal funds to Mississippi until it complied with court orders to protect African-Americans from violence and discrimination, Kennedy had replied that it was beyond his powers.

As 1963 began, thirty-four African nations had freed themselves from colonial bondage, but more than two thousand school districts remained segregated in the South. At the current rate of progress, civil rights leaders moaned, it would be 2054 before school desegregation became a reality, and 2094 before blacks secured equality in job training and employment. Meanwhile, African-American children were half as likely to complete high school as whites; had one third as much chance of earning a college degree; were twice as likely to be unemployed; and had only half the earning power and seven fewer years of life than whites. Kennedy would have to be pushed, and pushed hard. That required a confrontation forcing the national conscience to recognize the injustice of racism, and obliging the Kennedy administration to intervene on behalf of civil rights for blacks. No longer did King think that nonviolence alone would convert the oppressor. Instead, he would conduct "Project C" — for confrontation.

Not wanting Bull Connor, a candidate for mayor, to capitalize on his presence, King delayed the Birmingham campaign until after the March 5 mayoralty election and the anticipated birth of his fourth child, Bernice Albertine, that month. Because none of the candidates won a majority, the runoff between Connor and Albert Boutwell stalled the start of Project C until April 3. Following Connor's defeat, King and his task force arrived in Birmingham that day and immediately issued a manifesto specifically demanding an end to segregation in the downtown stores; adoption of fair hiring practices by those stores; and the establishment of a biracial committee to pursue further desegregation. Demonstrations would commence despite the fact that Connor was challenging the legitimacy of the election in the courts and refusing to give up control over the city's police and firemen, which left Birmingham paralyzed by two contending city governments, each claiming authority.

That evening the first of what would become sixty-five consecutive nightly mass meetings commenced. They all began with spirited renditions of "Woke Up This Mornin' with My Mind Set on Freedom" and the other freedom songs that constituted the very soul of the movement. These songs "bound us together," King noted, articulating "our deepest groans and passionate yearnings." By ending "on a note of hope that God is going to help us work it out," they brought "forth a marvelous, sparkling, fluid optimism" no matter how dark the situation. "The massive Birmingham Movement Choir and the Albany

Freedom Singers took the power of movement music to a near-celestial level," John Lewis later wrote, "rocking the walls of the churches in which they and the people lifted their voices." King lifted his voice above all, vowing that he would lead an economic boycott and demonstrations against the downtown merchants until "Pharaoh lets God's people go."

The next morning a small group of protesters staged sit-ins at the segregated downtown lunch counters, which led to their anticipated arrests. Several days of even smaller protests followed. Most of Birmingham's black businessmen and middle class wanted no part of King's crusade, and because of professional jealousy, fear of potential violence, or "otherworldliness," just 10 percent of the city's black clergy supported the campaign. Emory O. Jackson, the editor of the city's Negro newspaper, the *Birmingham World*, belittled SCLC's tactics, denounced Shuttlesworth as irresponsible, and dismissed King as a "glossy personality." Both the black Masons and the Baptist Ministers' Conference urged him to leave town. King did his best to drum up support. But fear of arrest and loss of employment kept even African-American supporters from responding to King's call for demonstrators, and Connor kept his temper in check. "You've got to find some way to make Bull Connor tip his hand," King demanded of Walker.

"I haven't found the key yet," admitted Walker, but Connor helped him on Palm Sunday. The police chief intercepted some fifty African-Americans marching on city hall, led by Martin Luther King's brother Reverend A. D. King, and for the first time Connor displayed his K9 corps of snapping police dogs. As police arrested the marchers, a black man with a knife lunged at one of the dogs. The dog attacked, pinning the man to the ground, giving the press a front-page story. Discomforted by the national media attention, Birmingham officials on April 10 secured a state court injunction barring further racial demonstrations.

King had to decide between defying a court order and getting arrested or leaving for a previously scheduled speaking tour that would raise extremely needed funds to bail several hundred of Birmingham's black protesters out of jail. The movement had promised the protesters bail, yet King had announced he would march and be arrested. "If

you go to jail," an aide pleaded, "we are lost. The battle of Birmingham is lost. We need a lot of money. We need it now. You are the only
one who has the contacts to get it." Moreover, Daddy King added,
there was a good chance Martin would be murdered if he went to jail.
But if he did not go to jail—after his public pledge to do so—his leadership might be undone, and judges could shut down any future
protests with the stroke of a pen.

"I sat in the midst of the deepest quiet I have ever felt," King later
wrote, "alone in that crowded room."

Claiming he needed to pray alone, King closed himself into an ad-
joining room. A half hour later, he returned wearing a denim shirt
and jeans, to express his solidarity with working-class blacks and his
support of a boycott of buying new clothes at downtown department
stores. "I don't know what will happen. I don't know where the money
will come from, but I have to make a faith act.

"The path is clear to me," he said. "I've got to march."

The sputtering campaign needed a spark. Circumstances required
King to provide it by going to jail. His faith would enable him to act
with his body, not just his voice. As a matter of conviction, "I am going
to march if I have to march by myself. If we obey it, then we are out of
business." The score of men in the room, "almost as if there had been
some divine signal," King wrote, then linked hands and sang "We
Shall Overcome."

King's announcement that he would violate "this immoral injunction" on Good Friday intensified the national spotlight on Birmingham. On April 12 the young preacher led some fifty hymn-singing
volunteers along a route to city hall lined by nearly a thousand blacks
chanting, "Freedom has come to Birmingham!" There, in the focus of
dozens of newspaper photographers and television cameras, an infuriated Bull Connor, surrounded by snarling police dogs, arrested the
marchers. A detective lifted King by the back of his belt and threw
him into a paddy wagon.

Singled out, King disappeared into "the hole," sealed off from
other prisoners and the outside world. Alone in a filthy, windowless
cell with a rusty, seatless toilet and nothing more than a cot of metal
slats, he experienced "the longest, most frustrating and bewildering
hours I have ever lived . . . I was besieged with worry." He hated the

loneliness and craved seeing his newborn daughter. Held in solitary confinement, staring at the scurry of roaches, he was filled with dread. He later wrote of his terror, "You will never know the meaning of utter darkness until you have lain in such a dungeon."

After two days of isolation, a jailer slipped him a copy of the April 13 *Birmingham News*. Under the sole dim lightbulb, he read the headline WHITE CLERGYMEN URGE LOCAL NEGROES TO WITH-DRAW FROM DEMONSTRATIONS. Eight local religious leaders re-proved King and his "outsiders" for their "extremism" in provoking "unwise and untimely" civil disturbances, and they pleaded with Birmingham blacks to withdraw support from the protests. He already knew that *Time* had entitled its article on the campaign "Poorly Timed Protest." *Newsweek* had described him as an extremist. Even his good friend the evangelist Billy Graham urged him to "put the brakes on."

But King would not retreat. He had done so in the past. Now he would speak as the apostle Paul to defend his actions and rebuke his critics. "Seldom, if ever," he began to scribble on the newspaper, "do I pause to answer criticism of my work and ideas."

What he wrote became an eloquent essay justifying the aims and strategy of the civil rights struggle. It directly answered the many Americans who questioned the movement's tactics and who wanted African-Americans to be patient and law-abiding. King had previously thought of writing a letter from jail, as Paul of Tarsus had done—an epistle for a particular place and time that had universal meaning for all times and places—and he poured his passion onto the margins of the newspaper, then onto scraps of paper supplied by a black jail trusty, and finally, onto a pad left by his attorney, Clarence Jones. Four days later, Jones had managed to secretly remove from the jail twenty handwritten sheets for Walker to begin editing.

More than a million copies of King's "Letter from Birmingham Jail" would be distributed in churches across the country. *Liberation*, *The Christian Century*, and *The New Leader*, among other national periodicals, eventually reprinted it in its entirety; many publications featured major excerpts. It would later be the centerpiece of King's 1964 book, *Why We Can't Wait*. Widely quoted, the epistle became a potent weapon in the battle to convince mainstream America to ac-

cept nonviolent direct-action civil disobedience. It did so by depicting
the black protesters—rather than the forces of "law and order," or so-
called moderates—as the true disciples of the Judeo-Christian heritage, the true adherents of the "democratic American way."

King first refuted the charge of being an "outside agitator." He was
there because they had promised to help their affiliate if called upon,
he maintained; they were invited, and they were keeping their promise. They were there, moreover, because injustice was there. Like the
prophets of old, he insisted, he must respond to the call for aid. We're
all interrelated, King wrote, interconnected. *"Injustice anywhere is a
threat to justice everywhere."* No American is an outsider anywhere in
the United States. As a Christian and an American, he contended, he
had the duty to combat injustice wherever it existed.

He next explained how the white leaders of Birmingham had left
African-Americans no alternative but to demonstrate. He detailed the
refusals to negotiate and the broken promises of the city leaders, juxta-
posing them against a portrayal of the dismal plight of black Birmingham. Deplore the conditions that brought about the demonstrations,
he rebuked moderates, not the demonstrations. Deal with the underlying causes, not the effects. *"Human progress never rolls in on wheels
of inevitability; it comes through the tireless efforts of men willing to be
co-workers with God, and without this hard work, time itself becomes an
ally of the forces of social stagnation."*

King painstakingly described the steps blacks had taken to determine that injustice existed; seek to negotiate in good faith; practice
nonviolence; and engage in direct action to dramatize the issue in a
manner that opened the door to sincere negotiation. *"We have not
made a single gain in civil rights without determined legal and nonviolent pressure,"* he stated. *"Lamentably, it is an historical fact that privileged groups seldom give up their privileges voluntarily . . .*

*"We know through painful experience that freedom is never volun-
tarily given by the oppressor; it must be demanded by the oppressed."*
Something had to be done, he reasoned, something to break the crust
of indifference that enabled white America to ignore such injustice.
Something had to be done to create a crisis so that Birmingham could
no longer evade a solution.

To those who asked African-Americans to wait, King retorted that "wait" generally meant "never." He had never *"yet engaged in a direct action movement that was 'well timed' according to the time-table of those who have not suffered unduly from the disease of segrega-tion."* African-Americans had waited 340 years for their constitutional and God-given rights. While nations of Asia and Africa moved with jetlike speed in gaining independence, King avowed, *"we still creep at horse-and-buggy pace toward gaining a cup of coffee at a lunch counter."*

> *Perhaps it is easy for those who have never felt the stinging darts of segregation to say, "Wait." But when you have seen vicious mobs lynch your mothers and fathers at will and drown your sis-ters and brothers at whim, when you have seen hate-filled police-men curse, kick, and even kill your black brothers and sisters; when you see the vast majority of your twenty million Negro brothers smothering in an airtight cage of poverty in the midst of an affluent society; when you suddenly find your tongue twisted and your speech stammering as you seek to explain to your six-year-old daughter why she can't go to the public amusement park that has just been advertised on television, and see tears welling up in her eyes when she is told that Funtown is closed to colored children, and see ominous clouds of inferiority beginning to form in her little mental sky, and see her begin to distort her little per-sonality by developing an unconscious bitterness toward white people; when you have to concoct an answer for a five-year-old son who is asking: "Daddy, why do white people treat colored people so mean?"; when you take a cross-country drive and find it necessary to sleep night after night in the uncomfortable corners of your automobile because no motel will accept you; when you are humiliated day in and day out by nagging signs reading "white" and "colored"; when your first name becomes "Nigger," your middle name becomes "Boy" (however old you are), and your last name becomes "John," and your wife and mother are never given the respected title of "Mrs."; when you are harried by day and haunted by night by the fact that you are a Negro, living con-stantly at tiptoe stance, never quite knowing what to expect next, and are plagued with inner fears and outer resentments; when*

you are forever fighting a degenerate sense of "nobodiness"—
then you will understand why we find it difficult to wait.

Connecting the civil disobedience of African-Americans to that practiced by the early Christians and the patriots at the Boston Tea Party, King presented his most systematic justification for protest demonstrations that broke the law. He defined a just law as a human code that conformed to the moral law or law of God, one that was rooted in eternal and natural law, one that uplifted the human personality. Conversely, an unjust law countered moral law; it degraded human personality, *"relegating persons to the status of things."*

Still fond of quoting prominent others, King adduced Saint Augustine "that 'an unjust law' is no law at all"; he cited Saint Aquinas on the primacy of natural law over man-made law; and he summoned Martin Luther for the word of God taking precedence over that of worldly princes. He pointed to Socrates' willingness to die rather than surrender "his unswerving commitment to truth," and he hailed the Constitution for affirming the "right to protest for right."

In sum, segregation that distorted the soul and damaged the personality was unjust; and it was right to disobey laws that were unjust as long as one did *"so openly, lovingly, and with a willingness to accept the penalty."* By engaging in civil disobedience and accepting imprisonment *"in order to arouse the conscience of the community over its injustice,"* you were *"expressing the highest respect for law."* Reminding his fellow ministers that the statutes of Hitler had been "legal," he highlighted the undemocratic nature of the segregation ordinances by pointing to the exclusion of blacks from the political process responsible for these state and local laws.

To those still unwilling to accept nonviolent civil disobedience as a just and necessary tactic, King underlined the alternative to his peaceful protests: *"Millions of Negroes, out of frustration and despair, will seek solace and security in black nationalist ideologies, a development that will lead inevitably to a frightening racial nightmare."* In other words, if not King and his interracial Christian followers, it would be Malcolm X and his Black Muslims. By 1963 Malcolm X—who mocked nonviolence, scorned integration, and insisted, "Our enemy is the white man"—had gained significant numbers of converts and far more sympathizers. King held the threat of black violence over the head of white America if it did not choose to follow him down the nonviolent path to ending racial discrimination and segregation. It would hardly be the last time that King promoted himself and his way as the alternative to the Black Muslims and black nationalism, or depicted his "middle way" as the only responsible, sound strategy.

Last, King scorched the gradualist approach to racial justice, which he saw as unjust procrastination. "*I have almost reached the regrettable conclusion that the Negro's greatest stumbling block is not the White Citizen Council-er or the Ku Klux Klanner, but the white moderate who is more devoted to 'order' than to justice.*" It was wrong "*to use moral means to preserve immoral ends.*" Instead, he wished that the moderates had commended the "*demonstrators of Birmingham for their sublime courage, their willingness to suffer and their amazing discipline in the midst of the most inhuman provocation.*" One day, he hoped, the South would recognize the nation's true heroes. They would be the nonviolent black protesters who rose up with dignity and refused to ride the segregated buses; who faced the jeering, hostile mobs; who willingly went to jail for conscience's sake.

"*One day the South will know that when these disinherited children of God sat down at lunch counters they were in reality standing up for the best in the American dream and the most sacred values in our Judeo-Christian heritage, and thus carrying our whole nation back to great wells of democracy which were dug deep by the founding fathers in the formulation of the Constitution and the Declaration of Independence.*" Imagining centuries of racial injustice remedied by nonviolent protest, King concluded with a vision of two societies fused into one, of the American melting pot fully realized. One day, he hoped, "*the dark clouds of racial prejudice will soon pass away and the deep fog of misunderstanding will be lifted from our fear-drenched communities, and in some not too distant tomorrow the radiant stars of love and brotherhood will shine over our great nation with all their scintillating beauty.*"

One could hardly imagine a more eloquent statement of King's goals, methods, and philosophy of nonviolence. A literary masterpiece, perhaps his one piece of writing that matched his oratory, "Letter from Birmingham Jail" made the achievement of civil rights for African-Americans essential to the fulfillment of America's highest ideals.

But it did not quickly become acclaimed, and it did not have any

effect in Birmingham. After nine days in jail, King agreed to be released on bail. A small, despondent crowd greeted him at the mass
meeting that night, and few attended the subsequent meetings. Although King's friend Harry Belafonte, the popular singer, had so-
licited some $50,000 for bail money, the numbers of prospective
protesters had dwindled to a trickle. The movement ran out of steam.

The African-American community in Birmingham proved no
more united than the one in Albany. Many of the more moderate,
middle-class blacks considered Shuttlesworth a dangerous firebrand or
loathed the religiosity of the protest movement. Many disagreed with
the use of direct action, preferring the NAACP's approach. Many dis-
liked the fact that King had come to Birmingham just as the city was
on the verge of getting rid of Bull Connor. In addition, more than a
few African-Americans in this tough town had no faith in nonviolence. "We had run out of troops," Walker recalled. "We had scraped
the bottom of the barrel of adults who could go." But King refused to
quit. "We've got to get going," he exhorted his aides. "The press is losing interest. We've got to do something to get their attention again."

To that end, the eccentric James Bevel hit upon the idea of using
high school students in demonstrations. A veteran of the sit-ins and
Freedom Rides who had spent two years organizing at the grassroots
level in Mississippi before joining SCLC, the impetuous twenty-six-
year-old Bevel, his shaved head topped by a skullcap or yarmulke to
express his affection for the Hebrew prophets, first had to convince the
skeptical Walker. A boy from high school, Bevel explained, "can get
the same effect in terms of being in jail, in terms of putting the pressure on the city, as his father—and yet there is no economic threat on
the family because the father is still in his job." Unlike their parents,
the students were free to fill the jails. They had no mortgage, no job to
lose, no children of their own. Gradually won over, Walker then convinced King, who, after vacillating, announced himself in favor of the
action that might turn an apparently hopeless cause into a victory.
The increasingly resolute King complimented Bevel on his "inspiration" and allowed the irrepressible minister to announce the special
march of high school students on Birmingham's D-day.

Bevel convinced the black DJs on Birmingham's radio stations,
local idols, to inspire their young fans to attend workshops and rallies

and to participate in the mass protests. On May 2 an astonished television audience watched more than a thousand black children, some just six years old, scamper out of Sixteenth Street Baptist Church to demonstrate and be arrested. In front of the news cameras, the young African-Americans sang freedom songs, chanted movement slogans, and knelt to pray as the police corralled them. They offered no resistance to Connor's surprised forces; instead, they clapped, danced, skipped, and laughed to the patrol wagons waiting to take them to prison. Hundreds of boys packed the city and county jails. Nearly as many girls were penned like livestock in the state fairgrounds.

Criticism of King and the "children's crusade" poured in from every quarter. Parents anguished about the safety of their kids. Conservatives denounced the tactic as exploitative. Radicals demeaned it as unmanly. "Real men," objected Malcolm X, "don't put their children on the firing line." Robert Kennedy seconded Malcolm X: "An injured, maimed, or dead child is a price that none of us can afford to pay."

Standing firm, the preacher retorted that the children had gained a "sense of their own stake in freedom and justice" by demonstrating. They had developed a heightened pride in their race and belief in their capacity to influence their future. King demanded of his critics: Where had this concern for black children suddenly come from? Where had it been for the previous two hundred years? Who had spoken up for the children born into slavery, who later had to live in ghettos of utter poverty, ignored by schools and social services, treated as less than human from the day they came into this world? Thursday evening another thousand children packed the cavernous Sixteenth Street Baptist Church to shout their approval of King's promise: "Today was D-day, tomorrow will be Double-D-day."

"There was an ugly overtone to the events today that was not present yesterday," the New York Times account of the May 3 demonstrations characteristically understated. To this point Connor had managed to copy the restraint of Pritchett, whom he had hired as a consultant. But with the jails full and the courts paralyzed, Connor had to stop the protesters, not keep arresting them. Observing the hundreds of students gathering at the church to demonstrate, the irascible Bull Connor abandoned restraint. He ordered his troops to bar the exits from the church, trapping about half of the young protesters inside.

Connor's forces then charged the young blacks who had run from the church into nearby Kelly Ingram Park. Swinging their nightsticks, the police beat both black demonstrators and onlookers. Attack dogs sank their fangs into three fleeing children. Horrified, enraged adults hurled bricks and bottles at the police.

"Let 'em have it," Connor commanded the firemen holding high-pressure hoses. With the sound of gunfire, jet streams of water roared from the nozzles, slamming African-Americans against buildings and relentlessly sweeping drenched children, like rag dolls, down slippery streets. The hundreds of pounds of pressure ripped the bark off trees and tore the clothes off screaming children, cutting through their skin and jerking their limbs weightlessly.

Then a group of policemen, each holding a German shepherd on a leash, stepped forward. All at once they released the snarling dogs to attack the young demonstrators and the neighborhood blacks who stood aside to watch. A widely published AP photograph showed a white policeman holding a black boy by the front of his shirt while a German shepherd sprang upward and buried its teeth in the boy's stomach. The photo immediately came to symbolize what was occurring in Birmingham. Those jailed that day brought the number of children arrested to some thirteen hundred. Because of them, King had, for the first time, followed the Gandhian principle: "Fill up the jails."

King had the confrontation he'd sought. On Saturday hundreds more students courted arrest, and thousands of adult blacks skirmished with police, pelting them with rocks. By then pictures and stories of the disorder in Birmingham had appeared on the front pages of newspapers everywhere. Television stations across the nation broadcast graphic, appalling scenes of police dogs lunging viciously at youthful demonstrators, of beefy police manhandling children not over seven or eight years old, of high-pressure hoses knocking girls and boys off their feet.

These images left an indelible memory on millions of viewers. They catalyzed a profound psychological revolution across black America, spurring unprecedented anger and resolve, and for most, terminating the ambivalence about King's leadership. The movement surged to life. It now took four churches to hold those attending the mass meetings. Those same images also aroused a surge of conscience, or guilt, in millions of previously indifferent whites.

King hoped that President Kennedy would now have to act. But the president continued to temporize. Though he admitted that the pictures of violence in Birmingham made him "sick," Kennedy claimed he had no legal authority to act in Birmingham. "I am not asking for patience," he went on. "I can well understand why the Negroes of Birmingham are tired of being asked to be patient." Yet he shrank from the prospect of using federal force to impose racial reforms. Worrying mostly about Birmingham's damage to America's international reputation, the president sought the quickest possible restoration of civil peace.

The legitimacy of African-American demands came in a distant second. Secretly, the president ordered Justice Department mediators to Birmingham to persuade the contending groups to negotiate a settlement. In addition, key administration officials began an intensive campaign to pressure Birmingham's most influential businessmen, the so-called Big Mules, to accept a compromise agreement.

Until the crisis ignited by the children's crusade, the Senior Citizens' Committee, covertly organized by the Birmingham Chamber of Commerce to deal with desegregation matters, had avoided even a hint of willingness to negotiate for over a month. Suddenly they wanted to talk. They felt the heat from Washington and feared that Birmingham was verging on a major bloodletting. The toll of the boycott by African-Americans mounted. Sales in April dropped by more than a third in the downtown stores, and May promised worse. Birmingham's economic elite began to negotiate in earnest on May 4, even agreeing to hold all-night sessions. The talks commenced, but neither side backed down. King ordered the demonstrations to resume.

At the mass meeting on Sunday evening, King compared the child protesters to "a young Jesus saying, 'I must be about my father's business.' These young people are about their father's business. And they are carving a tunnel of hope through the great mountain of despair." There were those who wrote history, he said to the students in attendance, but they were making it. "And you will make it possible for the historians of the future to write a marvelous chapter. Never in the history of this nation have so many people been arrested for the cause of freedom and human dignity." When the roars of approval subsided, he added, "You know, there are approximately twenty-five hundred people in jail right now," and he wanted more.

King got it. Monday, May 6, saw the most massive black protest yet. Flyers distributed outside of schools urged young blacks, "Fight for freedom first, then go to school. Join the thousands in jail who are making their witness for freedom . . . It's up to you to free our teachers, our parents, yourself and our country." Attendance in some schools plummeted nearly 90 percent. "When I say I'm going to fill up the jails," Bevel exulted, "I mean I'm going to fill up the jails."

The popular comedian Dick Gregory led the first group of demonstrators from the church. As the police hurried them into waiting paddy wagons, the students sang, "I ain't scared of your jail / 'Cause I want my freedom / Want my freedom / Want my freedom now." Another group being herded off to jail sang, "I ain't scared of your dogs / 'Cause I want . . ." Out spilled another: "I ain't scared of your hoses / 'Cause . . ." And yet another: "I ain't scared of no Bull / 'Cause I want my freedom / Want my freedom / Want my freedom now."

Twenty to fifty black students at a time defiantly offered themselves for arrest, and the huge crowd in the park roared its approval. Some took to singing their own ditty: "It isn't nice to go to jail / There are nicer ways to do it / But the nice ways always fail." By nightfall, more than twenty-five hundred black juveniles overflowed Birmingham's jails.

The audacity of the students and the public contempt heaped on him by their elders caused Connor to snap. After seizing more than a thousand young demonstrators, he turned his troops, shoving and kicking, on the crowd in the park. Once again, as the television cameras rolled and the photographers focused their lenses, police dogs leaped at the throats of taunting children, fire hoses bowled over rock-throwing adults, and Connor's minions clubbed black onlookers. *Life* magazine featured a double-page spread on the melee. The captured images looked like battle footage from a war.

Because of the media, especially television, Birmingham became a crisis that the entire country experienced. The contrast with the largely untelevised campaign in Albany could not have been sharper. TV cameras depicted the "shameful scenes" in Birmingham much more vividly than "any number of explanatory words," observed the president. Television proved its power to make history as well as record it. Never again would the importance of the media to the movement be in doubt.

A shocked nation demanded federal action, *now*, to stop the blood-bath. Kennedy's mediators pressed King to compromise on his demands for immediate desegregation and an end to discrimination in employment in the downtown stores. They cautioned him not to prolong the crisis in the expectation of intervention by federal troops. At the same time, administration officials pushed the city's business establishment to make concessions, not merely promises of future action, warning of the dire economic consequences of an all-out racial clash in Birmingham. But neither side budged. The talks went on, and so did the demonstrations.

On Tuesday, May 7, V-day, a larger number of students than ever before—and seemingly less disciplined—appeared on the streets. Rather than march from church and accept arrest, more than two thousand young blacks invaded downtown at noon. "There were square blocks of Negroes, a veritable sea of black faces," wrote King. Most of them staged sit-ins at restaurants or clogged the aisles of major stores. Others picketed. Some held pray-ins on the sidewalk. Several thousand adults paraded through the business section chanting, "We're marching for freedom!" and "The police can't stop us now. Even Bull Connor can't stop us now!"

Connor tried. With an armored police tank added to the arsenal, the police drove the marchers into the black ghetto, penning nearly four thousand in Kelly Ingram Park. Once more, high-pressure hoses were directed at the trapped African-Americans. A water cannon mounted on a tripod tore bricks loose from walls. The crowd shouted, gagged, screamed. SCLC aides circulating in the crowd pleaded for nonviolence. Few could even hear over the crashing water from the hoses, and those who could did not listen. The clash went on. Not until the crowd had been thoroughly dispersed did the German shepherds quit biting, the clubs stop crushing bones, and the hoses cease pummeling sprawled blacks along the sidewalks. Watching in despair, a reporter mumbled, "God bless America."

With Birmingham in upheaval, a secret emergency meeting of the Senior Citizens' Committee that Tuesday resolved to end the conflict. With the din of freedom chants in their ears as they lunched, the business leaders directed their negotiators to come to terms with the SCLC. They had calculated the business costs of Connor's stormtrooper tactics and agreed they must cease. A three-hour bargaining session, amid the premonition of a recurrence of violence, brought the two sides together on the desegregating of the downtown stores, the upgrading of black employment opportunities, and the creation of a biracial committee to resolve other racial matters. Although no accord was reached on dropping the charges against the twenty-five hundred arrested demonstrators, King decided that a final agreement was close enough to announce a one-day moratorium on protests. He did not want to risk further violence, and he placed a higher priority on a Kennedy commitment to a national civil rights bill than on scoring local points.

But the intensely dedicated Fred Shuttlesworth could not abide a compromise. He wanted King to rally mass-based support for still more demonstrations, to win an unconditional white surrender on the specific local demands. "Hell, no, we're not calling anything off, Martin," an infuriated Shuttlesworth erupted. "You know they said in Albany that you come in, get people excited and started, and you leave the town with sickness and death and lost jobs." Just out of the hospital and still on medication, having been battered by the high-pressure hoses, he raged, "But I live here, the people trust me, and I have the responsibility after SCLC is gone, and I'm telling you it will not be called off." He would not be mollified: "You're mister big, but you're going to be mister S-H-I-T. I'm sorry, but I cannot compromise my principles and the principles that we established." The forty-one-year-old minister insisted that he would rather "die in the streets" than accept King's terms.

Reasoning that further disorder would only play into the hands of die-hard segregationists who wanted no agreement whatsoever, King gradually convinced the overwrought Shuttlesworth to announce to the press, "The City of Birmingham has reached an accord with its conscience." The fitting rooms of the department stores would be desegregated immediately, to be followed, in phases, by lunch counters, water fountains, and restrooms; black salesclerks would be employed gradually; and a biracial committee would eventually work on up-grading and improving employment opportunities for Birmingham African-Americans. King backed down on the outright dismissal of all charges against the protesters and accepted a timetable for desegrega-tion in place of the stipulation that the changes take effect right away.

Although the token concessions may have been the best that SCLC could obtain at the time, King claimed "the most magnificent victory for justice we've ever seen in the Deep South." Addressing the final mass meeting, he credited the gains to the power of the move-ment: "These things would not have been granted without your pre-senting your bodies and your very lives before the dogs and the tanks and the water hoses of this city!"

Before returning to Atlanta, King again advocated reconciliation and brotherhood in Birmingham. But too many in the steel town, black and white, resisted both. The day after the announcement of the agreement, Connor and other Alabama politicians broadcast their de-nunciations of the biracial accord. They verbally assaulted the Senior Citizens' Committee, the Kennedy brothers, and King and the SCLC with equal venom. At nightfall, more than a thousand robed Klans-men gathered to hear further diatribes against the agreement. One speaker proclaimed, "Martin Luther King's epitaph can be written here in Birmingham." Shortly after, two dynamite bombs rocked the parsonage of A. D. King, Martin's younger brother, strewing glass and timber in every direction. Sullen neighbors milled about, muttering vows of vengeance. They threatened and jostled the police and fire department officers inspecting the rubble. The crowd grew quickly, and so did calls for retribution.

Then another bomb blasted a gaping hole in the Gaston Motel, King's and SCLC's headquarters in Birmingham. From the bars and pool halls in the ghetto, Birmingham's black underclass streamed into the streets. They pelted the police and firemen with stones and bot-tles. One officer was stabbed, and several others were assaulted. When King's aides asked that the people stop throwing rocks and go home, they responded, "Tell it to Bull Connor. This is what nonviolence gets you."

As more Saturday-night drinkers joined the rampaging mob, police reinforcements swarmed into the ghetto. Pandemonium reigned. Battles between the police and the crowd flared for several hours. White-owned stores were torched. Cars burned. An entire block blazed. "Let the whole fucking city burn," Walker heard a young black yell. "I don't give a good goddamn—this'll show those white motherfuckers!"

Parents of arrested children who had heard tales of brutality and mistreatment in the prisons, as well as others who had been so ground down by white oppression that they'd never countenanced King's preachments of nonviolence, felt emboldened to express their rancor. Young adult males in particular—the "desperate class" of school dropouts and unemployed, those who ignored the black church and were, in turn, ignored by it—seized the moment to flaunt their resentments. A few SCLC staffers struggled throughout the night to prevent greater carnage. Their dedication kept the surge of violence from becoming a deadly flood. Nevertheless, more than fifty blacks reported injuries, and *The Birmingham News* estimated property damage in the smoldering shambles at over $40,000.

King hurried back to Birmingham the next day to try to calm the ghetto and ensure that the accord held. He made the rounds of bars and pool halls, schools and churches. Stay on the nonviolent road to freedom, he beseeched over and again. "Don't stop," he urged. "Don't get weary. There is a great camp meeting coming." How long? Not long. "We shall overcome!" Remarkably, the furor subsided. City officials and business leaders began to implement the desegregation pact on schedule, and order returned to Birmingham.

But nearly a thousand protests convulsed more than a hundred towns and cities in the South that summer, leading to some twenty thousand arrests—over four times as many as in 1960. Despite falling short of SCLC's original demands, the Birmingham campaign exposed the vulnerability of the old regime and changed the "rules of the game" in race relations. The very audacity of taking on "Bull Connor's Johannesburg," the unprecedented "children's crusade," and the determination of black Birmingham to wage the struggle by whatever means they chose affected more African-Americans, more passionately, than any previous event. Whites could no longer assume the passivity of African-Americans. Of course, some blacks had always resisted, always been militant. Birmingham democratized that spirit, injecting the values once held by a few into the bloodstream of main-line black America.

The movement in Birmingham awakened blacks to a new sense of power. It ignited confidence in the potency of mass social protest to overcome white intransigence. If such a bastion of last-ditch segregation could be breached, why not . . . ? Demonstrations followed on a scale never seen before. The Birmingham campaign also spurred self-pride, black unity, a commitment to the struggle, and incredible courage. "The most important thing that happened," Wyatt Walker declared, "was that people decided that they are not going to be afraid of white folks anymore. Dr. King's most lasting contribution is that he emancipated black people's psyche. We threw off the slave mentality. Going to jail had been the whip which kept black folks in line. Now going to jail was transformed into a badge of honor." CORE's James Farmer referred to the change as "a spiritual emancipation." Many journalists termed it the emergence of a "New Negro," dwelling on his loss of fear, readiness to go to jail, and urgent call for "Freedom now!"

The children of Birmingham could well claim parentage of the adult New Negro. The images on TV of the brave youth facing down Connor's bullies had incensed and inspired thousands of older blacks to demonstrate. If children could court jail so that all blacks could be free, how could their elders do less? "Hey, if they are standing up to fire hoses and dogs down there," SNCC's John Lewis presumed, "the least we can do is march outside a restaurant up here. Where at the time we might have had seven or eight people on a picket line, now we were seeing fifteen, or twenty, or thirty. All because of Birmingham."

Simultaneously, the images of police violence against black children had engendered new depths of anger and widespread bitterness, dissolving apathy and helping spark a brush fire of "Birminghams." By the end of 1963, more than three hundred cities had accepted various forms of desegregation.

The nature of the struggle itself changed with the Birmingham protests. The militant "never" of hard-core segregationists was now matched by the blacks' own stridency. En masse, African-Americans forsook gradualism for immediacy. Tokenism no longer sufficed. "Freedom now" meant sweeping basic change without delay or dilution. The price of racial peace, African-Americans stipulated, must be the vote, decent housing and good jobs, an end to police brutality, and immediate desegregation of all schools and public accommodations.

King's crusade in Birmingham helped bring many of the poorest African-Americans into the marches, boycotts, and sit-ins. Their entry accelerated the radicalization of the movement's strategies and goals. Prior to 1963, the black unemployed and working poor, for the most part, had not joined African-American college students, professionals, and churchgoing women in the pursuit of symbolic and status gains. They had even less interest in or sympathy for the spirit of *satyagraha*. King's talk of love left them cold. Many snickered at his request that they nobly accept jailing and suffering. As the black struggle became more massive and encompassing—in part because of King—he would have to lead an increasingly impatient movement whose disobedience was becoming barely civil. Nonviolence was seen primarily as a practical tactic to gain media sympathy and white support, a means of casting the struggle as a drama of good versus evil. King the gentle Jesus had bested Connor the sadistic Satan.

In so doing, King and the movement forced the Kennedy administration to propose the first comprehensive civil rights bill, and made passage of the legislation feasible. King's nonviolent direct action had become the preferred tactic for black movements throughout the South. For at least the moment, King reigned. But not without rivals.

Not having originated in one ideological or organizational source, the civil rights movement had always been characterized by some degree of competitive rivalry. As King hurried to capitalize on the new spirit and the new participants in the movement, so did the leaders of CORE and SNCC and the NAACP, even the Urban League. Each group demanded more than it ever had, and more vociferously. Wrangling between the civil rights organizations added to the militancy of the movement. Each group sought the financial contributions necessary to battle racism successfully. Each wanted more influence in Washington and a larger standing in a particular local community. Each craved the approval of the masses and the active support of true believers. The competition was not new; prior to Birmingham, however, it had been muted. Despite tactical differences, the goals of all the major civil rights groups had remained similar. Their weakness relative to their opponents had placed a premium on cooperation or, at a minimum, absence of open vocal opposition.

No longer. After Birmingham, there was so much more to compete for, and more reasons to win at any cost. The pool of prospective members, of bodies to be utilized in demonstrations, and of committed activists willing to do whatever was required bloomed like a thousand flowers. The potential for white support likewise blossomed. King brought clergy who "had been preaching only a Sunday kind of love, out into the streets to practice a Monday kind of militancy." Birmingham swung open the door to huge financial contributions, alliances with labor and corporate leaders, and public endorsements and assistance from the nation's civic groups. Accordingly, each of the major black protest organizations tried to outdo the others and respond to the surges from local struggles. Each sought bigger victories in campaigns and endeavored to prove a greater commitment to the struggle. Each generated still further momentum and militancy in the movement.

Both King and the other civil rights leaders understood that the dedication and militancy would not be sustained for long. Delay was their enemy. They pressed for all, and now! They advocated as much as they could, as quickly as possible. The pressure had to be stepped up, King stressed, even when "the highest officials in the land [are saying] that we ought to stop."

A "great shout for freedom reverberated across the land," King noted. An army of millions of "strong, militant, marching blacks, flanked by legions of white allies," set its sights on "the realization of a new and glorious freedom."

No longer fighting a single battle here or there, the movement launched a full-scale offensive against racism along a broad front. After Birmingham, King pointed out, the "lament became a shout and then a roar and for months no American, white or Negro, was insulated or unaware."

Even the NAACP's Roy Wilkins walked a picket line. Scores of localities established biracial commissions, hired their first black policemen, registered African-Americans on the voting lists, and enrolled their children in previously all-white schools. And thousands of African-Americans in the North staged walkouts against de facto school segregation, picketed against discrimination in employment, and conducted rent strikes against racism in housing. Accounts of racial protest dominated the news.

"The sound of the explosion in Birmingham reached all the way to Washington," King observed. "It's just in everything," President Kennedy complained; "I mean, this has become everything." An aide to Robert Kennedy called it the most serious internal turmoil since the Civil War. The race issue could no longer be ignored. Birmingham had ended the invisibility of "the Negro and his problems" to most of the country. It had forced the president's hand. It had altered his view of what needed to be done and what, politically, could be done.

The crusade in Birmingham and the demonstrations that followed led Kennedy to do what he had, until now, refused to do—make a commitment to civil rights greater than any previous president. No longer able to deal with each grassroots protest piecemeal, the president needed to end the insurgency that was embarrassing the United States in the eyes of the world. The time had come to satisfy the millions of Americans protesting federal inaction and calling for an end to disorder. Additionally, he had to maintain African-Americans' confidence in government and their political support. He also believed it essential to dampen the explosive potential of racial violence, to forestall feared race wars across the South. Finally, the president realized the importance of assisting mainstream civil rights leaders in securing their objectives, lest the movement be taken over by irresponsible extremists. "If King loses," Robert reminded his brother, "worse leaders are going to take his place. Look at the black Muslims."

John Kennedy demonstrated his newfound commitment right after the Birmingham accord by asking Robert to work out the essentials of a civil rights bill. The president then took a strong public stand against Governor George Wallace on June 11, forcing him to capitulate to a court order admitting black students to the University of Alabama. That evening Kennedy gave a televised address on the race issue, terming civil rights a moral issue as old as the Scriptures and as clear as the American Constitution. He also warned that "events in Birmingham and elsewhere have so increased the cries for equality that no city or state or legislative body can prudently choose to ignore them." A greatly heartened King telegraphed the president that his

words constituted "one of the most eloquent, profound, and unequivocal pleas for justice and the freedom of all men ever made by any
president." A week later, King cried with joy when Kennedy proposed
comprehensive civil rights legislation based on "the proposition that
race has no place in American life or law." It validated and vindicated
the very essence of the black struggle in Birmingham.

King did not know then that the FBI had sent a dossier on his private comments and personal habits to the attorney general, who
routed it directly to the president.

5

REDEMPTION AND CRISIS,

1964

It may be true that the law cannot make a man love me, but it can stop him from lynching me, and I think that's pretty important.

⟿

Both John F. Kennedy and Martin Luther King had much more on their mind that summer than J. Edgar Hoover's prurient interests. The president focused primarily on the deteriorating effort of the United States to keep South Vietnam an independent, non-Communist nation; on reducing the likelihood of a nuclear war with the Soviet Union; and on prodding Congress to act on the major items of his domestic agenda, now stalled in committees.

The preacher redoubled his efforts to encourage dramatic nonviolent demonstrations by the movement. King's strategy of militant nonviolent direct action had proved effective in Birmingham. It had forced the president to introduce a comprehensive civil rights bill and had attracted national backing for substantial civil rights legislation. Now King needed to press Kennedy for a full-scale commitment to pass the civil rights bill by continuing to expose and highlight racial injustice. No longer expecting the weapon of love to produce racial reconciliation, or dallying while others set the agenda of the movement, King began to consider "a march on Washington with a quarter of a million people" that would include disruptive civil disobedience tactics.

The idea had been bandied about by civil rights leaders ever since 1941. A. Philip Randolph's threat of such a march had prompted President Franklin Roosevelt to issue an executive order desegregating the nation's defense industries and establishing a Fair Employment Practices Committee. In 1948 Randolph had again threatened a march to force President Harry Truman to end segregation in the armed services. In the winter of 1962–1963, Randolph and Bayard Rustin had proposed a two-day "mass descent" on Washington to draw attention to "the economic subordination of the American Negro" and the need for "the creation of more jobs for Americans."

The NAACP's Roy Wilkins and the Urban League's Whitney Young—doubting the effectiveness of street demonstrations—opposed the protest. But King, already advocating a "concrete, practical preferential program" for African-Americans, "a crash program of special treatment to atone for past injustices to Negroes," approved Randolph's march for economic justice. He envisioned the March on Washington for Jobs and Freedom as an expression of the Negro's dissatisfaction with America's treatment of black citizens, and as an opportunity to expand the civil rights agenda. King favored including nonviolent civil disobedience against the seat of government, even a sit-in on Capitol Hill.

The president would not countenance it. Behind the scenes, the administration orchestrated opposition to the march from religious, liberal, and labor groups, as well as mainstream Negro organizations. On June 22 Kennedy summoned the "Big Six"—King, Randolph, Wilkins, Young, James Farmer of CORE, and John Lewis of SNCC— to the White House. The president criticized the proposed march as poorly timed and counterproductive. "We want success in Congress, not a big show at the Capitol." The civil rights spokesmen who'd announced the march had blundered: "The only effect is to create an atmosphere of intimidation," argued the president, "and this may give some members of Congress an out . . . Some of these people are looking for an excuse to be against us; and I don't want to give any of them a chance to say, 'Yes, I'm for the bill, but I am damned if I will vote for it at the point of a gun.' "

Pulling out all the stops to dissuade them from encouraging blacks to march on Washington, Kennedy claimed to "have just seen a new poll — national approval of the administration has fallen from 60 to 47 percent," even though his approval rating at the time was, in fact, 61 percent; despite being very confident of beating Barry Goldwater in 1964, he lamented, "I may lose the next election because of this." Concluding with a lecture on the practicalities of enacting legislation, he stressed the need to "give Congress a fair chance to work its will." Vice President Lyndon B. Johnson backed him up: To get the votes necessary to pass the bill, he said, "we have to be careful not to do anything which would give those who are privately opposed a public excuse to appear as martyrs." Moreover, the expected southern filibuster would have to be overridden. To get the required two-thirds majority of all members present (or sixty-seven of the hundred possible votes) would necessitate an extraordinary bipartisan consensus.

Randolph rejected Kennedy's effort. It is too late to call off the march, he insisted. "The Negroes are already in the streets. It is very likely impossible to get them off. If they are bound to be in the streets in any case, is it not better that they be led by organizations dedicated to civil rights and disciplined by struggle rather than to leave them to other leaders who care neither about civil rights nor about nonviolence?" King agreed: The march would be "the means through which a people with legitimate discontents could channel their grievances under disciplined nonviolent leadership. It could also serve as a means of dramatizing the issue and mobilizing support in parts of the country which don't know the problems at first hand." To Kennedy's comment that the march was "the wrong kind of demonstration at the wrong time," King shot back, "Frankly, I have never engaged in any direct action movement which did not seem ill-timed. Some people thought Birmingham ill-timed."

The president smiled. "Including the attorney general."

John Kennedy then took King for a private conversation in the Rose Garden. "I assume you know you're under close surveillance." Not mincing words, he admonished King to get Jack O'Dell, until recently a Communist Party operative, off the SCLC payroll and to sever all ties with Stanley Levison — who denied ever being a member of the Communist Party but had been a party fund-raiser and had once managed the party's business ventures. The president feared that the FBI's increasing concern posed as much of a threat to the civil rights program as the march.

"You've read about Profumo in the newspapers?" the president asked, referring to a current scandal about British prime minister Harold Macmillan's war minister, John Profumo, having been caught in an extramarital affair with a young call girl who was also the mistress of a Soviet deputy naval attaché. "That was an example of friendship and loyalty carried too far," Kennedy murmured. "Macmillan is likely to lose his government because he has been loyal to his friend. You must take care not to lose your cause for the same reason."

Without letting King know that the Justice Department had agreed to Hoover's request to wiretap Levison, the president reiterated his alarm: "They're Communists. You've got to get rid of them." FBI revelations would harm not just King but the entire movement and the chance for civil rights legislation. "If they shoot you down, they'll shoot us down too. So we're asking you to be careful."

Robert Kennedy and Burke Marshall, the head of the Civil Rights Division of the Justice Department, had already taken King aside to warn him that he must get rid of Stanley Levison, "a paid agent of the Soviet Communist apparatus," and Jack O'Dell, whom Levison had "planted" inside the SCLC to influence the civil rights movement. The need to pass a civil rights bill, the Justice Department officials stressed, took precedence over King's friendships or desire for conclusive evidence.

That the president would get involved in such a middling matter bewildered King. To ensure Kennedy's support for the civil rights bill and subdue his opposition to the march, King promised to fire O'Dell. But for the sake of fairness, he wanted to see the evidence against Levison. "I know Stanley, and I can't believe this. You will have to prove it." President Kennedy ended the conversation with a promise that he would convey the proof, and with an oblique warning that sex and spying could ruin public men.

Leaving the White House, King joked to Andy Young that Kennedy had chatted with him in the Rose Garden because he feared the FBI had bugged his office. He paid little more heed to the president's warning than he had to the Justice Department's advice about

Levison and O'Dell. King maintained that a man's past was not important as long as he could now say he was not a Communist. "Then as far as I'm concerned, he is eligible to work for me." A week later, however, a *Birmingham News* reporter who was close to Robert Kennedy published a story that King had kept a known Communist on his payroll. Rumors about Communist influence on King, circulated by the FBI, also made the rounds of the Senate.

King grudgingly requested O'Dell's resignation. But he would not disavow Levison, his most trusted adviser. Levison had no ulterior motives and personal agenda, and King counted on him for frank opinions. But Levison urged King to end their communication, fearing it would hurt the movement. "I said it would not be in the interests of the movement to hold on to me if the Kennedys had doubts." The minister would not turn his back on a friend, however deeply involved in the Communist Party he once may have been. King thought it a matter of principle as well as friendship and believed he could fool the Kennedys by publicly breaking with Levison while privately remaining in touch.

It worked, somewhat. The attorney general publicly rebutted charges of Communist influence in the civil rights movement. "We have no evidence," Robert Kennedy informed the Senate, that any key movement leaders "are Communists, or Communist controlled. This is as true as to Dr. Martin Luther King, Jr., about whom particular accusations were made, as well as other leaders." Nevertheless, the attorney general asked J. Edgar Hoover to supplement the Levison surveillance with wiretaps on King and his attorney, Clarence Jones, whom the FBI suspected of being a Communist because of his mid-1950s involvement in the Labor Youth League.

Robert Kennedy's request was music to Hoover's ears. He quickly filed the formal requisitions for the two wiretap authorizations. For whatever reason, Kennedy second-guessed himself and signed off on only the Jones surveillance. Still, Hoover could not have been more delighted with what the FBI gleaned from the tap on King's attorney. In coarse, racy language, King confided to Jones the details of his furtive sexual affairs. A disgusted Hoover—a confirmed bachelor, perhaps asexual or homosexual—had proof that the sanctimonious preacher was not the moral leader he pretended to be. Unrelenting in his effort to destroy the promiscuous "tom cat" with "obsessive, degenerate sexual urges," Hoover quickly sent a dossier on King's private comments and personal habits to the attorney general, who routed it directly to the president.

Dimly mindful of the administration's machinations and desperate to have a massive demonstration of support for civil rights legislation, King and Randolph agreed that there would be no sit-ins or aggressive activity of any kind in the March on Washington for Jobs and Freedom. To procure the support of Wilkins, Young, and liberal whites, they also assented to rerouting the march: Instead of going to the Capitol to petition Congress, it would proceed from the Washington Monument to the Lincoln Memorial. The only placards allowed would be those with one of five officially approved slogans.

Now working with the White House, the United Civil Rights Leadership Council, representing the Big Six, coordinated arrangements for the march. With Bayard Rustin as its national organizer, the council enlisted the support of nearly two hundred liberal groups. It also encouraged President Kennedy, content with the notion of a law-abiding demonstration in favor of civil rights legislation, to hail the forthcoming march as in "the great tradition" of peaceful assembly "for a redress of grievances." A month later, Kennedy even worried that the march might not be massive enough, that the hundred thousand people might not appear.

The turnout on August 28, 1963, exceeded all expectations. Nearly a quarter of a million Americans, including some seventy-five thousand whites, descended on Washington by airplane and by foot, by twenty-two chartered trains, two thousand chartered buses, and thousands of car pools, in the nation's largest ever demonstration for black rights. The day became a celebration, a rally and a church picnic, a day of glorious music—sometimes solemn, sometimes joyous. African-American school bands alternated marching songs and hymns. Joan Baez chanted, "We shall overcome someday." Peter, Paul and Mary wondered, "How many times must a man look up before he can see the sky?" Bob Dylan rasped a ballad of the murder of the NAACP's Medgar Evers. Almost as one, the huge assemblage clapped to deep-throated Odetta's "If they ask you who you are, tell them you're a child of God," and shed a tear as Mahalia Jackson bellowed "I been 'buked and I been scorned" in a way that seemed to echo off the distant Capitol.

The marchers good-naturedly endured the heat and humidity of summertime Washington as well as the endless introduction of notables and clichés by a dozen speakers. The abundance of platitudes and absence of passion led some to nap, some to walk away. Others frolicked in the Reflecting Pool between the shrines of Washington and Lincoln. It did not matter. They had made their point through their presence, through their good temper and dignified demeanor. The several thousand federal troops stationed nearby would not be needed, much less the fifteen thousand paratroopers on standby in North Carolina. Nor, it soon became clear, was it necessary to institute a citywide ban on liquor sales and to prepare the courts for round-the-clock sessions to process offenders. To the millions of white Americans watching the live broadcast on the three networks, African-Americans appeared not as the criminals or servile fools usually shown on TV but as churchly crusaders in a heroic quest to be free and equal.

Late in the sweltering afternoon, Randolph introduced the Reverend Dr. Martin Luther King, Jr., as "the moral leader of our nation." King had been, as Wilkins put it, "assigned the rousements." King would not fail; he and his staff had worked for hours polishing the seven-minute speech to a high sheen the night before. As he walked to the podium, the cheers swelled.

The minister placed his text on the lectern, nodded his thank-you to the vast assembly, and inhaled slowly, deeply. "Fivescore years ago," he said on an exhale, reading from a prepared lecture that was as smooth in prose as it was rough in its descriptions of injustice. It emphasized white America's hypocrisy and reneging on promises to blacks. King reminded his audience in words reminiscent of the stone figure of Lincoln above him that the hopes generated by the Emancipation Proclamation had still not been fulfilled. To underscore how little had changed, how much American racism persisted, he peppered the passage with a *"One hundred years later"* refrain.

"One hundred years later, the Negro is still not free." His deep tones came in a slow cadence. Summoning images of shackled, hobbled black slaves, he claimed, *"The life of the Negro is still sadly crippled by*

the manacles of segregation and the chains of discrimination."
[YESSIR!] Forced to remain separated from whites, the Negro, an outsider, *"lives on a lonely island of poverty in the midst of a vast ocean of
material prosperity."* Still *"languished in the corners of American society,"* he *"finds himself an exile in his own land."* [TELL IT, DOCTOR!]
Presenting blacks as victims of white racism, King would not appease
those who sought relief from the mounting black struggle.

Launching a metaphor of America's obligation to blacks, King described the promises of the Declaration of Independence as *"a sacred
obligation"* that had proved to be, for African-Americans, *"a check
which has come back marked 'insufficient funds.' "* But, he said to roars
of agreement, *"we refuse to believe that the bank of justice is bankrupt.
We refuse to believe that there are insufficient funds in the great vaults
of opportunity in this nation."* [YESSIR!] They had come to collect on
the promise, he observed, looking as far into the distant crowd as possible, to cash the check *"that will give us upon demand the riches of
freedom and the security of justice."* "Sho 'nuff," a woman near the
platform shouted, laughing.

King melodiously praised the *"veterans of creative suffering,"* urging them to continue the struggle. *"Now is the time to make real the
promises of Democracy. Now is the time to rise from the dark and desolate valley of segregation to the sunlit path of racial justice. Now is the
time to open the doors of opportunity to all of God's children. Now is
the time to lift our nation from the quicksands of racial injustice to the
solid rock of brotherhood.* [NOW! NOW! NOW!] *This sweltering summer
of the Negro's legitimate discontent will not pass until there is an in-
vigorating autumn of freedom and equality."* [OH YES!] [FREEDOM!]
[NOW!]

King never mentioned patience. He spoke of neither cooling off
nor gradualism. *"Those who hope that the Negro needed to blow off
steam and will now be content will have a rude awakening if the nation
returns to business as usual.* [AMEN!] *There will be neither rest nor tranquility in America until the Negro is granted his citizenship rights.*
[YEAH!] [THAT'S RIGHT!] *The whirlwinds of revolt will continue to
shake the foundations of our nation until the bright day of justice
emerges."*

In deep, rising tones, King responded to those who asked, *"When
will you be satisfied?"*

We can never be satisfied as long as the Negro is the victim of the unspeakable horrors of police brutality. We can never be satisfied as long as our bodies, heavy with the fatigue of travel, cannot gain lodging in the motels of the highways and the hotels of the cities. We cannot be satisfied as long as the Negro's basic mobility is from a smaller ghetto to a larger one. We can never be satisfied as long as our children are stripped of their selfhood and robbed of their dignity by signs stating "For Whites Only." We cannot be satisfied as long as a Negro in Mississippi cannot vote and a Negro in New York believes he has nothing for which to vote. No, no, we are not satisfied and we will not be satisfied until justice rolls down like waters and righteousness like a mighty stream.

King hurled each image at the whites who thought blacks received the same general treatment as whites. With the certitude of the Gospels, he vowed to all who believed the race problem had been solved that there would be no stopping the movement until African-Americans gained their full and equal civil rights, until the nation's promise to blacks was fulfilled. Whoops and hollers of approval reached skyward. Keep protesting, he said. *"Go back to Mississippi, go back to Alabama, go back to South Carolina, go back to Georgia, go back to Louisiana, go back to the slums and ghettos of our modern cities, knowing that somehow this situation can and will be changed."* Until then, he cautioned the two thirds of the American public who disapproved of civil rights demonstrations, there would be no surcease from nonviolent direct action. His allotted seven minutes up, King felt impelled to keep preaching.

"Tell 'em about the dream, Martin," Mahalia Jackson shouted. Like others who frequently accompanied King, she had heard his peroration that unfailingly left the audience enraptured. He had used this climactic ending, based on a sermon of Prathia Hall, to great effect at a mass meeting in Birmingham in April and in addressing 125,000 supporters in Detroit in June. He had also freely employed for half a dozen years the "Let freedom ring" coda, taken almost verbatim from an address given to the 1952 Republican National Convention by Archibald Carey. Eager to energize the movement, to send it back to the struggle with positive resolve, King harkened back to those orations again with his extemporized conclusion.

Setting aside *"the difficulties of today and tomorrow,"* King pictured the better country the protesters sought. *"I have a dream,"* he proclaimed, envisioning a nation of racial justice and social harmony, *"a dream deeply rooted in the American dream."* Blending Amos, Isaiah, the Declaration of Independence, and "America," the dream harmonized King's program for racial change with America's most basic ideals. It both assuaged white fears about the movement and heartened the massive assemblage of civil rights activists, becoming more utopian and yet believable as the crowd's antiphonal responses surged from the Washington Monument to the monumental Lincoln.

"I have a dream that one day on the red hills of Georgia the sons of former slaves and the sons of former slaveowners will be able to sit down together at the table of brotherhood. I have a dream that one day even the State of Mississippi,"—then in the feverish grip of the Klan and Citizens' Councils—*"a state sweltering with the heat of injustice, sweltering with the heat of oppression, will be transformed into an oasis of freedom and justice."* [TELL US. I SEE IT!] In a nation with hundreds of laws in 1963 that defined what a person could do and be on the basis of race, King dreamed that his *"four little children will one day live in a nation where they will not be judged by the color of their skin but by the content of their character."* [YES! YES!]

Still more audacious, King dreamed that one day in Alabama, leaving no stone unturned to maintain the separation of the races, *"little black boys and black girls will be able to join hands with little white boys and white girls as sisters and brothers."* He lifted his voice to the sky. *"I have a dream today!"*

Spines tingled, eyes teared, and shouts of approval swelled as the preacher's rapture gloried in every valley being exalted, every hill and mountain being made low, the rough places made smooth, the crooked places straightened, the glory of the Lord revealed, and all flesh seeing it together. Tapping the wellspring for an end to evil and for a truly united country, the timbre of King's voice cut through the din of this Pentecostal moment. *"With this faith we will be able to hew out of the mountain of despair a stone of hope. With this faith we will be able to transform the jangling discords of our nation into a beautiful symphony of brotherhood. With this faith, we will be able to work together, to pray together, to struggle together, to go to jail together, to stand up for freedom together, knowing that we will be free one day."*

Each lilting passage had increased the crowd's roar. Seeking to raise it yet higher, King trumpeted: *"Let freedom ring!"* Let it ring from hills and mountains everywhere in the United States, he implored above the tumult, from every hamlet and city and state. When we do, he went on, raising his right arm in benediction, his voice almost meditative, *"all of God's children—black men and white men, Jews and Gentiles, Protestants and Catholics—will be able to join hands and sing in the words of the old Negro spiritual, 'Free at last, free at last, thank God Almighty, we are free at last.' "*

Waving to the multitude, the young minister stepped back to shouts of "Free at last! Free at last! Free at last!" "The Kingdom of God," Coretta Scott King remembered, "seemed to have come on earth."

King modestly credited the march's importance to "the enormous multitude" who had attended, to "the mass of ordinary people who stood in majestic dignity as witnesses to their single-minded determination to achieve democracy in their time." At least as vital, King's message and majestic delivery made the day historic. At a time when most Americans did not perceive the injustice or the immorality of the nation's racism, King depicted it at its most searing to the millions who had watched on television and to the many more millions who had heard it on the radio or would see it excerpted on the evening news. At a time when the sight of black kids and white kids going to the same school inflamed racist mobs, he demanded an end to all barriers separating the races. At a time when civil rights remained a highly contested matter, flying against the winds of public opinion, King confronted white America with the undeniable justice of African-American demands and succeeded in associating black rights with accepted values. By identifying the movement with America's most respected themes and thinkers, and by putting a distinctively Christian seal on the black struggle, the pastor changed previously indifferent white minds. No harmless dreamer, the preacher interpreted a vast social upheaval, slaying expectations of gradualism or of moderation if America failed to make good on its promises.

King's rhetoric did not touch all hearts. It changed neither votes in Congress nor the minds of those whites most opposed to racial equality.

Some blacks also poured scorn on King. One young black shouted, "Fuck that dream, Martin. Now, goddammit, *now!*" Malcolm X labeled the event the "Farce on Washington." He ridiculed it as "a circus, nothing but a picnic," growling, "Who ever heard of angry revolutionists swinging their bare feet together with their oppressor in lily-pad park pools, with gospels and guitars and 'I Have a Dream' speeches?"

SNCC staffers, livid that John Lewis had been forced to launder his remarks in deference to the demand of some of the march's white supporters, denounced the demonstration as "a victory celebration for the Kennedy administration." SNCC's executive secretary, James Forman, snapped that "fancy productions like the March on Washington tended to 'psych off' local protest and make people feel they had accomplished something—changed something, somehow—when, in fact, nothing had been changed."

President Kennedy, watching King on TV, contended, "He's damned good. Damned good." He greeted the civil rights leadership at the White House afterward by playfully mimicking, "I have a dream." King took the opportunity to emphasize to the president that the movement was especially interested in jobs and fair employment practices. Despite King's eloquent summons for America to be the best it could be, despite his having made the black struggle far more acceptable to white America—to the extent that any single utterance could—Kennedy demurred. Slow to recognize the social revolution under way, the president voiced his preference for caution and compromise.

Not far from the White House, the same speech frightened J. Edgar Hoover and his subordinates at FBI headquarters. Fearing King's increasing popularity, they ratcheted up their effort to discredit and destroy him.

Unaware of the FBI's vendetta, King neither altered his sexual activities nor rushed to capitalize on the march's momentum. The September SCLC retreat at the Dorchester Center, and the annual convention in Richmond, could neither settle on new targets for the movement nor decide how to pressure the foot-dragging Kennedy administration. King refused to commit the SCLC to a new direct-action campaign or to a voter registration drive. Reluctantly, he admitted that his leadership was "standing still, doing nothing, going nowhere."

Just three weeks after the idealism and optimism of the march, on September 15 a powerful dynamite bomb planted by "Dynamite Bob" Chambliss and three other Klansmen exploded at Birmingham's Sixteenth Street Baptist Church, shattering the face of Jesus Christ in a stained-glass window and killing four girls attending Sunday school. Bitter African-Americans took to the streets, pelting police with debris. One black youth was shot and killed while the police tried to disperse the crowd, and another died in a racial shooting just outside of town. King demanded a federal intervention in Birmingham, lest they "see the worst racial holocaust this nation has ever seen." The president responded merely with a statement decrying the bombing.

In his eulogy at the funeral for the girls, King connected their deaths "to every minister of the gospel who has remained silent behind the safe security of stained-glass windows . . . to every politician who has fed his constituents the stale bread of hatred and the spoiled meat of racism . . . to a federal government that has compromised with the undemocratic practices of Southern Dixiecrats and the blatant hypocrisy of right-wing Northern Republicans . . . to every Negro who passively accepts the evil system of segregation and stands on the sidelines in the midst of a mighty struggle for justice."

King pleaded with blacks to remain nonviolent. "We must not lose faith in our white brothers. Somehow we must believe that the most misguided among them can learn to respect the dignity and worth of all human personality." We must be concerned, he concluded, with not just "who murdered them, but about the system, the way of life, and the philosophy which produced the murderers." King had gradually become aware of a changing black mood. He understood that "the Negro in the South can now be nonviolent as a stratagem, but he can't include loving the white man." He recognized that there will be "more and more bitterness because things haven't moved fast enough."

Later that week King met with the president. "The Negro community is about to reach a breaking point," he warned. "If something isn't done to give the Negro a new sense of hope and a sense of protection, then we will have the worst race rioting we have ever seen in this country." JFK chose only to send a former secretary of the army and a former football coach to Birmingham to attempt to calm tempers.

Brooding over what to do next, King telephoned Clarence Jones to say that he wanted to converse with Levison secretly. When Jones relayed the request to Levison, the FBI overheard through its electronic surveillance of both men in New York. Hoover informed Robert Kennedy in October of the continuing King-Levison relationship and of Jack O'Dell being spotted at the SCLC office. The FBI chief insisted that King's connection to Levison made it imperative to wiretap King as a matter of national security.

President Kennedy's concern about the ruin of public men through sex and spying became reality. Fearful of the FBI's secret files on John Kennedy's sexual affairs with numerous women—especially those involving the mistress of a Chicago Mafia boss collaborating in a CIA plot to assassinate Fidel Castro and an East German woman suspected of espionage—Attorney General Robert Kennedy appeased Hoover by approving the wiretapping of King's home and office on October 10. Stretching the permission to include surveillance of King's hotel rooms, the FBI gained evidence of King's extramarital affairs that was even raunchier than the secondhand accounts collected previously.

Within the movement, there had always been whispers of King's "voracious" sexual carousing. Friends delighted in joking about his eye for pretty women. SCLC colleagues warned him to stop or at least be less recklessly conspicuous. He would not. Whatever the psychological or physical compulsions, King engaged in one-night stands and ongoing relationships. He rationalized his behavior as only doing what other prominent and powerful men did at that time. He saw his sexual self as that of a preacher in a black church subculture where women outnumbered men three to one and illicit sexual relationships between black clergymen and their female flocks were commonplace—more often than not a subject of amusement rather than reproach. He excused his actions by noting that men in the movement put their lives on the line and needed the respite from danger and turmoil provided by sexual release. Indeed, virtually all the movement's male generals sexually exploited the female foot soldiers. They considered it their due for leading the black liberation struggle. They were objects of adoration, of hero worship, and no shortage of women sought to bask in their spotlight.

Additionally, King hardly slept at home. Delivering 350 speeches in 1963, traveling 275,000 miles, and spending nine days in ten away from Atlanta weakened the sexual bonds in his marriage. The ceaseless travel, the omnipresent fears, and the constant temptations fueled King's sexual compulsivity, and his desperate hedonism magnified his overwhelming guilt.

Whatever the reasons for his adultery, King considered himself a sinner. Fully understanding that his sex life was inconsistent with his values as a minister and a Christian, he often made a kind of public confessional the subtext of his sermons. He preached the difficulty of struggling with sin, whether it be "slavery to drink, untruthfulness, the impurity of selfishness or sexual promiscuity . . . You knew all along that it was wrong and that it had invaded your life as an unnatural intruder." Tormented by his shortcomings, he frequently alleged that "each of us is something of a schizophrenic personality, we're split up and divided against ourselves. There is something of a civil war going on within all our lives . . ."

King admitted to his congregants that "each of us is two selves" and that the "great burden of life is to always try to keep that higher self in command. Don't let the lower self take over." But the injunction proved too hard for him. His rampant infidelity continued.

Briefly home in late November, King saw the first televised reports of John Kennedy being shot. He yelled to his wife, "Corrie, I just heard that Kennedy has been shot, maybe killed." She joined him and later recalled him saying, "Oh, I hope that he will live, this is just terrible. I think if he lives, if he pulls through this, it will help him to understand better what we go through." Following the flash that the president had died, Martin turned to Coretta: "This is what is going to happen to me. I keep telling you, this is a sick society." She could not reply. "I had no words to comfort my husband. I could not say, 'It won't happen to you.' I felt he was right. It was a painfully agonizing silence. I moved closer to him and gripped his hand in mine." Deeply hurt that the Kennedy family did not invite him to the funeral mass at National Cathedral, King flew to Washington alone and stood by himself in the crowd, praying, as the horse-drawn coffin of John F. Kennedy moved past.

A month later, top FBI officials met in an all-day conference "aimed at neutralizing King as an effective Negro leader." Assistant director of the Bureau, William Sullivan, reported to Hoover: "We will, at the proper time when it can be done without embarrassment to the Bureau, expose King as an immoral opportunist who is not a sincere person but is exploiting the racial situation for personal gain." The plan pleased Hoover. In addition to all the grudges he already bore against King, the FBI boss was enraged that King had been chosen *Time*'s Man of the Year as "the unchallenged voice of the Negro people—and the disquieting conscience of the whites." He sneered, "They had to dig deep in the garbage for this one," and he gave the go-ahead for his agents to install bugs in the hotel room that King had reserved for early January at the Willard Hotel, near the White House.

The collected tapes captured the sounds of King, some SCLC colleagues, and two women enjoying an exuberant two-night party. They gave Hoover just what he wanted to try to destroy King. The FBI prepared an eight-page synopsis of the partying and a "highlights" tape of clinking glasses, male-bonding humor, and sexual groans and shrieks. Sullivan, resolved to knock King "off his pedestal and to reduce him completely in influence," began shopping them around to "Washington insiders and influentials" who were friendly or beholden to the Bureau.

Meanwhile, King gradually settled on St. Augustine, Florida, as SCLC's next target. It would be the 1964 dramatization of day-to-day racial injustice in the South; it would intensify pressure on Congress to pass the civil rights bill. "When we are idle," King reported to the SCLC, "the white majority very quickly forgets the injustices which started our movement and only think of the demands for progress as unreasonable requests from irresponsible people." It was necessary "for us to remind the nation of the reason the Civil Rights Bill came into existence in the first place. For this task, we chose the Nation's Oldest City." SCLC hoped the protest would keep it from being overshadowed by SNCC's well-publicized Mississippi Freedom Summer.

King expected St. Augustine, a racial powder keg with a short fuse, to be another Birmingham. Given the combination of an ultra-far-right city government tied to a populous Klan and a spirited SCLC affiliate spearheading the drive for equality for the city's 25 percent black population, King hoped to produce another telling victory for his increasingly provocative brand of nonviolent direct action. He believed the city's reliance on tourism and dependence on federal grants to celebrate its quadricentennial in 1965 made it vulnerable to the adverse publicity that SCLC demonstrations would bring. And he fully expected violence by the thousand-strong armed KKK militia in the region known as the Ancient City Hunting Club. King counted on Holsted "Hoss" Manucy—a pig farmer, bootlegger, and Exalted Cyclops of the St. Augustine Klan, whose members had been deputized by the sheriff to maintain order—to succumb to brutality in response to SCLC's taunting tactics, just like Bull Connor.

Despite a long history of white racist violence and intimidation, King lamented, St. Augustine's African-Americans "have been left—by the most powerful federal government in the world—almost to their own resources." Nothing had been done when Klansmen savaged black students staging a sit-in; or when Dr. Robert B. Hayling, a black dentist and head of the local NAACP, and three other blacks had been abducted by the KKK, beaten unconscious, and nearly castrated and burned alive; or when Hayling's home had been bombed and the homes of two families trying to desegregate an all-white school dynamited. Cross burnings and the automobiles of blacks set ablaze illuminated the nighttime skies. And when the City Commission finally agreed to meet with black leaders to discuss their grievances, the African-Americans who appeared at city hall found only a tape recorder and instructions to tell the machine their problems for the commission's later consideration. Not until Easter Sunday 1964, when police arrested an interracial group featuring the elderly mother of the governor of Massachusetts, for trying to integrate a motel restaurant, did St. Augustine make national news. By then SCLC staffers had arrived to conduct workshops on nonviolence, and King had announced plans for a "long, hot, nonviolent summer" for the city.

In May, SCLC's Hosea Williams proposed a series of dangerous night marches to the historic Slave Market—the most obvious symbol of white oppression—to dramatize the plight of African-Americans in St. Augustine. SCLC knew that night marches had the highest potential for violence, and that racist violence against blacks elicited media attention in a manner that brought public sympathy and support. King approved the night marches along the dark and narrow streets.

He presumed violence against blacks would force the federal government to act on behalf of the civil rights of African-Americans, as it had in Birmingham.

The first marches, of mainly black students from high school and Florida Memorial College, attracted little attention. On the evening of May 28, however, a white mob armed with iron pipes and bicycle chains, in the presence of reporters and television cameras, set upon a march of several hundred African-Americans led by Andrew Young. After the whites had finished clubbing blacks who dropped to their knees to pray, the sheriff declared martial law, ordering that there be no more marches.

Telegraphing President Lyndon Johnson that "all semblance of law and order has broken down," King appealed for federal intervention. Although "we have witnessed raw and rampant violence even beyond much of what we have experienced in Alabama and Mississippi," he said, he would not call off the marches. "We cannot in good conscience postpone our nonviolent thrust merely because violence has erupted against us, but we sincerely believe that as American citizens our right to peaceably assemble must be guaranteed and not abridged because of the unrestrained lawlessness of the Klan."

The president shelved King's plea. Seeking election to the presidency in 1964, Johnson knew his all-out support of the civil rights bill pleased most African-American and liberal white voters and that it made no sense to give the Republican candidate, Barry Goldwater — who opposed civil rights legislation — any more of a boost among Democrats in the Deep South.

On May 31, King arrived in St. Augustine. Despite a local court injunction banning night marches, he called upon "all men of conscience" to join him in evening demonstrations until the city's hotels and motels, restaurants, swimming pools, and other public facilities immediately desegregated; to march until St. Augustine hired African-American police and firemen; and to protest until local officials established a biracial commission.

Instead of storming the barricades, King went to the federal courts to have the injunction invalidated. Addressing a mass church meeting, he commended the protesters, *the heroes of St. Augustine,* for remaining nonviolent, and he sought to bolster the commitment to nonviolence by other blacks in town. *"Soon the Klan will see that all of their violence will not stop us, for we are on the way to Freedom Land and we don't mean to stop until we get there."* [THAT'S RIGHT!] [IT'S TIME, YES!] King then commented on the frequent threats to his life. *"Well, if physical death is the price I must pay to free my white brother and all of my brothers and sisters from permanent death of the spirit, then nothing can be more redemptive. We have long since learned to sing anew with our foreparents of old: 'Before I'll be a slave I'll be buried in my grave and go home to my Father and be saved.'"*

The judge saved King, forbidding further interference with SCLC's night marches. "We are determined [that] this city will not celebrate its quadricentennial as a segregated city," King exhorted. "There will be no turning back."

To underscore his new resolve and kick the campaign into high gear, King decided to get arrested in the glare of the national media. On June 11, accompanied by a handful of protesters and a large entourage of reporters and TV cameras, King insisted on being served lunch at the segregated Monson Motor Lodge restaurant. The sheriff whisked him off to jail for violating Florida's "unwanted guest" law. That night, which King spent in solitary confinement, a white mob from the neighboring timberland and potato fields attacked some four hundred blacks who had been urged earlier by King to "march tonight as you've never marched before." He had encouraged them to believe "that the bruises of clubs, electric cattle prods, and fists hurt less than the scars of submission."

King again pleaded with Johnson for federal intervention, to no avail. The next day J. B. Stoner, the vice presidential candidate of the right-wing National States' Rights Party, arrived in St. Augustine to rouse racist sentiment. "Tonight we're going to find out whether white people have any rights! When the Constitution said all men are created equal, it wasn't talking about niggers. The coons have been parading around St. Augustine for a long time!" The whites of this city, he predicted, will no longer put up with King, "a longtime associate of Communists." Brandishing deer rifles, Hoss Manucy's vigilantes rushed to the old Slave Market.

King feared for his life. A fire had gutted his rented cottage. Secretly, the preacher allowed himself to be accompanied by armed bodyguards and moved from house to house. "This is the most lawless city I've ever been in," he reflected to a reporter. "I've never seen this kind of wide-open violence."

By mid-June the pressure of almost daily demonstrations and violence had taken a big bite out of the business community. On June 17 city merchants announced their promise to obey the civil rights bill, now nearing passage. Officials indicated they would set up a biracial committee if King and the SCLC left St. Augustine for a month. King would have no part of it. He had learned to put no trust in a segregationist's verbal promise. He and the SCLC would stay in St. Augustine and continue virtual round-the-clock protests until the city established the biracial committee and the Senate passed the civil rights bill.

The latter occurred two days later. After Senator Robert Byrd of West Virginia finally stopped chattering, ending an eighty-three-day filibuster, the Senate passed the Civil Rights Act, seventy-three to twenty-seven. But white racists would not relent in their efforts to crush the SCLC campaign in St. Augustine. The manager of the Monson Motor Lodge prevented the desegregation of its swimming pool by pouring muriatic acid on the blacks who dared to swim there. A crazed mob, males and females, attacked black bathers who had the audacity to engage in a "swim-in" to integrate the Atlantic Ocean. On June 25, eight hundred Klansmen, led by Manucy, attacked black demonstrators at the Slave Market. Armed with bats, cue sticks, logging chains, and tire tools, the whites bloodied the protesters while state troopers looked the other way through their gold-rimmed sunglasses. *The New York Times* reported, "Negro women had their clothes torn off while they were being clawed and beaten by screaming terrorists."

Hidden on a dark porch, a stricken King watched his followers "stumbling past him in the dim shine of the streetlights like the tattered remnant of a brigade filtering back from a battlefield disaster, girls in shredded clothes, sobs now lifting up from them, a few scattered screams like a long-pent breath at last released."

Back in the ghetto, a bandaged woman shouted, "They done it now. I say, if we got to fight, dammit, fight! If we got to die, dammit, die! To hell with this nonviolence!" SCLC aides scurried about, trying to prevent angry blacks from returning to the square with their guns. To prevent an outright racial war, King beseeched the crowd back into a church. There, Abernathy calmed the outraged gathering: "What happened tonight was one of the dark hours of our movement. You have passed through it. Their purpose is to break your spirit, to break your heart. But let them beat us, let them kick us—we will continue to present our bodies in peaceful witness for justice, we ain't gonna let nobody turn us 'round. And we will not turn to hate!" The assembled sang an old hymn, "Be Not Dismayed, What E'er Be the Tide, God Will Take Care of You." They lifted their voices, singing, "God will take care of you . . . in every way all through the day," and dispersed. They would remain nonviolent.

Following an announcement by the Florida governor on June 30 that he would create a biracial committee, King declared, "This is merely the first step in the long journey toward freedom and justice in St. Augustine, but it is a creative and important first step, for it at last opens the channels of communication." With the fig leaf of a fragile cease-fire, King departed for Atlanta and left the black community of St. Augustine vulnerable to recriminations. The intended brief campaign had dragged on far too long, costing SCLC too much.

King achieved a partial victory at best. He neither secured federal intervention nor improved the lot of the local black community. The SCLC neither left a grassroots movement in place nor initiated a follow-up campaign when the racial situation worsened. But the demonstrations kept America conscious of the violence and bloodshed that epitomized the reality and horror of racism. They pricked the conscience of the nation, speeding passage of the Civil Rights Act. The needs of the local black community counted for less. "Some communities," the preacher noted, "like this one, have to bear the cross."

On July 2, King joined other civil rights leaders at the White House to witness the signing of the 1964 Civil Rights Act by President Johnson. It prohibited racial discrimination in most places of public accommodation; authorized the government to withhold federal funds to public programs practicing discrimination; banned discrimination by employers and labor unions; created an Equal Employment Opportunity Commission; established a Community Relations Service to facilitate desegregation; and provided technical and financial aid to communities desegregating their schools.

Passage of the bill resulted, in part, from the militant nonviolent demonstrations in Birmingham, those throughout the South in the summer of 1963, the assassination of John F. Kennedy, and the marches in St. Augustine. They stimulated active assistance from the politically skilled Lyndon Johnson and bipartisan backing in Congress. The Civil Rights Act, King claimed, "was first written in the streets." It "was not a product of the charity of white America for a supine black America." The nonviolent direct-action protests enlisted scores of labor, civic, and church groups to lobby for the bill, which had become, in the words of Senate Minority Leader Everett Dirksen of Illinois, "an idea whose time had come." A massive constituency of conscience had sounded the death knell for de jure segregation in the South. Like no other American, King represented that constituency.

He now sought to use his influence in international affairs and electoral politics. In numerous speeches he repeated his prior calls for "a massive international boycott" and sanctions against South Africa for its repressive apartheid policies. In early July he appeared before the platform committee of the Republican National Convention to plead for a progressive civil rights policy. He considered the "voting record, philosophy, and program" of Barry Goldwater "anathema to all the hard-won achievements of the past decade." King made no effort to hide his opinion that the Goldwater candidacy was "morally indefensible and socially suicidal."

He began a five-day tour of Mississippi to show his support for Freedom Summer. He praised the massive voter education and registration effort undertaken largely by SNCC as "one of the most creative attempts I had seen to radically challenge the oppressive life of the Negro in that state and possibly in the entire nation." He endorsed the Mississippi Freedom Democratic Party (MFDP), which SNCC created because the regular Mississippi Democratic Party refused to allow blacks to participate in its precinct, county, or state conventions. In Greenwood, on the edge of the Delta, King made the rounds of cafés and honky-tonks, inviting everyone to the nighttime rally for the MFDP.

"Mississippi has treated the Negro as if he is a thing instead of a person," King told those crowded into the New Savoy Café. "But you must not allow anybody to make you feel you are not significant and you do not count. Every Negro here in Greenwood, Mississippi, has worth and dignity—because white, Negro, Chinese, Indian, man or woman or child, we are all the children of God. You are somebody. I want every one of you to say that out loud now to yourself—I am somebody . . . I am somebody . . . I am somebody." King repeated his message at the next café and the next. At the rally, he claimed, "We have a power that's greater than all the guns in Greenwood or the state of Mississippi, a power greater than all the guns and bombs of all the armies in the world. We have the power of our souls!"

SNCC field secretaries snickered: "De Lawd, De Lawd, De Lawd." They choked on the messianic terms used by Ralph Abernathy to introduce King. Unaware of the heightened number of death threats being directed at him, they resented the FBI protection given to King as he traveled in Mississippi. And they exploded at King's unwillingness to immediately begin another direct-action campaign. While CORE's Farmer and SNCC's Lewis would not accede to the president's plea to the Big Six for a cessation of demonstrations—to deny Goldwater any racial ammunition with which to attack Johnson—King sided with Wilkins, Young, and Randolph in support of curtailing "mass marches, picketing and demonstrations" until after the elections. King felt this action sanctioned him to go to the Democratic National Convention in Atlantic City and press for the seating of the MFDP delegates rather than the regular Mississippi Democratic Party delegates, despite Johnson's insistence that such a move would only alienate white southern voters and the politicians who represented them.

Appearing before the Credentials Committee, King argued, "I say to you that any party in the world should be proud to have a delegation such as this seated in their midst. For it is in these saints in ordinary walks of life that the true spirit of democracy finds its most profound and abiding expression." Facing the Mississippi regulars, he censured them for not admitting "a single Negro into a state university," for illegally excluding blacks from the electoral process, and for pledging "to defy the candidate and platform" of the national Democratic Party.

"The question cannot be decided by the splitting of legal hairs or by seemingly expedient political compromises," King insisted. The failure to give people the vote and the right to govern themselves "brings certain chaos" to the institutions that allow such injustice to prevail. The

MFDP, he concluded, *"has assumed symbolic value for oppressed people the world over."* Seating its delegation *"would become symbolic of the intention of this country to bring freedom and democracy to all people . . . It would be a beacon light of hope for all the disenfranchised millions of this earth, whether they be in Mississippi and Alabama, behind the Iron Curtain, floundering in the mire of South African apartheid, or freedom-seeking persons in Cuba who have now gone three years without elections. Recognition of the Freedom Democratic Party would say to them that somewhere in this world there is a nation that cares about justice, that lives in a democracy, and that ensures the rights of the downtrodden."*

Fannie Lou Hamer, a black Mississippi sharecropper, followed with a harrowing account of the "woesome times" brought on by her attempt to register to vote. Her effort to exercise the most basic right of citizenship had caused her to be thrown off the plantation she had labored on for eighteen years, to be shot at, and to be brutally beaten by Mississippi law officers until her skin turned blue and she could no longer walk. "Is this America, the land of the free and the home of the brave," she cried, "where we are threatened daily because we want to live as decent human beings?" An infuriated Lyndon Johnson hastily called a press conference to preempt the live coverage of the committee hearings.

The president remained fearful that a walkout by the Mississippi regulars would lead eight or ten other southern delegations to follow; or that it would cost him the cooperation of southern committee chairmen in Congress upon whom he counted for enactment of his Great Society programs; or that Robert Kennedy was orchestrating the conflict to trick him into defending the white regulars so Kennedy could then say that LBJ had turned against African-Americans. "I think this is Bobby's trap," he worried to a friend. He made sure that the undercover FBI squad assigned to King mounted surveillance of Kennedy as well. He demanded that Senator Hubert H. Humphrey settle the dispute if he wanted to be vice president, and persuaded Walter Reuther, head of the United Auto Workers, to hurriedly leave contract negotiations in Detroit and use his influence in the movement on behalf of Johnson. Reuther immediately warned Joseph Rauh, the Washington counsel for the UAW and acting MFDP counsel, that if he did not get the civil rights groups behind the president, he would lose his job with the union. At the same time, Reuther growled to King, "Your funding is on the line. The kind of money you got from us in Birmingham is there again for Mississippi, but you've got to help us and we've got to help Johnson."

Johnson supporters did everything possible to deny the MFDP the required votes of the Credentials Committee to plead their case before the entire convention. The pressure placed on the committee members, recalled one SNCC field-worker, was "something unbelievable. Every person on the list, every member of that Credentials Committee who was going to vote for the minority, got a call. They said, 'Your husband is up for a judgeship, and if you don't shape up, he won't get it. You're up for a loan. If you don't shape up, you won't get it.'"

Johnson insisted that the convention not signal to whites that militant blacks had taken over. He already felt vulnerable to Goldwater in the South because of signing the Civil Rights Act. He did not want to lose northern whites as well. Unionists were upset, he told Humphrey. "Think that nigra's going to get his job. They think a nigra's going to move next door to him." LBJ would not allow the MFDP to endanger his mandate for greatness. Accordingly, the president proposed a compromise he hoped would please most delegates and voters: two at-large seats with full voting privileges for the MFDP cochairs; the rest of the MFDP delegation seated as nonvoting "honored guests" of the convention; and a pledge to revise party rules to eliminate racial discrimination in delegations at all future Democratic conventions.

The MFDP faced the unpalatable choice of approving what it termed a "back of the bus" token compromise or condemning those, black and white, who had secured the most significant victories for civil rights since Emancipation. In heated exchanges, the civil rights leadership fought over the decision for nearly three days. King straddled, empathizing with those who opposed any compromise as a betrayal of the ideals of all those who had struggled, even died, for the right to vote, while granting the persuasiveness of the arguments that the compromise was a victory of sorts and that, pragmatically, blacks would profit most from an overwhelming Johnson victory over Goldwater. Politics, King reminded his colleagues, was the art of the possible. "We have to take the best we have and work to make it better." How could they hurt the chances of a president who had just produced a Civil Rights Act and the $1 billion War on Poverty, running against a racist, reactionary candidate? How could they spurn Hubert Humphrey, who had been the chief proponent of civil rights in the Senate for fifteen years and who would now be in line for the presidency? As a national black leader, the minister murmured, he would accept the compromise, "but if I were a Mississippi Negro, I would vote against it."

King's equivocation satisfied no one in the room. The ensuing debate pitted the practical against the idealistic, the moderates against the militants, the needs of the national movement against those of local movements, middle-class blacks against sharecroppers in the cotton fields, and it swirled with angry charges and recriminations. "We're not here to bring politics to our morality," SNCC's Robert Moses pointed out, "but to bring morality to our politics." Bayard Rustin responded that the movement must move from protest to politics to make "real gains and not only bear witness to injustice." "You're a traitor, Bayard!" shouted SNCC's Mendy Samstein. Others in SNCC derided the compromise as the "usual bone thrown to Negroes who showed signs of revolt." Roy Wilkins yapped back, "You have put your point across. You should just pack your bags up and go home." Fannie Lou Hamer, speaking for the MFDP grassroots delegates, chided Wilkins, "Give 'em two dollars and a car and they think they're fine." She insisted, "We didn't come all the way up here to compromise . . . We didn't come all this way for two seats."

SNCC's James Forman, eager for the fray, accused Wilkins of a "fuck-the-people" stance and then turned on King and SCLC. All the enmity between the young militants and the preachers, which had been simmering since the Freedom Rides and Albany, boiled over. "While you niggers been staying in fancy hotels eating chicken, we been sleeping on floors in Mississippi . . . Y'all come through with nice cars, make a speech and run back to your fancy churches in Atlanta. It's bullshit!" Forman left no doubt about SNCC's chagrin with the intermittent nature and itinerant style of King's involvement in the movement.

Charging a "sellout" by the white liberal establishment, the

MFDP delegation bolted the convention. Although the delegation had succeeded in making sure that lily-white delegations would never be seated at future Democratic nominating conventions, and had raised the vital issue of the right to vote—which the recently approved Civil Rights Act did not address—its members felt abandoned and betrayed by those they had considered allies. "I will have nothing to do with the political system any longer," Robert Moses commented to reporters. One SNCC field secretary, Cleveland Sellers, referred to the disillusioning episode as "the end of innocence," after which "things could never be the same." Another, Stokely Carmichael, bellowed, "If you try to work from within, you're going to be cheated. The only way the Negro can be effective is to wreak havoc from without." Some in SNCC celebrated their unwillingness to have anything more to do with white liberals, and some questioned the very idea of nonviolence and SNCC's interracial basis. Several hurried off to Africa to meet with revolutionary nationalists.

Without waiting to hear Johnson's acceptance speech, a despondent King went home. SNCC's personal attacks hurt. Splits in the movement troubled him. Having to compromise a moral crusade distressed him. Seeking solace, he toured Europe with his wife; upon their return, he checked in to an Atlanta hospital with a viral infection, high blood pressure, and twenty pounds of excessive weight. At low ebb, lying in a hospital bed, he answered a telephone call from Coretta: "Martin, you have been awarded the Nobel Peace Prize."

At thirty-five, the youngest recipient in the history of the award, King gathered his closest aides by his bedside to pray that SCLC would bear the heavy cross the prize bestowed and redouble its commitment and efforts. He told reporters he was accepting the award as a trustee on behalf of the entire civil rights movement, that history had thrust him into this role. "It would be both immoral and a sign of ingratitude if I did not face my moral responsibility to do what I can in this struggle." In an article for the Negro press, King described himself and the other civil rights leaders as the pilot, and the masses of Americans who had demonstrated and marched as the ground crew, without whom there would be no journey for human dignity and social justice. It was the nonviolent protesting people who had earned this prize, he reiterated. "When years have rolled past and when the blazing light of truth is focused on this marvelous age in which we are now living—men and women will know and children will be taught that we have a finer land, a better people, a more noble civilization—because of the ground crew which made possible the jet flight to the clear skies of brotherhood."

King then crisscrossed the nation to increase African-American voter turnout. He took heart in November's landslide victory for Johnson and the Democrats. He began to confer with associates on the details of an SCLC campaign for voting rights in Selma, Alabama. Finally, he flew to the island of Bimini for a brief vacation.

He wanted to relax and not obsess about his responsibilities and troubles, including those with J. Edgar Hoover. The FBI had maintained its surveillance on King and his aides. Throughout 1964 it had planted news stories that King still accepted "Communist collaboration and even Communist advice" and that he'd ignored his own promises to sever contact with "key figures in the covert apparatus of the Communist Party." The charges had become commonplace in Washington. At one point King fired back: "It would be encouraging to us if Mr. Hoover and the FBI would be as diligent in apprehending those responsible for bombing churches and killing little children, as they are in seeking out alleged communist infiltration in the civil rights movement."

Unable to accept such criticism from the likes of King, the FBI chief grew angrier. Abhorring the preacher's extramarital and interracial sexual liaisons as much as his radicalism, Hoover fumed, "I am amazed that the Pope gave an audience to such a degenerate." He grumped to his staff about the farce of such a "top alley cat" being awarded the Nobel.

On November 18, as King relaxed on the beach, Hoover met with a group of women reporters. He called King "the most notorious liar in the country." He repeated the allegation twice, encouraged the reporters to quote him, and added off the record that King, "one of the lowest characters in the country," was still "controlled" by Communist agents. King knew he faced the possibility of his private misdeeds becoming a public scandal and ending his career. He issued a statement that Hoover must have been "under extreme pressure" and had "apparently faltered under the awesome burden, complexities and responsibilities of his office." King concluded by extending an olive branch: "I have nothing but sympathy for this man who has served his country so well."

Privately, yet heard by the FBI on the wiretapped phones of King and his aides, the SCLC leaders scorned Hoover as old, broken-down, senile. They plotted to get President Johnson to dismiss or at least censure the Bureau head. Johnson, however, wanted no part of the battle. When one aide mentioned firing Hoover, Johnson ended the speculation: "I'd rather have him inside the tent pissing out than outside pissing in."

On December 1 a nervous King went to the office of J. Edgar Hoover, hoping for reconciliation. Accompanied by Abernathy, Young, and Walter Fauntroy of SCLC's Washington office, he quickly indicated to the director the necessity of the SCLC maintaining a good working relationship with the FBI. He said that any criticism of the Bureau or its chief attributed to him had to be a misquote or misrepresentation. King prattled about encouraging his supporters to cooperate with the FBI and said that he personally opposed communism as a "crippling totalitarian disease." For his part in the charade, Hoover rambled for the rest of the hour about past cases the FBI had solved, advised King to concentrate on getting his people registered to vote rather than to demonstrate, and explained that the Bureau had few black agents for the same reason Notre Dame lacked black football players—"their grades are never high enough." The politely insincere discussion accomplished nothing.

Vainly hoping he had pacified Hoover, King flew to London to begin his triumphal Nobel Prize tour. He identified the civil rights battles in the United States *with those in the far more deadly struggle for freedom in South Africa.* Praising the nonviolent leadership of Chief Lutuli, King lamented that Nelson Mandela and Robert Sobukwe were wasting away in the Robben Island prison. *"For it is we, through our investments, through our governments' failure to act decisively, who are guilty of bolstering up the South African tyranny."* We *"can join in the one form of nonviolent action that could bring freedom and justice to South Africa, the action which African leaders have appealed for: a massive movement for economic sanctions."* He promised to use his influence to spread the philosophy of nonviolence around the world, to speak out for a global war on poverty and for a planet free of war and nuclear weapons.

In Sweden, King contrasted Scandinavia's democratic socialism with American capitalism's unemployment, slums, poor education, and lack of free medical care. He called for an all-out world war against poverty. *"The rich nations must use their vast resources of wealth to develop the underdeveloped, school the unschooled, and feed the unfed. Ultimately a great nation is a compassionate nation."*

On December 10, in Oslo, King accepted the Nobel Peace Prize *"on behalf of a civil rights movement which is moving with determination and a majestic scorn for risk and danger to establish a reign of freedom and a rule of justice,"* and on behalf of nonviolence, which, not at all passive, was *"a powerful moral force which makes for social transformation."* He refused to accept, King said, *"that mankind is so tragically bound to the starless midnight of racism and war that the bright daybreak of peace and brotherhood can never become a reality . . . I believe that even amid today's mortar bursts and whining bullets, there is still hope for a brighter tomorrow . . . I have the audacity to believe that peoples everywhere can have three meals a day for their bodies, education and culture for their minds, and dignity, equality, and freedom for their spirits. I believe that what self-centered men have torn down, other self-centered men can build up . . . I still believe that we shall overcome!"*

The next evening King delivered his formal Nobel lecture. He again emphasized his acceptance of the prize on behalf of *"the real heroes of the freedom struggle,"* the *"devotees of nonviolence who have moved so courageously against the ramparts of racial injustice and who in the process have acquired a new estimate of their own worth."* He used the occasion to reiterate the freedom struggle's determined *"demand for dignity, equality, jobs, and citizenship,"* and then to speak at length about ending poverty in the United States and throughout the world, and about achieving disarmament and finding alternatives to war—the two themes that would dominate the last years of his life.

Returning to the United States, King reiterated the interconnections among racism, world poverty, and war. Feted at New York's City Hall, he lambasted America's nuclear weaponry, its economic inequality, and the paucity of its efforts to end poverty. Yet in a dark, confused world beset by dangers, King still had faith in 1964 that *"the kingdom of God may yet reign in the hearts of men."*

But not in J. Edgar Hoover's heart. As the historian Taylor Branch wrote, "King and Hoover looked at each other through opposite ends of a powerful telescope. To King, Hoover was a distant speck of white authority, hostile and yet necessary to hopes for justice in the South, whereas Hoover closely examined King's magnified pores." Never intending to relent, Hoover, in his first speech after meeting King, alluded to "morally corrupt charlatans" in the civil rights movement. A few days later, FBI agents mailed the Bureau's Christmas package to the King home. Known to Hoover's aides as the "suicide package," it contained a spool of magnetic tape replete with King's bugged sexual groans and dirty jokes and a note warning, "Your end is approaching." Describing the minister as a colossal moral fraud, a "dissolute, abnormal moral imbecile," and an "evil, abnormal beast," the anonymous letter concluded, "King, there is only one thing left for you to do. You know what it is . . . You are done. There is but one way out for you. You better take it before your filthy, abnormal fraudulent self is bared to the nation."

6

WE SHALL OVERCOME,

1965

The ultimate measure of a man is not where he stands in moments of comfort and convenience, but where he stands at times of challenge and controversy.

L ike a ticking time bomb, the FBI package lay amid a cascade of unopened holiday mail in the King household. Unmindful, Martin Luther King finalized plans for the Selma campaign as 1965 began. It would prove to be the civil rights struggle that brought the most public sympathy; unprecedented northern white support in public opinion polls and in protest demonstrations; and the quickest, strongest assistance from the federal government. In the process, however, all the fissures in the movement became major cleavages. A victim of its own success, the movement created aspirations it could not fulfill. As white racist violence did not abate, some in the movement became ever more disinclined to compromise and disdainful of white support. "The paths of Negro-white unity that had been converging," King reflected, "crossed at Selma and like a giant X began to diverge."

On the long road from Montgomery to Albany to Birmingham to St. Augustine to Selma, King and SCLC had learned much and changed considerably. The years of anguish and triumph gradually transformed their commitment to nonviolence from *satyagraha*—

peaceful persuasion intended to change the hearts and minds of oppressors—to *duragraha*, nonviolence as a means to coerce a requisite end. SCLC planning proceeded on the conviction that white savagery against unresisting civil rights protesters provoked the national outcry necessary to move the federal government to act. Confrontation and crisis, wrote historian Adam Fairclough, "would arouse the press, the pulpit, the politicians, and the president. The desire for such a confrontation determined both the target and the tactics."

Like no other black leader, King had been able to transform the mass arrests and violence by southern law-enforcement officers and white hoodlums into national and international publicity that forced a government response. Accordingly, nonviolence became provocation. As King privately outlined the scenario for Project Alabama: (1) "nonviolent demonstrators go into the streets to exercise their constitutional rights"; (2) "racists resist by unleashing violence against them"; (3) "Americans of conscience in the name of decency demand federal intervention and legislation"; and (4) "the Administration, under mass pressure, initiates measures of immediate intervention and remedial legislation." Publicly, King asserted, "When you give witness to an evil you do not cause the evil but you oppose it so it can be cured."

President Johnson had just told King that a voting rights bill would have to wait. He wanted the dust to settle from the Civil Rights Act, less than half a year old, and he needed southern votes for other Great Society programs. "And if I present a voting rights bill, they will block the whole program. So it's just not the wise and the politically expedient thing to do," Johnson explained. "I'm going to do it eventually, but I can't get a voting rights bill through in this session of Congress." Not content to let the president set the movement agenda, King and his aides responded positively to the request of Selma blacks for assistance in their voting rights drive. SNCC field-workers had faltered there and grudgingly given approval to SCLC to focus on Selma as the site for its campaign.

Selma's strong local movement, the Dallas County Voters League—led by Reverend Frederick D. Reese and NAACP veteran Amelia P. Boynton—made it attractive to SCLC. Moreover, Selma, birthplace of the Alabama Citizens' Council, epitomized the difficulties of blacks voting in the Deep South. Although a majority of the city's 28,500 population, African-Americans accounted for just 3 percent of those on the voting rolls. Only 1.9 percent of its eligible blacks were registered. Even worse, in the adjacent, overwhelmingly black counties of Lowndes and Wilcox, barely a single African-American could vote. In all three counties, the registrar's office was open only twice a month, and the registrars often came in late, took long lunch breaks, and went home early. Few blacks, no matter how highly educated, passed the required literacy test, in which registrars could quiz applicants about sixty-eight provisions of the Alabama state constitution.

Selma city ordinances made public meetings subject to surveillance and harassment, and if those methods failed, the gun, the club, and the cattle prod produced the fear that kept blacks from even trying to register to vote. When SNCC organized a "Freedom Day" on October 7, 1963, a local photographer, under orders from Sheriff James G. Clark, Jr., took pictures of the 250 blacks who had lined up to register, asking them as he did so what their employers would think of the pictures. Police beat SNCC workers who tried to bring food and water to those in line.

The SCLC expected the heavyset Dallas County sheriff to be every bit as vicious as Birmingham's Bull Connor. It counted on Clark's inability to rein in his hair-trigger temper. It depended on him to produce the notoriety and martyrdom necessary for the national support to enact a voting rights bill. SCLC staffers arriving in Selma were neither surprised nor disappointed when they encountered Clark wearing a huge button on his shirt: NEVER! He would be their perfect foil.

As Abernathy admitted, they sought to be "visibly abused." King repeatedly urged marchers "to let Clark show his true colors." Hopefully, added Andy Young, it would occur "on Main Street, at noon, in front of CBS, NBC, and ABC television cameras." That would give SCLC its dramatic crisis. Longing to prevent it, Selma's new mayor, a young refrigerator salesman named Joe Smitherman, and his city police chief, Wilson Baker, endeavored to get the burly Clark to follow the Albany model of polite but firm resistance. "We were determined," Baker said, "not to give them what they wanted."

"At the rate they are letting us register now," King declared at the

onset of Project Alabama at the Brown Chapel AME Church on January 2, 1965, *"it will take a hundred and three years to register all of the fifteen thousand Negroes in Dallas County who are qualified to vote.* [THAT'S RIGHT.] *But we don't have that long to wait!* [TELL THEM, DOCTOR.] [SPEAK! SPEAK!] *Today marks the beginning of a determined, organized, mobilized campaign to get the right to vote everywhere in Alabama.* [ALL RIGHT, YES.] *Give us the ballot! Give us the ballot!"* he shouted. *"We are not asking,"* he warned as applause shook the walls. *"We are demanding the ballot!* [YESSIR!] *To get the right to vote, we must be ready to march. We must be ready to go to jail by the thousands. We will bring a voting bill into being on the streets of Selma!"* [IT'S TIME. YES! YES!]

Before the campaign could heat up, King received a phone call from a distraught Coretta. Because of the Nobel Prize trip, she had just opened the package secretly sent by the FBI. She summoned him home to Atlanta immediately. There, he and his closest aides listened to the earthy tape and read the letter demanding his suicide. They heard King's unmistakable sexual groans and recognized that the bawdy comments of friends came from at least three different cities, implying a concerted, extensive surveillance campaign by the FBI. King dispatched Abernathy and Young to ask the FBI to halt its vendetta against him, but Assistant Director Cartha "Deke" DeLoach denied any interest by the FBI in King's private life.

"They are out to break me," King acknowledged grimly. "They are out to get me, harass me, break my spirit." He knew he would have to live the rest of his life with the fear of public disclosure and ruin. And without FBI protection, he understood the greater likelihood of his assassination. Despite the risk and immense strain, he refused to succumb or be intimidated by Hoover. His leadership of the movement would not be inhibited.

In mid-January he returned to Selma, where the campaign, as was typical, started slowly. SCLC led peaceful daily marches to the Dallas County courthouse to attempt to register blacks to vote, once even rousing more than a hundred black schoolteachers—who usually did not get involved in civil rights protests for fear of retaliation from the white school board—to march to the courthouse.

Although King, according to local black lawyer J. L. Chestnut, Jr., "gave the movement in Selma more legitimacy and raised the confidence factor" among local people, Sheriff Clark denied the SCLC the confrontation it needed. By the end of the month, more than two thousand blacks had been arrested, without the photographic incident to spark national outrage.

Frustrated by Clark's calm demeanor, King decided to lead a giant demonstration on February 1. Encouraging his followers "to march on ballot boxes until brotherhood becomes more than a meaningless word in an opening prayer, but the order of the day on every legislative agenda," King got himself arrested along with 770 other protesters, many of them schoolchildren. The next day Clark imprisoned yet another 520 blacks for parading without a permit. The day after, he arrested 300 more students. Clark had not behaved in a brutal manner, but the growing number of arrests did lead President Johnson to issue a strong statement in support of black voting rights. A federal district judge ordered Clark to desist from impeding prospective black voters from marching to the courthouse. Encouraged, Andrew Young—who had succeeded Wyatt Walker as SCLC's executive director—made the decision to suspend demonstrations.

King, in jail, would not go along. He ordered Young to reverse his edict. They needed to keep up the pressure, he reprimanded Young, to stay on the offensive. "It was a mistake not to march today. In a crisis we must have a sense of drama . . . We can't stop." On February 5 King left jail, asserting to reporters that he would go to Washington to ask LBJ for voting rights legislation.

Invited by SNCC for its own purposes, Malcolm X addressed a mass voter registration rally in Tuskegee on February 3, and another at the imposing double-towered Brown Chapel two days later. There, the slim, reddish-haired six-footer, his fist slashing the air, insisted that one had the right to use any means necessary to gain the right to vote. "I don't believe in any kind of nonviolence," he snapped. Noting that he could not visit King in jail because he had a plane to catch for a speaking engagement in London, Malcolm X instead met with Coretta. "I want Dr. King to know that I didn't come to Selma to make his job difficult." He calmly stroked his goatee. "I really did come thinking that I could make it easier. If the white people realize what the alternative is, perhaps they will be more willing to hear Dr. King."

In the process of re-creating himself and fundamentally altering his beliefs, Malik el-Shabazz, as he now called himself, would be shot down later that month in a hail of gunfire in Harlem's Audubon Ballroom. Saddened, King claimed that his longtime critic "was re-evaluating his own philosophical presuppositions and moving toward a greater understanding of the nonviolent movement and toward more tolerance of white people."

Whether the two adversaries would, or could, have become allies, no one knows for sure. Both men understood the "good cop/bad cop" roles they performed. They represented, according to theologian James Cone, "the 'yin and yang' deep in the soul of black America."

One grew up sheltered and inspired by a strong African-American family, church, and community; the other went from a broken home to a life of vice and crime—pimping, peddling drugs, stealing—and then to prison. One gave voice to those steeped in the southern black church who were yearning for a better life; the other expressed the reality of ghetto life for many northern blacks expecting nothing better. One spoke to middle-class Americans of both races, the other to the poorer, ghettoized black. One fought for desegregation, for "black-and-white together"; the other insisted on black nationalism and black separatism. One sought to overcome by nonviolence; the other mocked it as cowardly, vowing victory "by any means necessary." One struggled to reform and regenerate a racist society; the other demanded revenge and retribution for abuse. One spoke unashamedly of loving one's enemy; the other thought only fools "could love someone who has treated blacks as the white man has." One built consensus; the other polarized. One endorsed America's highest religious and democratic ideals; the other denounced them as evil. One's "American Dream" was the other's "American Nightmare." Malcolm called Martin "a fool," "a traitor," "a Reverend Dr. Chickenwing," and "a twentieth-century Uncle Tom." King did not respond in kind, attributing the Black Muslim's "demagogic oratory" to "a society whose ills in race relations are so deep-rooted that it produces a Malcolm X."

More immediately, King feared meeting a fate similar to Malcolm's. To reporters, he made light of the almost daily threats on his life. Yet he believed: "One has to conquer the fear of death if he is going to do anything constructive in life and take a stand against evil." Despite the mounting death threats and his concerns about the FBI,

King did not cease lecturing throughout the country, ministering to his flock in Atlanta, or protesting in Selma.

Over several more weeks of sustained demonstration, the continuing deadlock in Alabama gave cheer to neither side. As fatigue set in, King toyed with the notion of declaring victory and shifting the sputtering campaign to another site. Instead, he checked in to an Atlanta hospital, suffering from exhaustion. At the same time, Clark went into a hospital with chest pains. "The niggers are giving me a heart attack," he whined. In response, some two hundred black schoolchildren, either exemplars of nonviolence or adept students of strategy, prayed outside the hospital for Clark's speedy recovery.

"You should not only know how to start a good movement," King reasoned in endorsing a shift from Selma to Lowndes County, you "should also know when to stop." To get the voting rights bill, "we need to make a dramatic appeal through Lowndes and other counties because the people of Selma are tired." King also realized that many Selma blacks did not want to be used to gain SCLC's national objective of congressional action on black voting rights. They wanted to use their gradually increasing number of registered voters to exert influence on Selma officials and not just be foot soldiers in SCLC's daily marches. But King and SCLC needed Selma or similar locales as the stage on which to dramatize racist disfranchisement. The protests would be extended into the surrounding Black Belt counties "so as to let the nation and the press know that this movement is not losing momentum." King promised "a broader focus of civil disobedience," including dangerous night marches. But, still ailing, he returned to Atlanta to rest while his aides planned a February 17 nighttime march in nearby Marion in Perry County.

Rumors quickly spread that black participants in the next night's march planned to break James Orange, an SCLC aide, out of jail. As soon as the marchers left the Zion Chapel Methodist Church, state troopers first ordered that they turn around and then began assaulting the demonstrators. "They turned all the lights out, shot the lights out, and they beat people at random," recalled Albert Turner, the young head of the Perry County Civic League. "They didn't have to be marchers. All you had to do was be black." Jimmie Lee Jackson, a young black Vietnam veteran, was shot twice in the stomach as he attempted to protect his mother from a beating in a nearby café. Critically injured, Jackson died a week later. Turner described what had happened in Marion as one of "the most vicious situations that was in the whole Civil Rights Movement." The police were "intending to kill somebody as an example, and they did kill Jimmie Jackson."

Though there was no national outrage at Jackson's murder, his death provided the movement with a martyr and an audacious response. King thought blacks throughout Alabama should join a motorcade to the capital in Montgomery, to call Governor George Wallace to account. After preaching at Jackson's memorial service—where he excoriated the "timidity of a federal government that is willing to spend millions of dollars a day to defend freedom in Vietnam but cannot protect the rights of its citizens at home"—King left for a meeting with aides in New York City.

That night Bevel remarked to the mass meeting that, as Mordecai in the Old Testament had implored Esther to go to the Persian king to plead for her people, "I must go to see the king!" While those in Brown Chapel roared their approval, Bevel adopted a Selma woman's suggestion that they walk the fifty-four miles to Montgomery instead of driving. "The blood of Jackson will be on our hands if we don't march. Be prepared to walk to Montgomery!" Bevel beseeched. "Be prepared to sleep on the highway!" Without consulting King, Bevel announced to reporters that King would lead the march from Selma to Montgomery on Sunday, March 7.

"Such a march cannot and will not be tolerated." Governor Wallace threw down the gauntlet, adding that his state troopers would "use whatever measures are necessary to prevent a march."

SNCC's Alabama staff also opposed the march, criticizing it as a futile distraction and a publicity stunt by SCLC. To reporters, SNCC complained that it had performed the tough pioneering work while SCLC reaped the glory and the financial contributions. Rather than march, it preferred to intensify local protest efforts as a way of proving that the movement could not be intimidated.

King stood fast with Bevel. The march and a presentation of grievances to the governor would be a telling response to Jackson's death, would give outraged blacks a means to vent their anger, and at the same time would focus the national spotlight on the denial of the right of African-Americans to vote in the Deep South. "I can't promise you that it won't get you beaten," King admitted at Brown Chapel. "I can't promise you that it won't get your house bombed. I can't promise you won't get scarred up a bit. But we must stand up for what is right."

However, Sunday, March 7, found King preaching in Atlanta rather than marching in Selma. Given the attorney general's warnings of potential assassins in the area, as well as the FBI's assertion that it would neither protect King nor inform him of threats against his life, King gave in to the pleas of Hosea Williams and Jim Bevel that, for the sake of his safety, he not lead the procession. Instead, Williams and John Lewis (marching as an individual and not as SNCC chairman) led some five hundred supporters out of Brown Chapel. Carrying bedrolls and lunch sacks, they silently marched through the dreary neighborhood and then down Broad Street toward the Edmund Pettus Bridge, which spanned the muddy Alabama River on the route to Montgomery.

As the TV cameras whirred and news reporters took notes, the long double file approached the bridge named for a Confederate general, the gateway out of Selma. Blue-uniformed, helmeted state troopers, commanded by Major John Cloud, stood shoulder to shoulder across the four lanes of the highway just beyond the bridge, and some hundred of Sheriff Jim Clark's deputized possemen lined both flanks. Upon Cloud's order, Lewis and Williams came to a halt on the far side of the bridge. "This is an unlawful assembly," Cloud bellowed through his bullhorn. "You are ordered to disperse and go back to your church or to your homes." "May we have a word with the major?" Williams asked twice. "There is no word to be had," the major barked. "You have two minutes to turn around and go back to your church." The column held its ground. Suddenly, Cloud ordered: "Troopers forward!"

The state troopers rushed forward in a flying wedge, trampling the first score of marchers to the ground and continuing to bowl over one row of marchers after another, flailing with nightsticks. Then Clark's mounted posse, voicing a rebel yell and swinging bullwhips and rubber tubing wrapped in barbed wire, spurred their horses into the retreating marchers. "Get those goddamned niggers!" Sheriff Clark could be heard. "And get those goddamned white niggers!" As the white spectators lining the south side of the road whooped and cheered, the screaming marchers huddled together to avoid the horses' hooves. A gray cloud billowed over them. "Tear gas!" someone screamed. Coughing and crying, the marchers broke ranks and ran. As troopers and possemen pursued them, the choking, stumbling victims fled back to Brown Chapel.

"They literally whipped folk all the way back to the church," remembered one marcher. "They even came up in the yard of the church, hittin' on folk. Ladies, men, babies, children—they didn't give a damn who they were." Bedlam reigned. The parsonage became an emergency room for the score of African-Americans requiring treatment.

Sunday evening, news reports of the carnage spread across the country. Television had captured it graphically. The nation saw it and recoiled. It now understood the reign of terror by which southern racists kept African-Americans from voting. ABC interrupted its Sunday movie—about the horrors of Nazi genocide and war crimes—to broadcast fifteen minutes of footage of the police assault on the bridge. "The violence in Selma was so similar to the violence in Nazi Germany that viewers could hardly miss the connection," wrote Andy Young. Network news programs stunned viewers with repeated images of billowing tear gas, stomping horses, and law officers venting their fury on limping, bleeding black marchers. The pictures of "Bloody Sunday" created an uproar of indignation. What *Time* magazine termed "an orgy of police brutality" resulted in a broad consensus in favor of action by Washington. Demands for federal intervention besieged the White House. Fourteen students, insisting that the president send troops to Selma, staged a seven-hour sit-in at the White House, while hundreds more sat in the snow outside.

At Brown Chapel that evening, outrage made the demand for another march irresistible. "There just had to be a march," Young remarked, "some kind of nonviolent demonstration to get the expression out. If there wasn't, you would have had real violence." As we "looked around the room at the bandages and bruises, we knew we had to do something." SNCC reversed course, taunting King for avoiding the perils he had invited his followers to brave. Stung by the accusations of cowardice, King announced that he would lead a second march on Tuesday, March 9, and invited clergy from all over the nation to *"join us on Tuesday in our peaceful, non-violent march for freedom."*

In the vicious maltreatment of defenseless citizens in Selma, where old women and young children were gassed and clubbed at random, we have witnessed an eruption of the disease of racism which seeks to destroy all America. No American is without responsibility . . . The people of Selma will struggle on for the soul of the nation, but it is fitting that all Americans help to share the burden.

Some 450 rabbis, pastors, and nuns hurried to Selma. Thousands of other supporters converged on Washington to press Congress for voting rights legislation. And tens of thousands of Americans, white and black, joined sympathy demonstrations across the country.

Monday morning, SCLC attorneys asked U.S. district judge Frank M. Johnson for an injunction to prevent Governor Wallace and Alabama police authorities from blocking the proposed march. Viewed by the movement as a liberal judge with a decent record on civil rights, Johnson surprised the lawyers by enjoining the SCLC from undertaking the march until a formal court hearing, which he scheduled for March 11. Despite strong opposition from SNCC's James Forman, King decided to obey the federal courts. He had never defied a federal court order, and to do so now would mean a march without federal protection, likely to be attacked by Wallace's troopers. Most vitally, to defy the court order might destroy the movement's continued ability to work with President Johnson for a strong voting rights law.

Once again King found himself walking the narrow, precipitous path between those who held the key to the changes he sought and the activists who thought him too timid. He knew that what made him comprising and cowardly to SNCC made him responsible and respectable to the majority of African-Americans and liberal whites, without whose support there would be no civil rights advances.

King's emotions vied against his calculations. He could not "forget my agony of conscience for not being there when I heard of the dastardly acts perpetrated against nonviolent demonstrators." If SCLC did not march now, it would rob the campaign of its momentum, disappoint the hundreds of supporters who had traveled to Selma to march, and widen the rift between SCLC and SNCC, many of whose members he continued to admire.

"Mr. Attorney General, you have not been a black man in America for the past three hundred years," King replied to Nicholas Katzenbach when the attorney general urged that he not march. True to his conscience, King announced Monday night at Brown Chapel that he would be marching. "We've gone too far to turn back now. We must let them know that nothing can stop us—not even death itself." Freedom requires conquering the fear of death, he said. "Man dies when he refuses to stand up for what is right, for what is just, for what is true."

King felt responsible for nurturing the militancy of Selma's blacks, many of whom now demanded that he join them in marching across the bridge. He could not bring himself to desert the youthful followers he had energized, those jailed in earlier demonstrations who now proclaimed that they would march regardless of what King decided. To postpone the confrontation would leave him open to charges of being a toady of LBJ, a tool of the establishment. Worse, it might destroy the nonviolent protest movement.

Yet in no uncertain terms, President Johnson demanded that King obey the courts and postpone the march. On Tuesday morning Judge Johnson handed down an injunction against the march. Dozens of administration officials and congressional supporters pressed King to avoid a repetition of Bloody Sunday. The SCLC leader knew he could not forfeit their support by defying the federal courts, which had been the major ally of the civil rights movement since the *Brown* decision. Indeed, the movement's most basic appeal had been for legal rights. His goal remained effective voting rights legislation and enforcement, and it would not come to pass without the cooperation of Congress and the White House.

Later that Tuesday morning King met with LeRoy Collins, head of the federal government's new Community Relations Service, and agreed to a secret face-saving plan. In return for an agreement by Alabama authorities not to molest the marchers, King would lead his followers to the Pettus Bridge, stop when halted by the troopers, pause to pray briefly, and then lead the marchers back to Brown Chapel. "I'll do my best to turn them back," he mumbled.

To those waiting to march, who knew nothing of the agreement, King spoke in a different voice. "We have the right to walk the highways," he contended.

> I have no alternative but to lead a march from this spot to carry our grievances to the seat of government. I have made my choice. I have got to march. I do not know what lies ahead of us. There may be beatings, jailings, tear gas. But I would rather die on the highways of Alabama than make a butchery of my conscience by compromising with evil.

Nearly a thousand blacks and half as many white sympathizers, urged by King to "put on their walking shoes," proudly paraded out of the church after him. Six abreast, they sang stanza after stanza of "Ain't Gonna Let Nobody Turn Me 'Round" as King led them toward the line of Major Cloud's one hundred state troopers. "I am asking you to stop where you are," Cloud once again boomed into his bullhorn. "We are here to see that this march will not continue." King alleged: "We have a right to march." Cloud repeated his order, and the preacher responded with a request that his group might stop to pray. "You can have your prayer," the major sneered, "and then you must return to your church." Following a verse of "We Shall Overcome," the mile-long column of kneeling marchers prayed and then rose to follow King.

Instead of marching forward, King turned and walked back toward Selma. At that moment the state troopers departed from the agreed-upon scenario and ambled to the side of the road. Highway 80, the path to George Wallace's Montgomery, lay wide open. But no one crossed the bridge. Wave after wave of confused marchers walked to the spot where King had stood, then turned around and went back to Selma, still singing "Ain't Gonna Let Nobody Turn Me 'Round."

"All of a sudden I realized that the people in front were turning around and coming back," a white minister from Boston recalled, "and I was aghast. What is going on? Are we not going through with this confrontation? What's happening?" An embarrassed King ducked the questions in seclusion while aides tried to placate his disappointed and angry followers. Few could accept the hollow rhetoric that the marchers had made their point.

Yet King understood that the Bloody Sunday march made what followed merely ceremonial, barely relevant. The national conscience had been aroused, the commitment secured. The movement had already persuaded millions of middle-of-the-road whites to accept black enfranchisement. To now alienate the administration and public opinion would serve no purpose. An illegal march would only hurt the cause.

Nevertheless, SNCC activists heatedly denounced the "Tuesday Turnaround." They scorned SCLC for making a secret deal to terminate the march. James Forman pulled SNCC's staff out of Selma, accusing King of "a classic example of trickery against the people."

King would not be baited. If he admitted the compromise arrangement, it would confirm the worst fears of SNCC and others in the movement that he had become little more than a cowardly emissary of the Johnson administration. On the other hand, if he had denied the understanding with LeRoy Collins and claimed his intention to march to Montgomery, he would have been in violation of Judge Johnson's injunction and likely found in contempt of court.

So the preacher waffled, telling reporters, "We knew we would not get to Montgomery. We knew we would not get past the troopers. We did not disengage until they made it clear they were going to use force. We disengaged then because we felt we had made our point, we had revealed the continued presence of violence." One day he asserted that "no pre-arranged agreement existed," and he felt they had to march "even if it meant a recurrence of violence, arrest, or even death." The next day the pastor admitted that there had been a "tacit agreement," contending, "I did it to give them [his supporters] an outlet. I felt that if I had not done it, the pent-up emotions, the inner tensions . . . would have exploded into retaliatory violence."

Fortunately for King, white racist violence kept the spotlight on Selma and not on his fumbling rationalizations and justifications. On Tuesday evening, as militant blacks emitted their displeasure with King, a gang of whites attacked three white Unitarian ministers who had come to Selma to participate in the march. One of the victims,

Reverend James J. Reeb from Boston—where he worked on housing for the poor in a black ghetto neighborhood—suffered a serious blow to the skull with a club. Reeb died two days later, the result "of a malignant sickness in our society," King despaired, "that comes from the tolerance of organized hatred and violence."

Reeb's death, unlike that of the black Jimmie Lee Jackson, provoked a national outcry and renewed demonstrations across the country. Some fifty members of Congress immediately criticized the attack. More than six hundred pickets at the White House demanded federal intervention. Some ten thousand marched in Detroit, led by the mayor and Michigan's governor. At least fifteen thousand protested in Harlem, and an equal number rallied in Washington. Many more thousands of Americans sent letters and telegrams to their members of Congress and the president supporting voting rights legislation, a position echoed by most of the nation's press. Lawyers in the Justice Department and the White House sped up their efforts to finalize the administration's voting rights bill.

King had another Birmingham and, luckily, personal vindication. Gauging the national mood, he again blended militancy with responsibility and elevated a local conflict into a battle of universals. He made Selma a theater of divine revelation. And, as Adam Fairclough observed, by obeying Judge Johnson's injunction to postpone the march, King reemphasized his respect for the federal courts, maintained Lyndon Johnson as a crucial ally in the quest for black voting rights, and shielded himself from white racist charges that he had behaved irresponsibly. He had kept his followers out of a bloodbath without diminishing in the slightest the swelling demand, in and out of Congress, for voting rights legislation.

As the reaction to the police rampage at Selma exceeded the public outrage over Bull Connor's use of police dogs and fire hoses, so Lyndon Johnson responded far more decisively than had John Kennedy. On Saturday, March 13, Johnson conferred with George Wallace at the White House. With the six-feet-four LBJ towering over the diminutive governor, who sank low in a deep-cushioned couch, the president insisted that Wallace had wrongly denied blacks the most basic political right of all, the right to vote, and that the Alabaman's oath of office required him to protect, not attack, peaceful demonstrators. Then, with the cowed governor by his side, the president explained to reporters and a national television audience how heartfelt his reactions had been to the unfolding events in Alabama. He would submit a voting rights bill to Congress on Monday that would "strike down all restrictions used to discriminate and deny the right to vote." He commented, "What happened in Selma was an American tragedy. It is wrong to do violence to peaceful citizens in the streets of their town. It is wrong to deny Americans the right to vote. It is wrong to deny any person full equality because of the color of his skin."

Monday evening, before a television audience of more than seventy million, President Johnson addressed a joint session of Congress and expressed his unmistakable determination to secure passage of the voting rights bill. In his slow Texas drawl, he compared the struggle at Selma to those at Lexington and Concord and Appomattox, where "history and fate meet at a single time in a single place to shape a turning point in man's unending search for freedom." He contended that the "real hero of this struggle is the American Negro."

> His actions and protests, his courage to risk safety, and even to risk his life, have awakened the conscience of this nation. His demonstrations have been designed to call attention to injustice, designed to provoke change, designed to stir reform. He has called upon us to make good the promise of America. And who among us can say that we would have made the same progress were it not for his persistent bravery and his faith in American democracy?

Barely pausing for the waves of applause to end, the president moved beyond voting rights.

> Even if we pass this bill, the battle will not be over. What happened in Selma is part of the far larger movement which reaches into every section and state of America. It is the effort of American Negroes to secure for themselves the full blessings of American life. Their cause must be our cause too. Because it is not just Negroes, but really it is all of us, who must overcome

the crippling legacy of bigotry and injustice. And—we—shall—overcome!

Most in the movement could not have asked for more. In Montgomery, watching on television, King wiped tears from his eyes. He thought Johnson's speech "one of the most eloquent, unequivocal, and passionate pleas for human rights ever made by a president of the United States." A member of his executive staff gushed: "It was a victory like none other. It was an affirmation of the movement." SNCC, not surprisingly, arraigned it as empty symbolism. The president had merely "ruined a good song," muttered James Forman.

Tuesday, March 16, as SCLC lawyers submitted to Judge Johnson a plan detailing the proposed march from Selma to Montgomery, SNCC organizers mounted a series of militant demonstrations near the state capitol. When some six hundred protesters led by Forman sat in the streets to block traffic, a dozen mounted deputies attacked them with canes and whips. A livid Forman blamed King for the Dexter Avenue Baptist Church's decision to turn down the SNCC request to make its building the campaign headquarters. King hurried to Montgomery to meet with Forman and patch up SCLC–SNCC relations. Both spoke that night to a mass rally at Beulah Baptist Church. The former Chicago schoolteacher, dressed in the SNCC uniform—the overalls of a sharecropper—demanded a campaign of civil disobedience to tie up Washington. "If we can't sit at the table of democracy, then we'll knock the fucking legs off." King followed, asserting that "we cannot stand idly by and allow" brutal beatings. He proposed "a peaceful and orderly march on the courthouse in Montgomery" to demand an apology from the sheriff for the attack on the demonstrators. Next morning he and Forman led two thousand marchers to the courthouse, where the sheriff apologized for the brutality of his possemen and the civil rights leaders promised to apply for permits before they demonstrated again.

Relations between SCLC and SNCC, however, remained tense. King rejected the counsel of several aides that he break with SNCC. Instead, he sought out emissaries such as Harry Belafonte to try to mend frayed relations. And when Judge Johnson finally approved SCLC's plans for a five-day march to begin on Sunday, March 21,

King asked Bevel, Williams, and Young to spend several days trying to persuade SNCC to take part. Forman remained hostile. SNCC would not endorse the march. Anyone could participate as an individual.

Sunday morning, more than thirty-two hundred blacks and whites gathered on the unpaved street by Brown Chapel to begin the march. "You will be the people that will write a new chapter in the history books of our nation," King addressed the rabbis and ministers, student radicals and would-be novelists, nuns and grandmothers. "Walk together, children, don't you get weary, and it will lead us to the Promised Land."

The joyous throng surged forward, laughing, singing, barely noticing the white hecklers with crude placards reading MARTIN LUTHER COON or the record shop blaring "Bye Bye Blackbird." With helicopters clattering overhead, and the federalized Alabama National Guard, federal marshals, and FBI agents lined up along the route, the huge cavalcade tramped uneventfully for seven miles along Jefferson Davis Highway before reaching its first campsite. As the rest were bused back to Selma, three hundred marchers, the maximum allowed by Judge Johnson, bedded down in two large tents.

Paced by Jim Letherer, a one-legged man from Michigan walking on crutches, and Joe Young, a blind man from Atlanta tapping with a cane, the marchers covered sixteen miles on Monday, passing rickety black churches and dilapidated black schools, and another eleven miles in the rain on Tuesday—troops guarding their flanks, army patrols checking the bridges and road ahead, and a convoy of armed vehicles in their wake. Suffering, like others, from badly blistered feet, King rested on Wednesday morning, then flew to Cleveland for a fund-raising rally, where he compared the march to Gandhi's Salt March to the Sea.

In what was more a victory parade than a protest march, an exhausted Martin Luther King led some thirty thousand supporters the final few miles to the Alabama state capitol on Thursday morning. Their ranks included Selma protesters in soggy clothes and shoes caked with mud, and a galaxy of movement veterans, labor leaders, movie stars, and religious officials from across the United States. A stout white woman carried a sign: HERE IS ONE NATIVE SELMAN FOR FREEDOM AND JUSTICE. It was indeed another giant step forward in the long trek toward racial justice. Many sang out:

Keep your eyes on the prize, hold on, hold on.
I've never been to heaven, but I think I'm right.
You won't find George Wallace anywhere in sight.
Oh, keep your eyes on the prize, hold on, hold on.

Stanley Levison, who had flown down from New York, "was struck by the unfamiliarity of the participants. They were not long-committed white liberals and Negroes. They were new forces from all faiths and classes." "I was glad I had on dark glasses," recalled Price Cobbs, a black psychiatrist, because "tears were streaming down my cheeks. I just wasn't prepared for the overwhelming feeling of love. I didn't realize that people of every color, every background, could really feel together." Similarly, Coretta Scott King "kept thinking about how ten years earlier" the civil rights movement was virtually all black, and what a beautiful thing it was now to see whites and African-Americans "marching together." The sight of so many whites and blacks from every station of life, "brimming with vitality and enjoying a rare comradeship," led Martin to think "I was seeing a microcosm of the mankind of the future in this moment of genuine and luminous brotherhood." The joy with which they sang "We Have Overcome" suggested to him how much America had changed in the nine years since his epiphany in the kitchen several blocks away.

As the nation watched on television, and George Wallace peered through the slats of his office venetian blinds, King addressed the largest-ever civil rights rally in the South. Once again his oratory transformed the occasion. Once again he transformed his podium into a pulpit. *"They told us we wouldn't get here,"* he trumpeted. *"And there were those who said that we would get here only over their dead bodies, but all the world today knows that we are here and that we are standing before the forces of power in the state of Alabama saying, 'We ain't goin' let nobody turn us around.'"* [YEAH!] [THAT'S RIGHT!] As the familiar "amens" ascended, King claimed with *"conviction that segregation is on its death bed, and the only thing uncertain about it is how costly the segregationists and Wallace will make the funeral."* [THAT'S RIGHT, BROTHER.] [YES. YEAH.]

King called for more marches, everywhere: *"Let us march on segregated housing until every ghetto of social and economic depression dissolves and Negroes and whites live side by side in decent, safe, and* sanitary housing. *Let us march on segregated schools until every vestige of segregated and inferior education become a thing of the past.* [IT'S TIME.] [YES, DEFINITELY!] *Let us march on poverty until no American parent has to skip a meal so that their children may eat.* [ALL RIGHT!] *March on poverty until no starved man walks the streets of our cities and towns in search of jobs that do not exist.* [SURE.] [NOW!] *Let us march on ballot boxes until all race baiters disappear from the political arena.* [THAT'S RIGHT!] *Let us march on ballot boxes"*—he turned to the Capitol—*"until the Wallaces of our nation tremble away in silence."* Thunderous waves of applause immersed the crowd.

To shouts of "Yes, sir!" "Speak!" "Tell it, Doctor!," King recalled Selma. *"Once more, the method of nonviolent resistance was unsheathed from its scabbard, and once again an entire community was mobilized to confront the adversary. And again the brutality of a dying order shrieks across the land. Yet Selma, Alabama, became a shining moment in the conscience of man."* [SO RIGHT. SO RIGHT.] He heralded with confidence that *"we are on the move now,"* and will reach *"the land of freedom."* [NOW! NOW! NOW!] There, he foresaw *"a society at peace with itself, a society that can live with its conscience. That will be a day not of the white man, not of the black man.* [SPEAK, PREACHER.] *That will be the day of man as man.*

"How long will it take?" King asked, and answered, *"Not long."* He concluded with a rising climax that elicited louder and louder exclamations of approval:

> *. . . however difficult the moment, however frustrating the hour, it will not be long because truth pressed to earth will rise again. How long?* [NOT LONG.] *Not long, because no lie can live forever. How long?* [NOT LONG.] *Not long, because the arm of the moral universe is long but it bends toward justice. How long?* [NOT LONG.] *Not long. Because mine eyes have seen the glory of the coming of the Lord . . . Glory, glory hallelujah! Glory, glory hallelujah! Glory, glory hallelujah!* [GLORY. GLORY HALLELUJAH!] [HALLELUJAH!]

White violence had made this moment possible, and it struck again. Mrs. Viola Liuzzo, the white wife of a Detroit labor-union official and mother of five children, had come to Alabama, her husband said later, because "it was everybody's business—she had to go." After King's speech, she volunteered to drive some of the marchers back to Selma. As she returned to Montgomery with a young SCLC volunteer later in the night to transport a second group of demonstrators, a car filled with Klansmen pulled alongside. As Liuzzo glanced at the car, a gunfire blast shattered her side window, and shotgun pellets lodged in the base of her brain. She died instantly. King had indicated in his speech that day that "a season of suffering" still lay ahead, but he had not expected it that soon. The "dying order" of hard-core segregationists remained murderous. Yet, as the reporter covering the march for *Ebony* observed, two died that Thursday—Viola Liuzzo and Jim Crow.

Selma would prove to be King's, and the movement's, crowning moment, the passage of the Voting Rights Act the apex of their success. In less than a decade, they had gone from asking to be treated decently on segregated buses to demanding their full and equal rights as American citizens. In less than two years, they had rewritten American law to destroy de jure segregation and disfranchisement. The awesome power of nonviolent direct action to expose the injustice of racism to the nation had again been substantiated, and the foundations of white supremacy lay in ruins. As never before, it surely seemed as if God, History, and the United States government were committed to the movement and to King. They had achieved a national consensus in favor of civil rights and faced a divided, dwindling, and uncertain opposition. Blacks were not at the end of the road, but they were farther along, and the prospects for additional strides were greater than they had ever been.

King had again demonstrated his charismatic leadership and inspirational oratory. They enabled him, despite the embarrassing moments, to emerge from the Selma campaign with an enhanced reputation. In the eyes of the great majority, black and white, King was the foremost symbol of the movement, its main strategist and chief spokesman. The preacher's actions and words had steeled the resolve of African-Americans to struggle for every aspect of first-class citizenship. With the movement, King had taught blacks how to effectively confront those who oppressed them, how to take pride in their race, how to gain their rights as Americans. He had helped southern blacks "destroy barriers of fear and insecurity that had been hundreds of years in the making," added SNCC's Cleveland Sellers. "He made it possible for them to believe they could overcome."

Despite the equivocations, Martin Luther King had succeeded in exposing the plight of southern blacks and the horrors of racism, leading many in white America to view the civil rights movement as morally right and in line with America's highest ideals of freedom and equality. Never before—or since—in American history had a private individual, holding no governmental position, used body and voice to affect public opinion so decisively and thereby induce such social and political change.

On August 3, 1965, the House of Representatives passed the Voting Rights Act by better than a four-to-one margin. The Senate followed suit the next day. Signing the act that authorized federal examiners to register qualified voters and suspended discriminatory devices such as literacy tests, President Johnson proclaimed, "Today is a triumph for freedom as huge as any victory that has ever been won on any battlefield. Today we strike away the last major shackle of fierce and ancient bonds." Almost every major proponent of black rights agreed. Voicing their general sentiment, John Lewis characterized the act as a "milestone and every bit as momentous and significant . . . as the Emancipation Proclamation or the 1954 Supreme Court decision." The lock on the ballot box for African-Americans had been shattered.

Following the arrival of a federal examiner in Selma, the percentage of voting-age African-Americans registered in the city rose in less than two months from under 10 percent to over 60 percent. Whereas fewer than 22 percent of Alabama adult blacks could vote in 1964, 57 percent could in 1968. In Mississippi the percentage of adult blacks registered to vote leaped from less than 7 percent in 1964 to nearly 67 percent in 1968. In those four years, the number of African-American voters in the South tripled. American politics would never again be as it was in the early 1960s.

In the immediate aftermath of Selma, however, King faced the challenge of coming up with a program that would utilize the groundswell of support for civil rights and lead the movement to yet greater accomplishments. Many expected him to pull rabbits out of a hat once more. His aides, as Andy Young admitted, "really didn't know what our direction should be after Selma," but they had no shortage of suggestions. Young wanted SCLC to pursue voter registration in the area around Selma. James Bevel lobbied for a national boycott of Alabama's goods and products to force the state's white leaders to comply with the Voting Rights Act. Some favored a program of dialogue with poorer whites, to reduce racial fears and help individuals of both races get to know one another as real human beings. Hosea Williams sponsored SCOPE—the Summer Community Organization and Political Education Project—a plan to enlist a thousand northern college students to organize black voter registration drives in the Deep South and engage in citizen education, much like SNCC had done in the Mississippi Freedom Summer of 1964.

Conversely, Bayard Rustin saw class, not race, as the next great cause. He wanted King to switch from "protest to politics," to head a biracial political movement to restructure the American economy and society. The key to a "majority liberal consensus" that would pursue far-reaching economic changes, Rustin insisted, was a new, different movement that would join the forces of civil rights with the labor movement. Real equality for African-Americans, he maintained, could never be achieved "within the framework of existing political and economic relations." Only a political coalition that would support a radical program to "alter the social structure of America" could accomplish that.

Stanley Levison warned King of reaching beyond his grasp. The civil rights coalition that King led supported moderate, gradual reform, particularly "against terror, violence, deprivation of voting rights and elementary human rights." It was for gently altering old patterns, not for excessive upheavals. "It is militant only against shocking violence and gross injustice," claimed Levison. "It is not for deep radical change." Moreover, the American people were "not ready for a radical restructuring of its economy and social order." Levison urged his friend to pursue the changes "possible within the limits of the basic system we now have."

Ironically, he cautioned King not to make the mistake that American Communists made in the 1930s when they insisted that "no deep-going improvements were attainable without socialism." King, he said, must not force the nation to choose "between equality and freedom for Negroes with the revolutionary alteration of our society, or to maintain the status quo with discrimination. The American people are not inclined to change their society in order to free the Negro." They were ready for reform, not revolution.

King, characteristically, saw some merit in all the ideas bandied about by his advisers, and he found it difficult to propose a specific program for SCLC that embraced his global human rights vision and his desire to end black poverty and privation. Then events, rather than arguments, shaped his course. On August 11, just five days after Johnson signed the Voting Rights Act, the most destructive race riot since World War II exploded in Watts, a Los Angeles ghetto where a quarter of a million African-Americans lived.

Shortly before eight on a sultry summer Wednesday evening, an ordinary arrest for drunk driving brought a typical crowd of onlookers. Angry words between white police and blacks on the street was an everyday occurrence in the ghetto. On this night the arrested youth's mother scuffled with the patrolmen, the African-Americans observing the tussle responded with menacing jeers, and the policemen brandished their rifles and radioed for reinforcements. The black spectators refused to be cowed by a show of superior force, and pelted the newly arriving law officers with rocks and bottles. By ten the irate crowd had become a rampaging mob, overturning the cars of passing white motorists and smashing shopwindows. Looting began at midnight. For the next several hours, a few thousand African-Americans openly vented the fury they had so long repressed. Calm returned at dawn. The police confidently announced the riot's end.

But the mob reassembled the next evening. Many of the young blacks carried arms. In the littered streets of the ghetto, black violence raged. And it did not end with the light of day. Friday morning saw five thousand rioters roaming Watts. Some yelled, "Long live Malcolm X." Others shouted, "Burn, baby, burn," the slogan of a hip DJ, the Magnificent Montague. Disavowing King's vision in Montgomery of "luminous brotherhood," the residents of Watts battled their white oppressors. Some struck out at the Los Angeles Police Department for its brutality toward African-Americans; some at the indignities of de facto segregated, substandard housing; others at the lack of public transportation in the ghetto; and still more at the unemployment rate of 30 to 40 percent for adult black males.

Many looted and trashed. Some firebombed white-owned businesses, overturned cars, and attacked whites caught in the ghetto. A few returned police fire, sniped at them from rooftops, and ambushed firemen responding to the increasing number of fire alarms. Entire blocks were soon aflame. That afternoon National Guard troops rushed to Watts to restore order. They could not.

The number of rioters multiplied. The damage soared. By late Saturday some fifteen hundred law officers, augmented by fourteen thousand Guardsmen, struggled in vain to contain the insurrection of an estimated fifty thousand African-Americans. All traditional restraints on black anger had evanesced. The burning, looting, and shooting continued. By week's end, thirty-four had been killed, some nine hundred injured, nearly four thousand arrested, and an estimated $40 million worth of property destroyed.

The riot devastated King. He cut short a vacation to fly to Los Angeles. Accompanied by Rustin, King told newsmen he had come to help blacks in their negotiations with the Los Angeles mayor, Sam Yorty, and the police chief, William Parker. He deplored the rioting: "Violence is not the answer to social conflict, whether it is engaged in by white people in Alabama or by Negroes in Los Angeles." And he insisted that America must right the wrongs from which the violence sprang. "The economic deprivation, racial isolation, inadequate housing, and general despair of thousands of Negroes teeming in Northern and Western ghettoes are the ready seeds which gave birth to tragic expressions of violence."

The next day, August 18, he toured the destruction of Watts. Amid the fire-gutted stores and smoldering shops, he heard a youth say, "We won." Stunned, King asked, "How can you say you won when thirty-four Negroes are dead, your community is destroyed, and whites are using the riots as an excuse for inaction?" "We won," the young black replied, "because we made the whole world pay attention to us."

The comment underscored the depths of alienation King discovered among African-Americans in Watts. The repeated heckling he endured when addressing local residents shocked him. " 'I have a dream' . . . craa-ap," one youth mocked him. "We don't want dreams, we want jobs." The shouts of "Get out of here" and "We don't want you" would remain deep within King. So would the glee with which many of the rioters expressed their riot exploits. "They were destroying a physical and emotional jail; they had asserted themselves against a system which was quietly crushing them into oblivion and now they were 'somebody.' " He acknowledged that the gains made so far had profited the middle classes, not the masses. He felt the material and spiritual desolation of the ghetto, what he previously had grasped just intellectually.

"I'll never forget the discussion we had with King that night," Rustin recalled. "He was absolutely undone, and he looked at me and said, 'You know, Bayard, I worked to get these people the right to eat hamburgers, and now I've got to do something . . . to help them get the money to buy it.' " The long nighttime confab ranged over the ghetto's problems of joblessness and poverty, physical isolation and psychological hopelessness. It would be almost another epiphany for King. "I think it was the first time he really understood," concluded Rustin.

The next day King tried to explain it to Yorty and Parker. They rudely denied his claims of police brutality or of racial prejudice and discrimination against blacks; they condemned his proposal for a civilian review board to investigate charges against the police. When Rustin asked the police chief why he had demeaned blacks as "monkeys" and "criminals," Parker retorted that it was the only language that Negroes understood. Incensed at Parker's "blind intransigence and ignorance of the social forces involved" in the riot, King took pains to explain to newsmen that the riot had been "a class revolt of underprivileged against privileged."

African-Americans in Watts, King specified, had not benefited from the gains won by the movement in the South and had "been bypassed by the progress of the past decade." For them, "the main issue is economic." King described rioting as "the language of the unheard," the desperate cry of one "who is so fed up with the powerlessness of his cave existence that he asserts that he would rather be dead than ignored." He cautioned, "A mere condemnation of violence is empty without understanding the daily violence that our society inflicts upon many of its members. The violence of poverty and humiliation hurts as intensely as the violence of the club."

That Chicago blacks also began rioting after a fire truck accidentally struck and killed an African-American woman on August 12, as King struggled for solutions in Watts, only intensified his prophetic rage and confirmed his resolve to take the SCLC north. For two days and nights, the West Side of Chicago resembled the Watts battlefield. Thousands of blacks looted and burned white-owned stores and battled police and National Guardsmen.

Since "Chicago has been pleading with us to come on in," King told the SCLC staff at a three-day emergency meeting a week later, he knew where he had to go next. He saw Chicago as yet another Birmingham. If SCLC could solve the problems in America's most "ghettoized" city, he observed, it could solve them anywhere. But Rustin rebuked him for being out of his depth: "You're going to get wiped out." Others expressed concerns and reservations, especially in terms of alienating SCLC's white supporters and forfeiting financial contributions. Despite the dissents, King would neither tarry nor allow others to decide. He would risk more than he ever had before.

SCLC would turn north. It had become morally imperative for King to focus on the myriad problems of northern blacks — de facto school segregation, police brutality, unequal job opportunities, and substandard housing and racist real estate practices. The effectiveness of nonviolent direct action to produce concrete results had to be re-proved. Blacks needed a vent for their maddening frustrations, or the smoldering cities of America would go up in flames. "The present mood dictates that we cannot wait," King declared. "This is where our mission is, we have received a calling," he confided to Rustin: "God has dictated this move."

In less than a decade, King had gone from politely asking that blacks be allowed to sit in the front of the bus to demanding "a social revolution" for "basic structural changes in the architecture of American society." His long-held goals of economic justice and world peace, often sloughed off for more immediate African-American needs, as well as for political expediency, now became his foremost concerns.

THE ROAD TO JERICHO
VIA CHICAGO,
1966

In the end, we will remember not the words of our enemies, but the silence of our friends.

━━

Hoping that the rabbits he had pulled out of his hat in the South would do the trick in Chicago, King considered his mission to the "have-nots" everywhere a moral imperative. The "shock and horror of Northern riots exploded before our eyes and we saw that the problems of the Negro go far beyond mere racial segregation," he would say over and over again, until the end of his days. He would not rest on his laurels. He wanted to prove that Chicago—home of the nation's largest black nationalist organization and a bastion of white working-class racism—was "the metropolis where a meaningful nonviolent movement could arouse the conscience of this nation to deal realistically with the northern ghetto."

King would not desert the battle. His Social Gospel commanded that he combat economic injustice as well as racism. The struggle would profoundly transform him, setting his agenda for his final campaign against the evils of poverty, racism, and war.

King initially believed that key allies would join his Chicago crusade. The Windy City's churches, affluent blacks, and wealthy white liberals had been the source of much of SCLC's fund-raising, and

King expected their assistance. He counted on white liberals nation-wide—the "coalition of conscience" that had backed his efforts in Birmingham and Selma—to do the same in Chicago. Given the concentration of power in Mayor Richard Daley's hands, King thought winning over the all-powerful Democratic boss, who had supported national civil rights legislation, would lead to the rooting out of racial discrimination throughout the city. He assumed Daley could use his political clout and well-oiled political machine to purge the city of racism.

King also expected assistance from the Johnson administration. The president had, after all, declared a "war on poverty." And he had not stopped there. In a nationally televised address to Congress on March 15, 1965, Johnson said the nation must go beyond the goal of opening doors of opportunity to "give all our people—black and white—the help that they need to walk through those gates." In a June 4, 1965, address at Howard University, the president emphasized that African-Americans must be granted preferential treatment to compensate for generations of inherited disadvantages. "The next and most profound stage of the battle for civil rights," he said, must concentrate on achieving equality of living conditions. "Not equality as a right and a theory, but equality as a fact and a result."

King shared the president's belief that the time had come to move from opportunity to achievement. He banked on the million blacks in Chicago to make that a reality. James Bevel, who started mobilizing in Chicago right after Selma, promised King a "massive disciplined organization" for the Chicago campaign. "We are going to create a new city," Bevel exulted. "Nobody will stop us."

But they would. King did not fully understand the dynamics of Chicago's complex African-American community, or how to counter Mayor Daley's slipperiness. King would soon discover that "Egypt still exists in Chicago but the Pharaohs are more sophisticated and subtle." Chicago was not Birmingham or Selma; the same strategy and tactics would not suffice. King would have to learn that much more than miles separated the church-oriented South from the despair-ridden ghettos of the North. In addition, he did not anticipate how rapidly the race riots would shift white opinion against African-American demands, and how most whites would soon want a brake upon rapid black progress. The young minister did not foresee how much the war in Vietnam would separate him from the president, solidify Daley's alliance with Johnson, and distance the chief executive from his own Great Society. Nor, initially, did King fully grasp the magnitude of the problems he sought to solve. With more courage than cleverness, he pressed ahead.

Having "been called by God to go to Chicago," the preacher arrived in January 1966. He met with the Coordinated Council of Community Organizations (CCCO), a federation of some thirty neighborhood civil rights groups that had been involved in nonviolent protest against de facto segregation in Chicago's public schools for three years. Unable to force Daley to fire school superintendent Benjamin Willis, its preeminent demand, the CCCO had formally invited King and the SCLC to help organize a massive boycott of Chicago's segregated public schools to campaign for "quality integrated education."

Instead, the SCLC and CCCO merged forces under the banner of the Chicago Freedom Movement, King explained, to "put an end to the black ghetto as an island of poverty in the midst of a sea of plenty." He announced to reporters that the SCLC had chosen Chicago because the city's slums were "the prototype of those responsible for the Northern urban race problem . . . Our primary objective will be to bring about the unconditional surrender of forces dedicated to the creation and maintenance of slums." The elimination of the ghetto superceded the elimination of segregated neighborhood schools.

As the *Chicago Defender* headlined, DR. KING WILL OCCUPY CHICAGO SLUM FLAT IN NEW RIGHTS DRIVE / HE'S OUT TO CLOSE GHETTO, King moved into a North Lawndale tenement at 1550 South Hamlin Avenue in the heart of Chicago's West Side on January 16 in order to dramatize the primitive squalor in which so many black Chicagoans lived. He would have to pay ninety dollars a month for a cramped, decrepit apartment—more than white renters in nearby communities paid for larger, modern apartments. "You can't really get close to the poor without living and being here with them," he explained as news photographers recorded the scene. "I have to be right here with the people."

Despite the slumlord dispatching a work crew to repair the apartment's worst faults and to fix some of the items in violation of the city's building code, Coretta King remained horrified with the urine-smelling tenement. "It was grim," she recalled: no lock on the front door; an entry-level dirt floor; dark, creaky flights of stairs; a constant smell of stale beer and rotting rubbish; drunks coming in from the street to relieve themselves in the hallway; a center of drugs and prostitution on the corner of Hamlin and Sixteenth Street. Coretta and Martin would soon see how very many of the neighborhood's tenements were even worse. On the West Side, some three hundred thousand blacks lived lives of desperation, and on the South Side, twice as many blacks endured slum conditions at least as depressing and dehumanizing.

King thought the system of "internal colonialism" flourishing in the slums "not unlike the exploitation of the Congo by Belgium." It opened only 1 percent of Chicago's residential listings to African-American applicants and charged blacks inflated rents for substandard housing in segregated neighborhoods, where inferior schools prepared them for only the least skilled, lowest-paying jobs, thereby perpetuating African-American powerlessness and poverty. The recently completed Robert Taylor Homes, twenty-eight sixteen-story public housing buildings, contained two of the three poorest census tracks anywhere in the United States. In what the Chicago Urban League termed the "color tax," black slum residents had to pay 10 to 20 percent more for inferior goods than what whites paid in suburban stores. African-Americans knew this but, unable to afford a car, could not shop in the outlying areas not served by public transportation. In a vicious cycle, the poverty and racist exploitation suffered by one generation bred the poverty and racist exploitation of the next, in a city where blacks outnumbered those in the state of Mississippi.

If perchance an African-American escaped this fate and earned enough to afford a decent dwelling, he or she faced Realtors who would not sell or rent to a black; racial-restrictive covenants that forbade home owners in given neighborhoods to sell to African-Americans; and banks and mortgage companies that refused to make loans to blacks who sought to purchase homes in white areas. To combat this pervasive racial discrimination, Bevel confidently assumed that TV pictures of the slums of Chicago would show the nation that the "real estate dealers in Chicago are the equivalent to Wallace and Jim Clark in the South." Only gradually would SCLC and King recognize that "deep prejudices and discriminations exist in hidden and subtle and covert disguises" in the North, and that the "eradication of slums housing millions is complex far beyond integrating buses and lunch counters."

On his first night in Lawndale, King held a "hearing" in a local church. One "Slumdale" resident after another repeated the litany of complaints he had heard in Los Angeles: overcrowded and substandard housing, poor schools, lack of health care, and unemployment. King responded: "I say to the power structure in Chicago that the same problems that existed, and still exist, in Watts, exist in Chicago today, and if something isn't done in a hurry, we can see a darker night of social disruption." He announced plans to organize blacks "to make Chicago a model city. Remember, living in a slum is robbery. It's robbery of dignity and the right to participate creatively in the political process. It's wrong to live with rats."

In response, Mayor Daley politely received King at city hall, assured him that the city's slum eradication program would solve the problem, and shrewdly announced the forthcoming resignation of Superintendent Willis—the CCCO's galvanizing issue. Not for the last time, Daley proved a more formidable opponent than a belligerent sheriff beating defenseless blacks. Nevertheless, King resolutely announced that he would focus on the issue of open housing. The Chicago movement's slogan would be "The Campaign to End Slums." King took heart in President Johnson's call for housing legislation in his January 1966 State of the Union message. He was even more excited by the Model Cities plan that the president proposed. The bill submitted to Congress called for $2.3 billion to convert America's slums into "masterpieces of civilization."

Mayor Daley, on the other hand, kept King off balance. He flatly denied any segregation in Chicago or "any reason for breaking the law" to protest. He claimed, and was echoed by his black machine within the Democratic machine, that the city was making great strides in solving whatever minor problems needed solution, and there was no need for interference from "outsiders." Chicago African-American congressman William Dawson condemned King as a foolish outside agitator. "What does he mean coming in here trying to tell our citizens that we are segregated? Chicagoans know what's best for Chicagoans." Black alderman Thomas Keane, head of the City Council, blasted King as "a disrupter of society." One of the so-called Silent Six, the six African-American aldermen who kept black Chicago in line for Daley, Keane publicly charged that King "is trying to destroy what we built."

Three days after moving to Chicago, King announced he would lead a rent strike unless Chicago's slumlords immediately began to renovate their properties. King foresaw patient block-by-block organizing to build grassroots support for a "Slum Union" or "Union to End Slums." The "union" would then bargain with absentee slumlords to improve housing conditions and, if necessary, conduct strikes and boycotts to force the desired changes. King would also lead southern-style nonviolent direct action by the masses to protest "the slow, stifling death of a kind of concentration camp life" in the ghetto.

The preacher envisioned a protest campaign to secure for African-Americans the blessings of decent housing, good education, and equal opportunities. He continued to hope that his strategy might eventually "create the beloved community," that by "rejecting the racism, materialism and violence that has characterized Western civilization," the movement would usher in a "world of brotherhood, cooperation and peace."

To that end, the Slum Union plastered END SLUMS placards throughout the West Side. They contained Bevel's slogan "We Are Being Robbed" and called for a rent strike; but, unwilling to organize people "on the basis of their hate," the Chicago movement also sought to teach nonviolent civil disobedience and to emphasize the structural bases of black oppression. It wanted ghetto residents to know that "the struggle to which they are being called is not merely the besting of an enemy, but the renewal and re-democratization of the social order itself."

SCLC found it hard going. In the more secular urban North, the African-American church lacked the influence and prestige it had in the South. "We were particularly disturbed by the youth gangs," recalled Abernathy. "Those hard-eyed black boys had no respect for anything or anybody. To them a preacher was the next worse thing to a policeman, and religion was for old folks and suckers, both of whom they regarded with a fine contempt."

King would neither give in nor give up. Night after night he sat on the soiled linoleum of his creaky floor with leaders of Chicago's many black youth gangs—the Blackstone Rangers, Cobras, East Side Disciples, Roman Saints, and Vice Lords. Over sandwiches, they talked long into the night, mostly about the nature and power of nonviolence. Facing young men who looted helpless merchants, who raped and robbed, even murdered, their own neighbors, King described nonviolence as a positive strategy rather than a failure to fight. "Power in Chicago," he told them, "means getting the largest political machine in the nation to say yes when it wants to say no." He wanted their cooperation to maintain a nonviolent movement, and he succeeded in getting about two hundred gang members to form nonviolent brigades and participate in demonstrations.

King had less success than Malcolm X in getting ghetto youngsters to clean up their act. It tore him up to see organized crime seducing black youth into a world of narcotics and prostitution with little or no police interference. In vain, he sought to prevent a generation of African-Americans from surrendering to the self-destructiveness of drugs and gang warfare.

The movement made little headway. Bevel's team of organizers on the West Side canvassed door-to-door "with nothing seemingly happening" to destroy the slums; and Jesse Jackson, SCLC's fastest-rising new recruit, went in another direction on the South Side—mobilizing Operation Breadbasket, a project to use selective black consumer buying, or boycott, campaigns to procure African-Americans jobs in the ghetto. Both groups ignored CCCO and further divided the Chicago Freedom Movement's limited and dwindling resources. "We haven't gotten things under control," Andrew Young conceded. "The strategy hasn't emerged yet."

Most vitally, Daley denied the movement the crude, violent opposition that had dramatized racial injustice in the South. A far cry from Birmingham's Bull Connor, the jowly Daley undermined King with a series of cosmetic improvements in the ghetto, a well-publicized investigation of code violations in the slums, and frequent press releases indicating that the mayor shared King's goals and hoped the preacher would join him in making Chicago an even greater city. Andy Young complained that, as soon as the movement tried to organize a community, "Daley's forces would come in and offer a preacher a contract for subsidized daycare in his church." That would end the minister's cooperation with the movement.

In fact, most of the community's black clergy joined with the local politicians in opposing King. His most vociferous black critic, Reverend Joseph H. Jackson, encouraged their disparagement. Pastor of Olivet Baptist Church, the largest black church in Chicago, and president of the five-million-strong National Baptist Convention (NBC), the "Negro Pope" held animosity toward King that stemmed in part from King's past efforts to depose him as the NBC president, and in part from Jackson's political conservatism and disapproval of the tactic of mass civil disobedience. Jackson's unrelenting attacks on King would severely injure the movement.

So would the reproach of Chicago's black strivers. King made little headway with African-American professionals, city employees and ward heelers in Daley's machine, or entrepreneurs—many of whom depended on the mayor to support their businesses. Many of them favored either the doctrine of self-help preached by Reverend Jackson or the legalistic tactics of the city's NAACP, which had pointedly refused to join the Chicago Freedom Movement. "Do not stand by and be a conscientious objector in this war to end slums," King pleaded. But Chicago's black elite remained AWOL.

More significantly, few of the city's half a million impoverished blacks responded to King's organizing efforts. Most refused him the reverential deference he received in the South. His rhetoric fell on deaf ears. He could not find the words that would arouse the black ghetto dweller without simultaneously frightening whites to death. "I found myself fighting a daily battle against the depression and hopelessness which the heart of our cities pumps into the spiritual bloodstream of our lives."

Equally disappointing to King, the support he expected from Chicago's white religious groups and labor unions never materialized. The liberal Catholic Interracial Council had little influence on the predominantly Catholic population of Chicago, and Archbishop John Cody, who had been briefed by the FBI on King's Communist ties and "hypocritical behavior" in sexual matters, kept his distance. Although a few local labor leaders supported King, the city's most powerful workers' organization, the Chicago Federation of Labor and the Industrial Union Council (CFL-IUC), closely tied to Richard Daley, disdained the Chicago Freedom Movement. Many of its rank and file would be conspicuous in the mobs that assaulted King and his followers.

Checkmated by Daley, King rashly moved to seize a slum tenement on North Kenmore Avenue on the West Side. He had heard about a sick baby in a run-down building with no heat and impulsively announced on February 23 that the SCLC would take the property into "trusteeship." The rent collected from the building's four tenants would go for renovations rather than to the landlord. When challenged on the legality of his action, King responded, "I won't say that it is illegal, but I would call it supralegal. The moral question is far more important than the legal one."

To his embarrassment, the landlord turned out to be an eighty-one-year-old invalid about as poor as his tenants. The octogenarian soon died, and a black judge, denouncing King's tactic as "theft," voided the tenement seizure. It was hardly the dramatization of exploitative slum landlordism King had hoped for. Levison fumed that SCLC had come across as "a gang of anarchists."

Meanwhile, Mayor Daley masterfully outflanked King and the Chicago Freedom Movement by conveying his determination to do all that King wanted—but without protest demonstrations and threats. In March he coopted the city's leading clergy by inviting them to join his effort to rid Chicago of slums, then by announcing the coming construction of thousands of new public housing units and the renovation of thousands of existing slum dwellings. Daley confidently predicted the end of Chicago's slums within four years. City hall's barrage of promises and federal anti-poverty projects left the Chicago Freedom Movement at an impasse. For King, "it was like fighting a pillow." Dejected, he admitted to reporters, "we are not omniscient or omnipotent." He pleaded for public support, but by May his campaign was on life support and about to expire.

His effort at long-term community organizing a failure, King turned back to mobilizing a dramatic direct-action campaign—the newsworthy spectacle the media expected and the kind of event that made best use of his charismatic leadership and evangelical oratory. King announced a mass rally at Soldier Field for late June to start the campaign's "action phase." "We've been studying to see exactly what's needed and now we've emerged with concrete demands. Chicago will have a long hot summer, but not a summer of racial violence. Rather, it will be a long hot summer of peaceful nonviolence."

A far more radical King would emerge. More than decisively shifting the movement from south to north, King talked unabashedly of escalating the struggle for black equality from an attack on state-sanctioned denials of basic civil rights to an assault on social and economic inequities. No longer just decrying legal barriers to full citizenship rights, King now demanded the expansion of equality into what was considered the private realm of American life. He sought equality of results, not just equality of opportunity. "Social peace," he insisted, "must spring from economic justice." The Chicago Freedom Movement's slogan—"Ending the Slums"—became the far more grandiose "Creating the Open City." The key lesson of the Albany campaign—focus on a single, achievable goal—was ignored. The time had come, King maintained, for "a massive assault upon slums, inferior education, inadequate medical care . . . the entire culture of poverty."

As King began preparations for the "open city," the national news reported on June 6 that James Meredith, the hero of the desegregation of the University of Mississippi, had been shot on the second day of his "Walk Against Fear"—his solo trek from Memphis to Jackson, Mississippi, to encourage blacks to vote and to demonstrate that African-Americans would no longer be intimidated by white violence in the South. The SCLC staff immediately agreed that the walk to the Mississippi state capital must continue. Anything less, King reasoned, would add to African-American fear and be a mortal blow to the entire nonviolent struggle for black equality.

Meeting in Meredith's Memphis hospital room, King and Floyd McKissick, the newly elected head of CORE, and Stokely Carmichael, who had replaced John Lewis as chairman of SNCC that May, agreed that the march—now named the Meredith March Against Fear—would highlight the evils of racism in the Deep South.

The three movement leaders and a small group of marchers then headed for the spot on Route 51 where the shooting had occurred, to take up Meredith's march. During a confrontation with Mississippi highway patrolmen, anger erupted, and some black marchers talked openly of forgoing nonviolence. "I'm not for that nonviolence stuff anymore," said one. "This should be an all-black march," another said. No whites: "This is our march!" still others yelled. "We Shall Overcome" became "We Shall Overrun." Some sang, "Jingle bells, shotgun shells / Freedom all the way / Oh what fun it is to blast / A trooper man away."

"I should have known that in an atmosphere where false promises are daily realities," King wrote, "where deferred dreams are nightly facts, where acts of unpunished violence toward Negroes are a way of life, nonviolence would eventually be seriously questioned. I should have been reminded that disappointment produces despair and despair produces bitterness, and that one thing certain about bitterness is its blindness."

Returning to Memphis that night, the march leaders met at James Lawson's Centenary Methodist Church. They were joined by Roy Wilkins and Whitney Young. The NAACP and Urban League heads wanted the march to drum up support for the 1966 Civil Rights Act, which included provisions for open housing and the protection of civil rights workers. Carmichael, the twenty-four-year-old black Robespierre who now led SNCC, would have none of their limited, lobbyist approach to racial equality. "I'm not going to beg the white man for anything I deserve," he lashed out. "I'm going to take it." Screaming and cursing at Wilkins and Young, Carmichael would not allow the march to endorse the president's bill; he also demanded that the march exclude whites and be protected by the Deacons for Defense and Justice, a heavily armed paramilitary group from Louisiana.

Carmichael's rant epitomized the dashed dreams and loss of faith pervading SNCC. The new SNCC stance had been gradually emerging since at least 1962, when some field secretaries argued for a more militant strategy than voter registration. This approach gained force in Montgomery in 1963 and during the 1964 Mississippi Freedom Summer, when SNCC field secretaries saw the many articulate and self-assured white volunteers overwhelm the poorly educated local blacks in the movement. Also precipitating change was the failure of white liberals and the old-line civil rights groups to stand by the Mississippi Freedom Democrats at the Democratic National Convention. Some in SNCC went on a trip to Africa and returned seeing themselves as a part of a worldwide revolutionary struggle of national and racial liberation. They turned from King's notions of redemptive suffering and racial integration to Malcolm X's ideas of racial separatism and liberation "by any means necessary."

In their eyes, King had discredited himself by not going on the Freedom Rides, failing to abide by the "Jail, not Bail" principle in Albany, leaving jail too quickly in Birmingham, and worst of all, avoiding Bloody Sunday and turning around on the Edmund Pettus Bridge. Their new hero, Malcolm X, appealed to the growing number in SNCC, such as Carmichael and James Forman, who had grown up in the North and found more inspiration in the writings of Frantz Fanon and Che Guevara than in the religiosity of the southern black church. The Watts riot in August 1965 completed SNCC's transformation, convincing a majority of the field secretaries that the end of legal segregation and disfranchisement in the South did nothing to address the problems of urban blacks suffering from poor education, substandard housing, police brutality, and unemployment. It was time to give up on the nonviolent quest for racial integration and reconciliation, and instead pursue a separatist path to gaining power. The time of offering love in return for hate was over. The time had come for power to confront power.

Disgusted by Carmichael's outburst, Wilkins and Young left Memphis. King had to try to constrain Carmichael's bellicosity by himself. Tempering the call for armed protection by the Deacons for Defense and Justice, which McKissick had seconded, King pleaded for nonviolence as a pragmatic necessity. "I can't imagine anything more impractical and disastrous for any of us, through misguided judgment, to precipitate a violent confrontation in Mississippi. We have neither the resources nor the techniques to win." It was not a matter of using a gun to protect your home from attack, King argued, "but whether it was tactically wise to use a gun while participating in an organized demonstration."

Violence would eclipse the moral issues, King maintained, becloud Mississippi injustice, and give authorities an excuse to wipe the marchers out. He insisted on keeping the march interracial, reminding them of "the dedicated whites who had suffered, bled, and died in the cause of racial justice." To "reject white participation now," he persisted, "would be a shameful repudiation of all for which they had sacrificed."

King's pleas resulted in an agreement that the march be interracial and nonviolent, but the manifesto issued the next day bore the stamp of Carmichael. It characterized the march as "a massive public indictment and protest of the failure of American society, the Government of the United States, and the State of Mississippi to 'Fulfill These Rights' "—the name of the recent White House Conference on Civil Rights. It highlighted the failures of the Johnson administration and called upon the president to send federal registrars to Mississippi and to support the $185 million Freedom Budget proposed by A. Philip Randolph for anti-poverty and social welfare programs.

Dismayed by the refusal of Meredith, Wilkins, Young, or Charles Evers—head of the Mississippi NAACP—to sign on, King nevertheless felt he had to continue the march. "Martin saw the gunning down of Meredith not just as an effort to stop one man," wrote Coretta King, "but to intimidate the whole Movement for equality in Mississippi." Without a right flank, King could no longer be the man in the middle, the "conservative militant." He could not dissuade Carmichael and McKissick from minimizing white participation, allowing the Deacons for Defense and Justice to protect marchers, and using the march as a means to organize local blacks in towns along the way.

Dividing his time among Mississippi, Atlanta, and Chicago, King could do little to forestall Carmichael's instigation of racial polarization and conflict. Matters came to a head on June 16, following the arrest of the cocky Carmichael in Greenwood for erecting a sleeping tent on the grounds of a black school after being ordered not to do so by Mississippi state troopers. Word of his arrest brought out a large and angry crowd to a protest rally that night, and after he was released on bail, he gave free vent to his emotions. "This is the twenty-seventh time I have been arrested," Carmichael shouted from a flatbed truck, "and I ain't going to go to jail no more." With a raised arm and clenched-fist salute, he exclaimed, "We're asking Negroes not to go to Vietnam and fight but to stay in Greenwood and fight here."

Having already spread the word to his followers that "Black Power" would be their slogan, Carmichael hurled defiance. "The only way we gonna stop them white men from whippin' us is to take over," he boomed. "We been saying freedom for six years and we ain't got nothin'. What we gonna start saying now is Black Power!" As he repeated rhythmically, "We . . . want . . . Black . . . Power!" the crowd chanted, "That's right! Black Power!" Carmichael shouted, "That's what we want. Now, from now on, when they ask you what you want, you know what to tell them. What do you want?" His followers roared, "Black Power!" "What do you want?" "BLACK POWER!" "What do you want? Say it again!" "BLACK POWER! BLACK POWER! BLACK POWER!"

Hurrying back from Chicago, King faced SNCC's fury. Their shouts of "Black Power" drowned out SCLC's chants of "Freedom Now." Preachments of nonviolence brought forth boasts that "white blood will flow." Talk of Christian love stimulated clamoring to "seize power." Although avoiding any public reaction to the SNCC slogan, King privately implored Carmichael to abandon it because the term "carried the wrong connotations," implying hostility to whites, and it weakened the movement by widening the rifts.

Carmichael would not back down. He knew the slogan invited misinterpretation and ignited dissension. Yet his mantra remained "Power is the only thing respected in this world, and we must get it at any cost." King considered pulling SCLC out of the march but instead issued a mild statement that the term "is unfortunate because it tends to give the impression of black nationalism." Seeking to minimize the difference between Carmichael and himself, the pastor implied it was merely a matter of semantics and style.

Carmichael, however, relished feeding rhetorical red meat to the media. "Stokely Starmichael," as some called him for his eagerness to court the press, countered every effort by King to dilute the threat. In a slashing style reminiscent of Malcolm X, he poured oil on the fire with each public challenge to African-Americans to "stop begging and take power—black power." Rather than advocating nonviolence, he exhorted, "It's time we stand up and take over. Take over. Move on over, or we'll move on over you." Cleverly, Carmichael used King's presence at the march to gain the fullest press coverage for his own views.

At a contentious mass meeting in Yazoo City, SNCC's followers booed when King began to speak. It hurt. He understood their cry of rage yet insisted African-Americans must pursue "power that is moral, that is right and that is good," not just "power for power's sake." Blacks "are ten percent of the population of this nation" and could not win their freedom by a violent struggle. It would only bring unnecessary deaths. "There's going to have to be a coalition of conscience, and we aren't going to be free here in Mississippi and anywhere in the United States until there is a committed empathy on the part of the white man." With all his customary passion, King related the talk of power to the need for power to bring about "the creation of the Beloved Community," and ended with a ringing "We can't be stopped. We are going to win right here in Mississippi."

For the next five hours, King huddled with Carmichael and McKissick and their staffs in a small Catholic parish house, pleading with them "to abandon the Black Power slogan." He emphasized the need for a program, not merely "an unfortunate choice of words" that conjured fears of black violence and black domination. King suggested "black consciousness" or "black equality" in its place. Absolutely not, Carmichael shot back: The movement needed a rallying cry.

King conceded the point. "But why have one that would confuse our allies, isolate the Negro community, and give many prejudiced whites, who might otherwise be ashamed of their anti-Negro feeling, a ready excuse for self-justification?" Each proponent remained adamant. The interminable argument ended with only the barest of compromises that both sides stop chanting their slogans.

Carmichael confessed with his most ingratiating of smiles that he had deliberately cried "Black Power" on the march to force King to take a stand and thereby give the slogan a national forum. King laughed. "I have been used before. One more time won't hurt."

For the rest of the night, King lay sleepless. However much he admired and liked Carmichael, he found nothing amusing in SNCC's anti-white, hostile rhetoric. Yet, he admitted, "I could not for the life of me have less than patience and understanding for those young people. For twelve years, I and others like me had held out radiant promises of progress . . . Their hopes had soared." They were booing him now because "we were unable to deliver on our promises."

Shaken, dejected, frustrated, King refused the order of a sheriff in Canton that he not raise a tent on the grounds of a black elementary school. "It's an all-Negro school—our school—and we won't be denied." Despite the urgings of John Doar, the Justice Department civil rights chief, as well as school and city officials, that the marchers leave the school grounds, King held fast. Suddenly, without warning, Mississippi lawmen unleashed a barrage of tear-gas canisters.

"Cover your face with a handkerchief," King shouted. "Nobody leave. Nobody fight back. We're going to stand our ground." In vain, he tried to lead them in singing "We Shall Overcome." The gagging marchers either fled or braved the swinging clubs and whips of two hundred gas-masked patrolmen. It was a rout. With Carmichael choking and hysterical from the gas, and McKissick "almost incoherent with rage," King calmed the frightened marchers gathered in a church sanctuary, gently admonishing them to defeat violence with nonviolence.

To King's chagrin, the governor of Mississippi insisted, "We aren't going to wet-nurse a bunch of showmen all over the state," and Attorney General Katzenbach blamed the marchers for "trespassing" where they had no right to be. "The federal government makes my job more difficult every day," King stated as President Johnson refused to reply to his plea for intervention. "The government has got to give me some victories if I'm going to keep people nonviolent," King told a reporter. "Much of the responsibility is on the white power structure to give meaningful concessions to Negroes . . . I know I'm going to stay nonviolent no matter what happens. But a lot of people are getting hurt and bitter, and they can't see it that way anymore." That included Andy Young: "I didn't say it, but I thought to myself, 'If I had a machine gun, I'd show those motherfuckers.'"

The dispirited march in the Delta heat concluded with a rally at the state capitol in Jackson on Sunday, June 27. The majority of Americans appeared to be fed up with protest marches, and few reporters or white supporters attended the ceremony. Most of those who had answered the call in Selma stayed home. While competing chants of "Black Power" and "Freedom Now" resounded, marchers waved placards reading MOVE OVER OR WE'LL MOVE ON OVER YOU. McKissick proudly proclaimed 1966 the year of Black Power, and

Carmichael demanded that blacks build enough power to bring whites "to their knees every time they mess with us."

King, bereft of allies in the federal government, resurrected his "dream" that "one day, right here in this state of Mississippi, justice will become a reality for all." It had a hollow ring. The marchers drifted away. Three days later, CORE officially adopted Black Power as its strategy. "The only way to achieve meaningful change," McKissick declared, "is to take power." SNCC and CORE left SCLC to foot the bill for the march, and each of the major civil rights groups announced separate voter registration drives in Mississippi. They would no longer work with one another.

King later wrote that because "Stokely Carmichael chose the March as an arena for a debate over black power, we didn't get to emphasize the evils of Mississippi and the need for the 1966 Civil Rights Act." He blamed Carmichael for allowing Mississippi to "get off the hook" and condemned SNCC's concept of Black Power as irrationally defeatist, "a nihilistic philosophy born out of the conviction that the Negro can't win. It is, at bottom, the view that American society is so hopelessly corrupt and enmeshed in evil that there is no possibility of salvation from within."

In its place, King proposed the "pooling of black economic resources in order to achieve legitimate power" and employing "black political resources in order to achieve our legitimate goals." "Power, properly understood," he wrote, "is the ability to achieve purpose. It is the strength required to bring about social, political, or economic changes. In this sense power is not only desirable but necessary in order to implement the demands of love and justice." He especially embraced a concept of Black Power that highlighted what he called "psychological freedom." King believed that the accent on racial pride and racial identity, on self-esteem and self-affirmation, would bring blacks inner emancipation.

However much King publicly rationalized the anger of black militants as "the feeling that a real solution is hopelessly distant because of the inconsistencies, resistance, and faintheartedness of those in power," he also criticized SNCC's Black Power for its lack of an effective program. To as many as would listen, he enumerated the reasons why he chose desegregation over black separatism; coalition with liberal whites over black nationalism; nonviolence over armed self-defense; hope over despair; and love over hate. In no uncertain terms, he criticized SNCC's inflammatory rhetoric and dehumanization of white people, even those white radicals who endorsed its agenda. However culturally and psychologically empowering, he maintained, it would be interpreted as anti-white separatism and as an endorsement of hatred and armed violence. It would shatter the possibility of a progressive interracial alliance for fundamental change. "What is needed is a strategy for change, a tactical program that will bring the Negro into the mainstream of American life as quickly as possible."

Harkening back to Gandhi's movement in India, King contended that the struggle for black equality must be rooted in love, nonviolence, and hope. "When hope dies, a revolution degenerates into an undiscriminating catchall for evanescent and futile gestures. The Negro cannot entrust his destiny to a philosophy nourished solely on despair, to a slogan that cannot be implemented into a program." Echoing his rhetoric in the Montgomery bus boycott, King proclaimed, "I must oppose any attempt to gain our freedom by the methods of malice, hate, and violence that have characterized our oppressors. Hate is just as injurious to the hater as it is to the hated." One of the few who agreed was Chicano labor leader César Chávez. "I am convinced that the truest act of courage, the strongest act of manliness," he insisted when explaining why he was fasting rather than fighting, "is to sacrifice ourselves for others in a totally nonviolent struggle for justice. To be a man is to suffer for others."

But too few agreed. While liberal whites and black moderates quickly joined the chorus of Black Power critics, hardly any promoted King's middle way. As the fate of the civil rights movement hung in the balance, the liberals' silence destroyed the dream. When it mattered most, President Johnson turned his back on King. As historian David L. Lewis observed, "It required a special kind of moral irresponsibility and political arrogance for a President to write off the single civil rights leader who combined the virtues of mass appeal, however diminished, and ideological responsibility at the precise moment when racial polarization in the United States was rapidly accelerating. Lyndon Johnson was that kind of President." As limited in generosity as he was imposing in manner, Johnson spited King for his criticism of the war in Vietnam.

Divided against itself and bereft of allies, the black struggle for justice and equality would never again be what it had been for a decade.

Adrift and despondent, King contemplated giving up. But he could not do that. Far more than ever before, he had to make the Chicago campaign a success. Nothing less could save the movement's adherence to nonviolent direct action and rebut the advocates of both black separatism and white resistance. Yet "Creating the Open City" still lacked a sharp focus and coherent strategy. Although boldly proclaiming that "there is nothing more effective than the tramp, tramp, tramp of marching feet," and assembling 163 organizations to begin the action phase of the campaign, King still had not devised a way to combat the complexity of Chicago's omnipresent racial injustice.

For the July 10 rally at Soldier Field, SCLC assembled a smorgasbord of immediate demands. They included the nondiscriminatory listing and showing of properties by real estate brokers, an end to discriminatory loan practices by banks, a civilian review board to hear complaints of police brutality, and an enormous increase in the number of low-cost public housing units to be built by the Chicago Housing Authority. They also called for a guaranteed annual income for the poor from the federal government and the desegregation of the Chicago school system, where 90 percent of African-American children attended all-black schools, despite the absence of any laws or regulations mandating segregation. To back up its demands, SCLC announced "a series of direct actions which will make the injustice so clear that the whole community will respond to the need to change."

In nearly hundred-degree clammy heat, some thirty thousand Chicagoans streamed into the huge Soldier Field on the shore of Lake Michigan to kick off the nonviolent direct-action campaign. Once again, King echoed Montgomery: "We are here today because we are tired . . . tired of being seared in the flames of withering injustice." With the Meredith March still uppermost in his mind, King blended Black Power's tactical militancy with a stress on maintaining white support. He spoke of racial pride, of black "as beautiful as any other color," while reminding the rally that "freedom is never voluntarily granted by the oppressor; it must be demanded by the oppressed."

Urging the assembled "to fill up the jails of Chicago, if necessary, in order to end the slums," King then reiterated his conviction that "Our power does not reside in Molotov cocktails, rifles, knives and bricks." He still believed "nonviolence is a powerful and just weapon. It cuts without wounding. It is a sword that heals." It had been the "major factor in the creation of a moral climate that has made progress possible." Finally, King rebuked those who preached black separatism and hatred of whites. The achievement of goals, he proclaimed, required the support of many whites, and there remained many whites "who cherished democratic principles above privilege." He urged both blacks and whites to "see that we are tied in a single garment of destiny. We need each other."

Just five thousand followed King on the three-mile trek to city hall. With Mayor Daley out of town, King taped the Chicago Freedom Movement demands on the door, much as Martin Luther in 1517 had nailed his 95 Theses to the door of All Saints Church in Wittenberg, Germany, igniting the Protestant Reformation. But King's symbolic gesture, reminiscent of his namesake, had little effect; there would be no reformation in the ways of Chicago politicians, bankers, or Realtors. The next morning, July 11, Daley met with King and, as usual, exuded sweet reason, claiming to crusade against urban decay and to want King's help, indicating that much of what King proposed he had already planned.

King no longer would accept vague suggestions of agreement. He insisted on concrete proposals, and when Daley demurred, King announced to the press that the mayor did not understand the "depth and dimension" of racial injustice in Chicago, and that the Chicago movement would escalate the confrontation. That night SCLC indicated it would begin the direct-action phase of the campaign. Its first target would be housing discrimination in Gage Park, one of Chicago's many exclusively white neighborhoods. "Dr. King is very sincere in what he is trying to do," Daley said, seeking to undercut King with the press. But "at times, he doesn't have all the facts on the local situation. After all, he is a resident of another city."

As SCLC and city hall shadowboxed on Tuesday, July 12—the fifth consecutive day that the temperature soared above ninety degrees, and the ninth time so far that month—black kids from the housing projects on the West Side frolicked in the "pool" created from water pouring out of several open fire hydrants. The police effort to close the hydrants led to pushing and shoving, then to hurling bricks

and bottles, attacking passing white motorists, smashing store windows, and looting. King rushed to the boisterous scene. Amid the
sounds of gunfire, he pleaded for nonviolence. Many laughed at him;
few heeded his call. Powerless to quell the disturbance, King and the
SCLC staffers abandoned the streets to the youth gangs, who threw
firebombs at police cars and shot at firemen from rooftops. Calm returned with daylight. But the locking of hydrants by city officials so
that blacks could not open them led to another night of rioting, then
another.

Shaken by the tumult, King called an emergency meeting of the
city's clergy. Nonviolence was "in deep trouble," he pleaded. "I need
some victories. I need some concessions." He urged them to use all of
their influence to convince the white establishment that "if they drain
the steam out of the nonviolent movement and give no concessions
they are planting the seeds for a Watts-like situation." Rising to a
higher level, the preacher reminded them that "genuine peace is not
the absence of tension, but the presence of justice." King repeated
what he had said after Watts: "Riots grow out of intolerable conditions.
Violent riots are generated by revolting conditions and there is nothing more dangerous than to build a society with a large segment of
people who feel they have no stake in it, who feel they have nothing
to lose."

As the riot spread, King invited the heads of the Cobras, Roman
Saints, and Vice Lords to his apartment. They immediately let him
know their preference for Black Power and for Stokely Carmichael,
who had arrived in Chicago and told them, "The only nonviolence
we need is nonviolence among ourselves. We've been shooting and
cutting the wrong people." Undaunted, King spent five hours dis-
cussing nonviolence with the leaders of the youth gangs most responsible for the violent rioting on the West Side.

Always the preacher, King kept preaching to the gang leaders,
notwithstanding the knives and guns stuffed in their pockets. Roger
Wilkins—a Community Relations Service director sent by President
Johnson to investigate the riot's causes—silently observed King's "sem-
inar in nonviolence" in the unbearably hot, cramped tenement flat.
Hour after hour he watched a profusely perspiring King "trying to
convince these kids that rioting was destructive and suicidal; and that

the way to change a society was to approach it with love of yourself and of mankind, and dignity in your own heart." Wilkins knew "there was no glory in it. It was just the most bone-racking kind of drudgery. He dealt with those kids with a reverence for their humanity, dignity, belief in their importance that he communicated to them, and with the patience of a saint." At three A.M. the gang leaders left, promising to give nonviolence a try.

King also wrung concessions from Daley to attach sprinkler nozzles on hydrants, to request federal funds to build some swimming pools in the ghetto, and to create a committee to advise the police department on how to improve its relations with the African-American community. It was not much. It barely constituted a start toward a meaningful agreement. But with the gangs off the streets, and four thousand National Guardsmen on them, the riot ended.

A fragile cease-fire tentatively cooled Chicago's tempers. King and Daley continued sparring. Despite the courageous efforts by King and his staff to get people off the streets and back in their homes, the mayor and his allies blamed them for inflaming the animosities that had led to the riot. Most of the local and national media followed suit. King, in turn, heaped responsibility for the riot "upon the shoulders of those elected officials whose myopic social vision had been further blurred by political expedience rather than commitment to the betterment of living conditions and dedication to the eradication of slums and the forces which create and maintain slum communities." It fell on deaf ears. "The trouble here is that there has been no confrontation," remarked Andy Young, "the kind where they interrupt the network TV programs to say that Negroes in such-and-such a white area are doing something." A crisis was necessary, King agreed, to make the city end its slums, "to make Chicago an open and just city."

To provoke the confrontation necessary to force concessions from unwilling city authorities, King again announced the start of demonstrations in Chicago's all-white communities. "We do not seek to precipitate violence," he insisted publicly. But by shifting the movement's goal from eliminating slum conditions in black neighborhoods to fighting the de facto housing segregation in ethnic white neighborhoods, King reckoned on the certainty of violence. He knew that peaceful civil rights demonstrations no longer made front-page news.

In demanding open housing, the item on the civil rights agenda most stridently denounced by whites, the Chicago Freedom Movement courted racist violence. It counted on the white working class in Gage Park, Belmont Cragin, Bogan, Marquette Park, and South Deering—many of whom had previously fled an expanding black ghetto—to react vociferously to its demands and marches through their neighborhoods. To most of Chicago's whites, open housing was "forced housing," a violation of their property rights and liberty. They believed "one's home was one's castle" and that government should not have the power to tell them to whom they must sell or rent their property. It was a private matter, unlike voting rights. Indeed, no fair-housing measures had ever been approved in a public referendum anywhere in the United States by 1966.

King knew that challenging residential segregation meant a battle on the most intractable front of American apartheid. There was little that the working class in its ethnic neighborhoods and the affluent in their suburban enclaves would not do to block entry to blacks. King also knew the movement's goals could begin to be met only if the media portrayed African-Americans as the innocent victims of brutal white supremacists.

Thursday, August 4, King addressed a crowd of some two thousand at the New Friendship Missionary Baptist Church. The preacher began by explaining, "*Stay in your place in the North means stay on the reservation. Stay in your place in the North means to be content with the low-paying job . . . Stay in your place means that you must be content with overcrowded, inadequate schools.*" King refused to stay in that place. "*My place is in the sunlight of opportunity. My place is in the security of an adequate quality education.*" "My place!" the crowd knew to shout in response as it moved to King's rhythm. "*My place is in comfort and in the convenience and in the nobility of good, solitary living conditions and in a good house.*" When King roared, "*My place is in Gage Park,*" the audience roared back its agreement. He would lead the next day's showdown. "*My brothers and sisters,*" he concluded, "*I still can sing 'We Shall Overcome.'*"

Friday morning, King led five hundred followers on a march through Marquette Park and Chicago Lawn to the Southwest Side community of Gage Park. As soon as the march began, a rock struck

King in the head, causing him to stagger to the pavement. He insisted on continuing to lead the march, and as the demonstrators headed up California Avenue, they encountered hundreds of furious whites. A sign read THE ONLY WAY TO STOP NIGGERS IS TO EXTERMINATE THEM. Some whites waved Confederate flags, chanting, "We want King! We want King!" Others threw bottles and bricks. Many howled, "Nigger go home," "White power," and "Kill Martin Luther Coon." Someone hurled a knife at King. It missed its target but struck a white marcher in the shoulder. Soon hundreds of whites clogged the street, forcing an end to the march.

About four thousand rowdy whites in the mainly Lithuanian-American enclave of Marquette Park then assailed the demonstrators in their pell-mell retreat. Often egged on by their parents—in a frenzy that the sale of a house or two to blacks would turn their neighborhood into a slum and wipe out a lifetime of saving—rowdy young men hurled rocks and cherry bombs at the marchers, injuring sixty people. When the beleaguered protesters finally reached the street where they had parked, their car tires had been slashed and car windows smashed, and about a dozen autos had been set on fire or pushed into a lagoon.

Such fury rattled many of the demonstrators. They were used to facing mobs of fifty or a hundred or so, Andy Young remarked, not thousands. "The violence in the South always came from a rabble element. But these were women and children and husbands and wives coming out of their homes [and] becoming a mob—and in some ways it was far more frightening."

"I had never seen, even in Mississippi," King lamented to reporters, "as much hatred and hostility on the part of so many people." But he would not be frightened away. "We shall have to keep coming back until we are safe from harassment. Until Negroes can move into the neighborhoods, the tenets of freedom will continue to decay."

Two days later, about a thousand protesters marched for open housing in Belmont Cragin on Chicago's Northwest Side. A huge crowd of white hecklers shouted the customary invectives, but this time the police—criticized by King for being "either unwilling or unable to disperse the riotous mobs"—restrained the white onlookers. The presence of large numbers of police creating a wall between the protesters and the neighborhood whites in subsequent demonstrations similarly dampened spirits and made the marches far less bloody— and newsworthy. Nevertheless, the activists continued their protest. "We march, we return home emotionally drained," one noted, and "from some inner reservoirs replenish our strength and go back."

At the mass meeting on August 8 at the Warren Avenue Congregational Church, a fervid Jesse Jackson stunned the crowd of five hundred before him by declaring, "I'm going to Cicero." Even the threat of death, he insisted, should not deter them from marching on all-white Cicero, the site of a vicious race riot in 1951 and the preeminent symbol of northern bigotry. Instinctively, James Bevel ascended the podium, further tantalizing the congregation: "If the people of Cicero are going to buy guns because Negroes are coming there, it won't make any difference." As the crowd cheered, he intoned, "They can buy tanks and they can arm every child, but we're going to Cicero." Although taken by surprise by the announcements, King, in Atlanta preparing for the SCLC annual convention, added that he himself would lead the march to Cicero if Chicago did not combat housing bias.

Meanwhile, the mayor and his juggernaut of a political machine, knowing that most Chicagoans opposed the provocative marches, went on the offensive against King. Virtually every Chicago politician, from aldermen to state senators to congressional representatives, condemned the protests as causing needless turmoil and not furthering social justice. The conservative *Chicago Tribune* thought the marches were a plot to "sabotage" the city. Chicago's *American* labeled them "a deliberate attempt to perpetuate violence." Even the liberal *Chicago Daily News* insisted that King "call off the marches entirely and turn to more constructive pursuits."

In no uncertain terms, Chicago's ABC-TV affiliate demanded in an editorial aired seven times that King "cease these demonstrations." Similar summons for a moratorium on marches came from many of the city's most eminent academics, labor leaders, and clergy, including Chicago's Catholic archbishop, who called for demonstrations to give way to negotiations. Most whites, even those who favored desegregation in the South, did not want integration in their own lives. By 1966, 85 percent of whites thought demonstrations were "hurting the

Negro cause." A majority of whites thought that the administration had pushed civil rights "too fast" and considered King "irresponsible."

Despite the incredible pressure on him to desist, King replied, "We must condemn those who are perpetuating the violence," not those who engaged in the pursuit of their constitutional rights. The demonstrations would continue. On August 12 a six-hundred-strong open housing march on the Southwest Side's Bogan community brought out hundreds of hecklers and signs reading JOIN THE WHITE REBELLION. Two days later, more than a thousand demonstrators participated in simultaneous marches through Jefferson Park on the Northwest Side, and to Bogan and Gage Park on the Southwest Side. In addition to encounters with angry local residents, the marchers now faced scores of extremist outside agitators. George Lincoln Rockwell and his henchmen in the American Nazi Party, robed Ku Klux Klansmen, and demagogues from the National States' Rights Party vied to take advantage of the uproar over open housing marches. City fears of an all-out race war mounted.

Behind-the-scenes maneuvering by Mayor Daley and the Commission on Human Relations led the Chicago Conference on Religion and Race (CCRR) to call for a peace conference, with itself as the mediator. Knowing that each successive demonstration brought less and less white support, King went along with the proposal, hoping he could gain meaningful concessions. Meeting on August 17 in the Cathedral House of St. James Church, Chicago's oldest Episcopal congregation (1857), King and his associates sat around a horseshoe of tables with the mayor and some fifty key representatives of white Chicago's power elite. In response to King's "Leadership has got to say that the time for change has come," the chair of the Chicago Commission on Human Relations presented an eleven-point plan that called for a moratorium on "marches into neighborhoods" and pledges by various civic and community agencies to work for equal opportunity in housing. A ten-hour discussion by the Summit Conference ensued. Much of it involved threats and accusations.

With the meeting near collapse, King sought to instill calm. *"Our marching feet have brought us a long way, and if we hadn't marched, I don't think we'd be here today."* He went on, *"If you are tired of demonstrations, I am tired of demonstrating. I am tired of the threat of death.*

I want to live. I don't want to be a martyr. And there are moments when I doubt if I am going to make it through. I am tired of getting hit, tired of being beaten, tired of going to jail." The important thing "*is not how tired I am; the important thing is to get rid of the conditions that lead us to march.*" We should be here, he said, "*to discuss how to make Chicago a great open city,*" not how to end marches. "*We don't have much money. We don't really have much education, and we don't have political power. We have only our bodies and you are asking us to give up the one thing that we have when you say, 'Don't march!' We cannot do this. A doctor doesn't cause a cancer when he finds it. In fact, we thank him for finding it, and we are doing the same thing. Our humble marches have revealed a cancer.*"

We are not the ones who have been violent, King concluded. "*Maybe we should begin condemning the robber and not the robbed . . . No one here has talked about the beauty of our marches, the love of our marches, the hatred we're absorbing.*" He urged the negotiators to continue the dialogue. "*We don't see enough to stop the marches, but we are going with love and nonviolence.*"

Although city officials agreed to reasonable changes, the Realtors refused to budge. They did not see themselves in the business of solving social problems. The protest leaders proved equally adamant. They insisted on specific commitments, not professions of goodwill, despite not having a foolproof plan for successful residential desegregation. There would be no agreement that day. A Summit Conference subcommittee would continue negotiating, and the movement would continue demonstrating.

The next night King addressed more than a thousand civil rights adherents packed into the Greater Mount Hope Baptist Church and another thousand outside the church listening via a public address system. He insisted that, just as white southerners were wrong in predicting that whites "*would never sit on buses by Negroes,*" so white northerners would be proved wrong in their assertions of the immutability of housing segregation. He rejected accusations that the Chicago movement was provoking disorder. We "*haven't caused the hatred. We've just brought to the surface hatred that was already there.*" [TELL IT, DOCTOR!] He pledged to make Chicago an open city, because "*it's practical,*" "*it's sound economics,*" and "*it's right.*" It was wrong that he could not *"live somewhere because of the color of my skin."* [YESSIR! YESSIR!] He would no longer tolerate housing discrimination. *"It humiliates me, it does something to my spirit and to my soul, and I'm not going to take it any longer."* The roar of his followers swelled. *"I'm going,"* King shouted above the thunderous ovation, *"to live wherever I want to live.* [THAT'S RIGHT!] *I'm tired of marching for something that should have been mine at first.* [AMEN, AMEN, AMEN.] *I'm tired of living every day under the threat of death. I have no martyr complex. I want to live as long as anybody in this building tonight, and sometimes I begin to doubt whether I'm going to make it through."* Weary to the bone and soul, he ended, *"I don't march because I like it. I march because I must."*

Having failed to get an agreement at the negotiating table, Mayor Daley obtained an injunction on August 19 restricting the size and time of marches due to their constituting a clear and present danger of riot. He went on TV to criticize civil rights leaders for being more interested in demonstrating in the streets than in finding solutions at the conference table. Daley skillfully undercut King's framing of the conflict as a case of right against wrong, instead depicting it as a matter of abstract rights versus the safety and well-being of the city. The mayor's appeal for civic order trumped the preacher's quest for social justice. Within the week, the Chicago City Council formally endorsed the injunction by a vote of forty-five to one. The Chicago and national media added their voices to the chorus calling for an end to marches and demonstrations, and public opinion turned sharply against further protests.

King publicly denounced the injunction as "unjust, illegal, and unconstitutional. We are prepared to put thousands in the streets if need be. The city hasn't seen the number of people we can put there." But on the advice of his lawyers, he chose to fight the ruling in court, not defy it. In the meantime, he wondered, how could the checkmated movement increase the pressure to get a decent settlement? "We're not hopeful," admitted Andy Young. "We haven't been able to put enough pressure on yet." In desperation, King announced on August 20 that the Chicago Freedom Movement would lead a massive march on Sunday, August 28, through the all-white suburb of Cicero, beyond the jurisdiction of the injunction. The governor of Illinois immediately placed the National Guard and state police on high alert. "We can walk in outer space, but we can't walk the streets of Cicero without the National Guard," King retorted. "We're not only going to walk in Cicero," he added a few days later, "we're going to work and live there." Nothing promised a greater likelihood of brutal white violence.

Meanwhile, the Summit subcommittee inched closer to an agreement. The prospect of a civil rights march in Cicero, the most truculent of all-white suburbs, led Chicago officials to offer substantive compromises. The civil rights delegation, fearing that further provocative demonstrations would lead to a race riot or a permanently divided city, indicated its willingness to settle for the best deal possible. Although some of the activists thought that the concessions did not go far enough and the demonstrations should continue, most believed the time had come to stop the protests in exchange for practical steps toward the eventual end of housing discrimination. King agreed. He understood that the movement could not keep large demonstrations going with the school year about to start; that the injunction severely hampered his freedom of action; that he should neither forfeit good relations with those whites still supporting him nor exacerbate a growing "white backlash"; that many blacks who had followed him now wanted some concrete achievements to compensate for their labors; and that an accord would boost the stock of nonviolence. The pragmatist trumped the moralist.

On Friday, August 26, the full Summit Conference of seventy-nine participants reconvened in the stately Walnut Room of the Palmer House Hotel. Despite continuing misgivings within the Freedom Movement and by the Realtors, the Summit Conference unanimously approved an agreement that stipulated the following: the public support of open housing legislation by the Chicago Real Estate Board; the suspension or revocation of the licenses of real estate brokers who violated the city fair-housing ordinance; the selection of scattered lower-density public housing sites by the Chicago Housing Authority; the lending of mortgage money to qualified families by savings and bankers' associations, without regard to race; nondiscriminatory housing assignments for welfare recipients from the Cook County Department of Public Aid; a pledge to promote fair housing by all the major Chicago organizations and institutions; and the creation of a leadership council for Metropolitan Open Housing to oversee the fulfillment of the entire agreement. The Chicago movement protests would end; there would be no march on Cicero "so long as these pledged programs are being carried out." King then delivered a brief benediction, reminding everyone that the agreement was a beginning, not an end. "Our people's hopes have been shattered too many times, and an additional disillusionment will only spell catastrophe. Our summers of riots have been caused by our winters of delay." We must, King concluded, "make this agreement work."

Before the press, King praised the fair-housing provisions of the agreement as "the most significant program ever conceived" for open occupancy. "The total eradication of housing discrimination has been made possible." He informed his Atlanta congregation that it was the "most significant and far-reaching victory that has ever come about in a northern community on the whole question of open housing." He took pride that "The whole power structure was forced by the power of the nonviolent movement to sit down and negotiate and capitulate and make concessions that have never been made before."

More soberly, King's lieutenants admitted that the movement had no real choice but to accept the agreement. The great mass of Chicago's blacks showed no stomach for the fight. They "have a greater feeling of powerlessness than I've ever seen," commented Hosea Williams, "they are beaten psychologically. We are used to working with people who want to be free." SCLC had neither the bodies to fill up the jails nor the treasury to pay the fines incurred for violating the injunction. "It was a choice of going into Cicero and having all-out war, which I don't think we were prepared for," Andy Young added, "or taking this agreement . . . We were realizing along with the rest of the country that the movement had passed the stage of easy solutions."

Despite SCLC's bailing out, a small contingent of CORE and SNCC radicals, protected by nearly twenty times as many National Guardsmen and state troopers, marched in Cicero. To no avail, they endured a heavy downpour of rocks and bottles and went home to condemn King for the agreement's lack of specific timetables and absence of enforcement mechanisms. Some accused King of abandoning "the poor Negro," of "selling out" for a superficial media triumph. Other militants denounced King for failing to initiate a major campaign of civil disobedience and for failing to go to jail in Chicago. SNCC circulated flyers reading, "Daley blew the whistle and King stopped the marches."

Many Chicago African-Americans, conversely, believed something good would come from the accord. They understood that the comprehensive and intertwined nature of the problems made them impossible to solve overnight, and that a negotiated settlement inevitably meant accepting less than what the people needed and deserved. King had driven an unwilling Daley to the conference table, and merely getting the leaders of the white establishment to sign their names to a document admitting that housing in Chicago was segregated and unjust and required change was a victory. For the first time, a civil rights campaign had succeeded in focusing national attention on the deeply rooted problems of the black slums and had proved beyond doubt that racism was a national problem. "We are all," the editors of *The Saturday Evening Post* confessed, "let us face it, Mississippians."

King's criticisms and proposals would be echoed by the president's National Advisory Commission on Civil Disorders following 1967's "long hot summer." Much of what he pleaded for would make its way into new housing ordinances subsequently enacted by Chicago and by Illinois, and into 1968's federal Housing and Civil Rights acts— which called for the construction of millions of new housing units in minority areas; struck down racial-restrictive covenants; attacked redlining; and prohibited property owners with more than four rental units from discriminating on the basis of race. Moreover, Operation Breadbasket, begun in 1966 by the SCLC, would prove to be enormously successful in Chicago, and eventually other cities, in attaining thousands of jobs for blacks.

In the short run, the "white backlash" to the civil rights movement set the course. Although King warned, "If these agreements aren't carried out, Chicago hasn't seen a demonstration," Daley refused to honor his commitments. The mayor maintained that the agreement's binding proposals were only suggestions. His press secretary even confided that Daley's "idea of affirmative action was nine Irishmen and a Swede." Desperately, King tried to mount an African-American voter registration drive to end Daley's grip on the black vote. It failed. Mayor Daley easily won a fourth term by piling up a four-to-one margin in the Negro wards. At the same time, Congress killed an open housing bill. The nation had no intention of responding positively to King's cries for full equality for blacks. In fact, polls indicated that 85 percent of whites thought blacks were protesting and demanding too much.

An increasingly skeptical King reassessed his basic assumptions. He ceased speaking as a reformer simply seeking adjustments in American society. He no longer believed liberalism could respond adequately to the needs of African-Americans and the poor, and he no longer spoke of the inherent goodness of whites or tried to reach the "coalition of conscience," the "great decent majority." The depth of white hatred in Chicago appalled him, as did the indifference or obstinacy of the government and white liberal opinion. Most Americans, he concluded, are at best "unconscious racists." Rather than seeing racism as simply irrational prejudice by individuals, King described it as the systematic exploitation of the African-American minority by the white majority. Only collectivist solutions could end it. Henceforth, he would focus on the underlying causes of racism and attack it at its roots. He would demand "a restructuring of the very architecture of American society." As the advocate for the powerless and impoverished, the preacher would not relent.

> I choose to identify with the underprivileged. I choose to identify with the poor. I choose to give my life for the hungry. I choose to give my life for those who have been left out of the sunlight of opportunity. I choose to live for and with those who find themselves seeing life as a long and desolate corridor with no exit sign. This is the way I'm going. If it means suffering a little bit, I'm going that way. If it means sacrificing, I'm going that way. If it means dying for them, I'm going that way, because I heard a voice saying, "Do something for others."

King would heed his inner voice.

SEEING LAZARUS,

1967–68

Our lives begin to end the day we become silent about things that matter.

⟍

G rief would shadow King's spirit in the last year and a half of his earthly journey. In the fall of 1966, Stokely Carmichael reaped headlines and political havoc by increasingly portraying Black Power as a rejection of both white society and King's nonviolence, and by depicting the score of ghetto riots that summer as revolutionary violence to overthrow a reactionary society. Meanwhile—capitalizing on the backlash against racial violence and "crime in the streets"— Republicans, most of them right-wing conservatives, replaced forty-seven Democratic incumbents in the House and three in the Senate. At the same time, King watched the war in Vietnam ominously expand, multiplying the numbers of Americans shipped home in body bags—16 percent of them black in 1966—and causing appropriations for the war on poverty to be slashed by a third.

King despaired a "white society more concerned about tranquility and the status quo than about justice and humanity." As never before, Coretta thought him morose. He smoked constantly and overate heedlessly. His depression, she recalled, was "greater than I had ever seen before." He brooded that "people expect me to have answers and

I don't have any answers." Worried that Black Power had made him irrelevant, he feared a looming race war.

Unlike most mainstream civil rights leaders, King did not jump on the anti–Black Power bandwagon. Instead, he decried the "white backlash" and insisted, "America's greatest problem and contradiction is that it harbors 35 million poor at a time when its resources are so vast that the existence of poverty is an anachronism." He called for mass protests until the government provided a guaranteed annual income of $4,000 to every American adult. He proposed that SCLC organize "the poor in a crusade to reform society in order to realize economic and social justice."

King mused to his aides that the only way to get the nation to address poverty might be to get large numbers of very poor people to march on Washington. "We ought to come in mule carts, in old trucks, any kind of transportation people can get their hands on. People ought to come to Washington, sit down if necessary in the middle of the street and say, 'We are here; we are poor; we don't have any money; you have made us this way; you keep us down this way; and we've come to stay until you do something about it.' "

"There are few things more thoroughly sinful than economic injustice," King thundered to a church convention in Texas. Laying bare his troubled soul, he vouched, "Christianity has always insisted that the cross we bear precedes the crown we wear. To be a Christian one must take up his cross, with all its difficulties and agonizing and tension-packed content, and carry it until that very cross leaves its mark upon us and redeems us to that more excellent way which comes only through suffering."

King knew he would suffer. He knew what he must do. But, not knowing how to do it, he called for a staff retreat at the Penn Center on St. Helena Island, South Carolina, to mull over SCLC's future. He admitted his chagrin that the movement's "legislative and judicial victories did very little to improve the lot of millions of Negroes in the teeming ghettos of the North" and his despair that "the roots of racism are very deep in America." To his seventy-five staff members, King expressed his conviction that "something is wrong with the economic system of our nation." He emphasized the need to pursue "substantive," not "surface," changes that would make "demands that will cost the nation something."

Few of his aides and advisers saw it King's way. Hosea Williams wanted SCLC to concentrate on voter registration in the South; Jesse Jackson thought it should devote its resources to an expanded Operation Breadbasket in northern cities. Stanley Levison admonished King that whites were not ready for "deep radical change," and to maintain that black equality could be achieved only "with the revolutionary alteration of our society" was "poor tactics." Others feared King's increasing economic radicalism would frighten potential donors and foundations and worsen the serious money problems SCLC already faced. The lack of support for a mass-action campaign focused on economic justice and the incessant clash of executive staff egos further depressed King, as did the constant fund-raising trips to keep the financially sinking SCLC afloat. They left him little time for reflection, and for home and family. Despite his awareness of FBI surveillance, King's need for respite, for solace, increased his thirst for sexual liaisons.

Perhaps in atonement, King openly trumpeted his prophetic rage at the military conflict halfway around the world that had replaced civil rights as the nation's most pressing concern. Leaving for Jamaica in mid-January 1967 for a month of solitude to work on his next book, *Where Do We Go from Here*, King happened upon "The Children of Vietnam," an illustrated article in the January *Ramparts* magazine. Suddenly, he stopped, recalled his aide Bernard Lee:

> He froze as he looked at the pictures from Vietnam. He saw a picture of a Vietnamese mother holding her dead baby, a baby killed by our military. Then Martin pushed the plate of food away from him. I looked up and said, "Doesn't it taste any good?" and he answered, "Nothing will ever taste good for me until I do everything I can to end the war."

Upon seeing the pictures of children maimed and murdered by the United States, King committed himself to whatever was necessary to oppose the war. He would "no longer remain silent about an issue that was destroying the soul of our nation."

He knew this meant incurring the wrath of the president of the United States. He knew it would deprive the civil rights movement of his precious time and energy. He knew it would cause a drop in contributions to the SCLC—already 40 percent lower than a year earlier. He knew it would mean allying himself with radicals whom most Americans despised, and that it would destroy whatever slim chances remained for the kind of massive federal expenditures required by the ghettos. But King had crossed his Rubicon.

Considering himself a "realistic" rather than a "doctrinaire" pacifist, King believed "the potential destructiveness of modern weapons of war totally rules out the possibility of war ever serving again as a negative good." An alternative must be found, he wrote. "The choice today is no longer between violence and nonviolence. It is either nonviolence or nonexistence." Accordingly, he spoke out first against the Vietnam War at Howard University in March 1965, just as President Johnson began his escalation of the conflict. To audiences that year in the Roxbury neighborhood of Boston and in Petersburg, Virginia, King declared that the war must be stopped and called for a negotiated settlement. When it was extremely unpopular to do so, he stated, "We must even negotiate with the Vietcong." Going further yet, he suggested that Americans travel to Vietnam to rebuild some of the villages they had destroyed.

However, in August 1965, when King sought the backing of SCLC's board for his idea to send personal letters to all the leaders involved in the war, urging a speedily negotiated settlement, the board demurred. It recognized King's right to speak as an individual but affirmed that SCLC existed for the purpose of securing the civil rights of Negroes. The board said that SCLC's "resources are not sufficient to assume the burdens of two major issues." SCLC would not get involved in foreign affairs.

Despite the rebuke, King called on the president to "seriously consider halting the bombing" of North Vietnam and to state "unequivocally" his willingness to negotiate with the Vietcong. Taking his Nobel Peace Prize to heart, valuing the importance of his reputation as a proponent of nonviolence, resenting the patronizing attitude of the administration that he was "out of his depth" on foreign policy, and foreseeing that the war abroad would be paid for by starving social programs at home, King pressed on with his intention to plead with all the warring parties to settle their differences at the conference table. To those who wanted him to stick to racial matters, he repeated, "Injustice anywhere is a threat to justice everywhere" and "Justice is indivisible." He could not be for democracy and humanitarianism and not be against colonialism and imperialism. "I will not stand by when I see an unjust war taking place and fail to take a stand against it."

But Lyndon Johnson had had enough. He gave King the cold shoulder at the Voting Rights Act signing ceremony in August. The following month he directed UN ambassador Arthur Goldberg to meet privately with King, inform him that secret negotiations were under way and peace was quite near, and that any public criticism "would give aid and comfort to the enemy and stiffen" its diplomatic position. At the same time, Johnson had one of his senatorial cronies, Thomas Dodd of Connecticut, publicly blast King for having "absolutely no competence" to speak about foreign affairs and for unpatriotically aligning himself "with the forces of appeasement." The news media seemed to see it all through Johnson's eyes. In an article entitled "Confusing the Cause," *Time* declared that King should stop meddling where he did not belong. King, other columnists echoed, had no business speaking about foreign affairs. Public opinion polls indicated that most blacks and whites agreed.

Dismayed by the president's offensive and by the public disapproval of his antiwar activities, a frustrated King decided to call it quits. He could not fight the war while fighting for civil rights. "I'm already over-loaded and almost emotionally fatigued," he confided to friends, and "can't battle these forces who are out to defeat my influence . . . to cut me down." He needed to "withdraw temporarily," to "gracefully pull out so I can get on with the civil rights issue." Most of the SCLC staff, following Andy Young in thinking antiwar activists "a bunch of crazies," breathed a sigh of relief.

Yet King's conscience churned away. Quietly, he turned to James Lawson, who journeyed to Vietnam in 1965 on a peace-seeking mission and then helped form the Southern Coordinating Committee to End the War in Vietnam, and to James Bevel, who preached that the "Lord can't hear our prayers here in America because of all the cries and moans of His children in the Mekong Delta." Constantly urging King to take a more radical stand on Vietnam, Bevel claimed that the Lord had appeared to him sitting on the dryer in his Chicago laundry room, "saying, 'My children are dying in Vietnam, my children are

suffering. They are your brothers and sisters too. You must help them.' "
Mostly, King listened to his wife on Vietnam. A committed pacifist,
Coretta Scott King had joined the Women's International League for
Peace and Freedom as a student at Antioch, continued her peace activities later in the National Committee for a Sane Nuclear Policy,
and picketed the White House over Vietnam even before Martin first
spoke against the war. Her views on the war in Vietnam, more than
anyone else's, nurtured his beliefs.

"I did not march, I did not demonstrate, I did not rally," he later
wrote about the remainder of 1965. "But as the hopeful days became
disappointing months, I began the agonizing measurement of government promising words of peace against the baneful, escalating deeds
of war. Doubts gnawed at my conscience." Certainly, King told an
aide, "the position of our government is wrong and it is getting
wronger every day."

Lashing out at the administration's efforts to muzzle critics of the
war, to depict advocates of negotiation "as quasi-traitors, fools, or venal
enemies of our soldiers and institutions," King declared to a New York
audience that he would not be silenced. He quoted Amos on justice,
Isaiah on renouncing violence, and Micah on beating swords into
plowshares. As a minister, "I am mandated by this calling above every
other duty to seek peace among men and to do it even in the face of
hysteria and scorn."

As 1966 began, the Georgia state legislature barred SNCC's Julian
Bond from taking his elected seat because of SNCC's call for young
blacks to take up civil rights work rather than submit to the military
draft. King left no doubt of his resolve by adding his voice and prestige
to the campaign to get Bond seated. "We are in a dangerous period
when we seek to silence dissent," King told newsmen, adding that "in
my current role as a pacifist I would be a conscientious objector." In
his next Sunday's sermon, King proclaimed, "Our hands are dirty"
in Vietnam, and depicted dissent and nonconformity as the essence of
true Christianity.

Later in the spring, King won the approval of the SCLC board for
a resolution that branded as "immoral" the U.S. support of South
Vietnam's military junta; called on President Johnson to "seriously ex-
amine the wisdom of prompt withdrawal" from the war; and condemned the conflict "on the grounds that war is not the way to solve

social problems" or ensure America's interests. "The intense expectations and hopes of the neglected poor in the United States must be regarded as a priority more urgent than pursuit of a conflict so rapidly
degenerating into a sordid military adventure." The following month,
on CBS's *Face the Nation*, King renewed his public demand for a halt
to the U.S. bombing of North Vietnam. In August another SCLC
board resolution denounced Johnson's "relentless escalation" of the
war and demanded that he immediately and unilaterally deescalate
the conflict. Late in the year King sadly told a Senate subcommittee,
"The bombs in Vietnam explode at home; they destroy hopes and pos-
sibilities for a decent America."

Yet King now largely confined his comments about the war to its
damaging impact on the civil rights movement, then followed them
with longer periods of silence on the issue. Torn between his conscience and his fear of alienating the movement's key political allies
and financial supporters, he sought, in the words of a former SCLC
staffer, "to walk a tortuous middle path." He would continue to oppose the war, but tentatively, guardedly—not in a headline-grabbing
manner.

The graphic illustrations of the horrors of war in *Ramparts* ended
King's reticence. He no longer considered either Johnson or the Democrats in Congress dependable allies. Berating himself for pulling his
punches, he informed his aides that he would take a more active role
in opposing the war, no matter the cost.

Making his first public appearance in over two months at an antiwar rally in Los Angeles in late February 1967, King lambasted Johnson's Vietnam War policies for morally isolating the United States.
"We are engaged in a war that seeks to turn the clock of history back
and perpetuate white colonialism." He decried the American military's atrocities, "our paranoid anti-Communism," and "deadly Western arrogance." Unable to bear "the betrayal of my own silences,"
King thundered that it was time to halt the bombing, negotiate with
the Vietcong, and "deal positively and forthrightly with the triple evils
of racism, extreme materialism and militarism . . . We must demonstrate, teach, and preach until the very foundations of our nation are
shaken."

Several days later, at a meeting in New York, Whitney Young berated King. "The Negro is more concerned about the rat at night and

the job in the morning than he is about the war in Vietnam," the head
of the Urban League declared. "If we are not with him [Johnson] on
Vietnam, then he is not going to be with us on civil rights." "Whitney,
what you're saying may get you a foundation grant," King shot back,
"but it won't get you into the kingdom of truth." Livid, Young pointed
to King's ample stomach. "You're eating well." The two former com-
rades in the movement, now politically far apart, had to be physically
separated. King telephoned Young hours later to apologize for the outburst, to no avail. They renewed the argument, neither man backing
down or changing the other's mind.

King had little more success with the SCLC board or his closest
advisers. He reminded the board of "those little Vietnamese children
who have been burned with napalm," and observed that African-
Americans were paying the heaviest price for the war, in both battlefield casualties and cutbacks in social welfare programs. But some
preachers thought he was imposing his views like a bishop, and the
board refused to adopt King's resolution committing the SCLC to active opposition to the war. Nor could he sway Levison, Rustin, and his
closest aides to take part in the upcoming April 15 protests against the
war. Bevel, alone, advocated King's participation. All the rest derided
his joining a "squabbling, pacifist, socialist, hippie collection." Warned
by Levison that it would cause a severe drop in contributions, King
replied, "I don't care if we don't get five cents in the mail. I am going
to keep preaching my message." He patiently explained, "At times you
do things to satisfy your conscience, and they may be altogether unre-
alistic or wrong tactically." The war was so evil that "I can no longer
be cautious about this matter. I feel so deep in my heart that we are so
wrong in this country and the time has come for a real prophecy and
I'm willing to go that road."

He would go alone, if need be. As he told a reporter for *The New
York Times*, "We are merely marking time in the civil rights movement
if we do not take a stand against the war." America must realize that
international violence was just as immoral as racial segregation. "It is
out of this moral commitment to dignity and the worth of human personality that I feel it is necessary to stand up against the war in Vietnam."

In late March, King and Dr. Benjamin Spock led five thousand
demonstrators in downtown Chicago, the first antiwar march of King's

career. There, he railed at the cruel irony of blacks and whites dying together "for a nation that has been unable to seat them together in the same schools."

On April 4, 1967—exactly a year before he would be slain in Memphis—King addressed some four thousand congregants in New York's stately Riverside Church. *"A time comes when silence is betrayal,"* he began, reading remarks written largely by Professor Vincent Harding of Spelman College. King declared his opposition to his government a *"vocation of agony."* But *"my conscience leaves me no other choice."*

In measured rhetoric that would be reported around the world, King enumerated the many reasons the war in Vietnam must be ended. First, U.S. military intervention in Vietnam had *"broken and eviscerated"* the war on poverty *"as if it were some idle political plaything of a society gone mad on war."* Like *"some demonic destructive suction tube,"* it had robbed funds from domestic programs and sent poor black youth to fight and die out of all proportion to their numbers. In addition, *"I knew that I could never again raise my voice against the violence of the oppressed in the ghettos without having first spoken clearly to the greatest purveyor of violence in the world today— my own government."* His Christian ministerial role and convictions required him to adopt a broad world perspective rather than a narrow American one. Furthermore, a moral obligation *"to work harder than I had ever worked before"* to end war had been *"placed upon me in 1964"* by the Nobel Peace Prize.

King harshly condemned America's puppet government in South Vietnam as a vicious dictatorship and questioned the very basis of U.S. foreign policy. Given America's neocolonialism, he thought Vietnam was no aberration. He pictured America siding with *"the wealthy and the secure while we create a hell for the poor"* of Vietnam, and he demanded once again that the United States end all its bombing and negotiate with the Vietcong. King also insisted on a date by which all foreign troops would be out of Vietnam, and he asked all young men to declare themselves conscientious objectors if drafted.

This business of burning human beings with napalm, of filling our nation's homes with orphans and widows, of injecting poisonous drugs of hate into the veins of peoples normally humane, of

*sending men home from dark and bloody battlefields physically
handicapped and psychologically deranged, cannot be recon-
ciled with wisdom, justice, and love. A nation that continues year
after year to spend more money on military defense than on programs of social uplift is approaching spiritual death . . . Somehow this madness must cease.*

"*The war in Vietnam is but a symptom of a far deeper malady
within the American spirit,*" King concluded. It was time, he said, that
America led a world revolution against "*poverty, racism, and militarism.*" If "*we are to get on the right side of the world revolution, we as
a nation must undergo a radical revolution of values. We must rapidly
begin the shift from a 'thing-oriented' society to a 'person-oriented' society.*" His voice resounding in the immense Gothic cathedral, the
preacher declared, "*If we do not act, we shall surely be dragged down
the long, dark, and shameful corridors of time reserved for those who
possess power without compassion, might without morality, and strength
without sight.*" He closed with Amos' "*justice will roll down like waters
and righteousness like a mighty stream.*"

Given that 73 percent of Americans in the spring of 1967 supported the war, and only 25 percent of African-Americans opposed it,
the speech ignited a firestorm of criticism. Virtually every American
newspaper and magazine rebuked King. Typically, *The Washington
Post* declared the speech "unsupported fantasy," adding that King had
gravely injured the civil rights movement and himself. "Many who
have listened to him with respect will never again accord him the
same confidence. He has diminished his usefulness to his cause, to his
country and to his people." Under the title "Dr. King's Error," *The
New York Times* belittled King's intelligence and claimed that he had
done "a disservice" to both the civil rights and peace movements.
Even Negro-owned newspapers such as *The Pittsburgh Courier* accused him of "tragically misleading" African-Americans, and the
NAACP adopted a resolution stating that his effort to join the civil
rights and peace movements was "a serious tactical mistake" that
served neither cause.

Newsweek denounced his demagoguery; *Time* complained that he
had set back the cause of Negro advancement; *U.S. News & World Re-*

port accused him of "lining up with Hanoi"; and *Life* magazine arraigned him for uttering "a demagogic slander that sounded like a script for Radio Hanoi." Baseball legend Jackie Robinson, African-American senator Edward Brooke of Massachusetts, and African-American Ralph Bunche, the UN undersecretary-general, added their public criticism of the speech.

"What is that goddamned nigger preacher doing to me?" Johnson raged. "We gave him the Civil Rights Act of 1964, we gave him the Voting Rights Act of 1965, we gave him the War on Poverty. What more does he want?" The preacher would never again be invited to the White House. Henceforth, King would be on the outside, in a picket line, shouting peace chants through the wrought-iron gates.

Adding to Johnson's anger, adviser John P. Roche told the president that King had "thrown in with the commies." He confided that "Communist-oriented 'peace' types have played him (and his driving wife) like trout," and pronounced him "quite stupid." J. Edgar Hoover similarly informed Johnson, "Based on King's recent activities and public utterances, it is clear that he is an instrument in the hands of subversive forces seeking to undermine our nation." Hoover insisted that King was being handled and steered by Stanley Levison and Harry Wachtel, "two of the most dedicated and dangerous communists in the country." After talking with the White House press secretary, the prominent black journalist Carl Rowan penned an article for the widely read *Reader's Digest* that attributed King's "tragic decision" to denounce U.S. policy in Vietnam to Communist influence. As a consequence, Rowan concluded, King had "alienated many of the Negro's friends and armed the Negro's foes."

Reacting to the onslaught and Levison's private critique of the speech as unbalanced and poorly thought out, King told his longtime friend that he knew his words would be unpopular, but *"I really feel that someone of influence has to say that the United States is wrong."* He understood that he had gone *"beyond the point that anyone has done who is of influence. I have just become so disgusted with the way people of America are being brainwashed."* So he would keep repeating, *"Injustice anywhere is a threat to justice everywhere."* He would not segregate his moral concerns: *"Justice is indivisible."*

In 1967, for the first time since King's rise to prominence, he failed to make the Gallup Poll's list of the ten most popular Americans. That did not matter.

> *Cowardice asks the question, "Is it safe?" Expediency asks the question, "Is it politic?" And Vanity comes along and asks the question, "Is it popular?" But Conscience asks the question, "Is it right?" And there comes a time when one must take a position that is neither safe, nor politic, nor popular, but he must do it because Conscience tells him it is right.*

He continued speaking in the same vein and accepted the position of cochairman of Clergy and Laymen Concerned About Vietnam (to put the "protest" back in "Protestant"). On April 15, chanting, "Stop the bombing, stop the bombing, stop the bombing," King led a procession of 125,000 marchers from Central Park to UN Plaza for the Spring Mobilization to End the War in Vietnam. His address recapitulated many of the points he had made at the Riverside Church, and appearing on CBS's *Face the Nation* the following morning, he reiterated that "something must be done on a much more massive scale to oppose" the Vietnam War.

Despite unceasing censure, King remained true to his convictions. He began planning for a Vietnam Summer, to mobilize ten thousand student volunteers to build mainstream opposition to the war, and he announced his formation of Negotiations Now, to garner one million petition signatures calling for immediate peace talks. He lauded Muhammad Ali's conscientious resistance to military service and barnstormed the country calling for "teach-ins" and "preach-ins" against the war.

At a second SCLC staff retreat at Frogmore in May, King spoke of his own vacillations on the war. "My name then wouldn't have been written in any book called *Profiles in Courage*. But now I have decided. I will not be intimidated. I will not be harassed. I will not be silent. And I will be heard." His radio program, *Martin Luther King Speaks*, aired on a dozen major stations around the country, attracting a weekly audience of more than two million. He advocated imposing strong sanctions against the apartheid regime in South Africa; admitting the People's Republic of China to the United Nations; adopting a

Marshall Plan for the Third World; and tying "the peace movement to the civil rights movement or vice-versa," even if it meant a complete break with the Johnson administration. Coretta felt it was "the beginning of a larger work for him which would develop into something greater than we could conceive at the time. All along in our struggle one phase had led to another."

But King could not stop the war. Nor could he prevent the growing white backlash and black militancy that fed upon each other. People expected him to have answers, Martin told Coretta, but he had none. He was emotionally spent from the unrelenting attacks on his antiwar activities, the stepped-up FBI vendetta against him, and the vicious ridicule of his nonviolent beliefs by numerous proponents of Black Power. He was weary from the unceasing pressures of fundraising and from being on the road five and six days a week—making speeches, attending conferences, answering the press, backslapping strangers who might offer a donation. He craved surcease from the interminable wrangling of his aides, the low morale of the field staff, the worsening financial situation of SCLC, and the wide-open battles between competing organizations in the rapidly disintegrating civil rights movement.

In July 1967 the black ghettos exploded in the most intense and destructive wave of rioting the nation had ever experienced. Unprecedented numbers of blacks in some threescore cities, north and south, coast to coast, took to the streets, looting and burning, throwing Molotov cocktails, and firing upon police. To stop the rioting in Newark, New Jersey, the police and National Guard killed twenty-five blacks and wounded or arrested another thirteen hundred. In Detroit, where nearly four thousand fires destroyed thirteen hundred buildings, most of the forty-three deaths and many of the thousand wounded came at the hands of untrained and jittery National Guardsmen. All told, the long hot summer of 1967 resulted in at least ninety deaths, more than four thousand wounded, and nearly seventeen thousand mostly black arrests. "There were dark days before, but this is the darkest," a dispirited King told Levison as he watched his "dream turn into a nightmare."

King placed the ultimate blame for the riots on white America. "The turmoil of the ghetto is the externalization of the Negro's inner torment and rage. It has turned outward the frustration that formerly was suppressed in agony." He pleaded for an immediate program to end unemployment, beseeching Washington for a New Deal effort to provide a job to everyone who needed work. Unless the government acted at once, he declared, "this tragic destruction of life and property" would spread. Neither Congress nor the president responded. King feared time was running out for America and all he believed in. He had to act.

His preoccupation with Vietnam became a preoccupation with leading a massive crusade of urban civil disobedience. King sought to force the nation to attack the root causes of black nihilism. Despite racial matters having changed more in the previous decade than in any decade since the Civil War, King knew much more was needed. As he had written just after the Watts riot in 1965, the "explosive Negro community in the North has a short fuse and a long train of abuses." He wished to "transmute the deep rage of the ghetto into a constructive and creative force." He had to salvage nonviolence as a strategy for change. King had already called for a "radical redistribution of power." On various occasions during the spring, he had insisted that America's "moral sickness," its "repulsive moral disease," necessitated radical measures.

"I didn't get my inspiration from Karl Marx," King liked to say. "I got it from a man named Jesus." Publicly, he avoided using the word "socialism." He feared giving his enemies—whether in the White House, the FBI, or the economically conservative black church— cause to claim he was a Communist or a Marxist. But many of his speeches clearly expressed his preference for what Coretta described as the egalitarian Christianity and democratic socialism that King had long held dear.

He had already called for a Bill of Rights for the Disadvantaged similar to the GI Bill of Rights. Justified by "the robberies inherent in the institution of slavery," it advocated preferential employment practices and home and business loan subsidies for African-Americans. Writing in Why We Can't Wait (1964), King insisted that the "relevant question" was how "can we make freedom real and substantial for our colored citizens? What just course will ensure the greatest speed and completeness? And how do we combat opposition and overcome obstacles arising from the defaults of the past?" Harkening back to what Indian prime minister Jawaharlal Nehru had told him about the preferential treatment given to untouchables in applying for jobs and education, King answered: "Compensatory consideration for the handicaps he has inherited from the past," preferential treatment that would equip blacks to compete on a just and equal basis. "Giving a man his due may often mean giving him special treatment."

In *Where Do We Go from Here?* (1967), his final book, he pictured "the good and just society" as neither capitalism nor communism but "a socially conscious democracy" that would close the gulf "between superfluous wealth and abject poverty" and end "cut-throat competition and selfish ambition." It "is morally right," King declared, "to insist that every person have a decent house, an adequate education, and enough money to provide basic necessities for one's family."

The year before, he had told the SCLC staff, "You can't talk about ending slums without first saying profit must be taken out of slums." King cautioned that "this means we are treading in difficult waters, because it really means that we are saying that something is wrong with capitalism." He had no blueprint but was sure "God never intended for some of his children to live in inordinate superfluous wealth while others live in abject, deadening poverty." Maybe, he concluded, "America must move toward a Democratic Socialism." He often used the example of Sweden as a model that the United States should follow.

Throughout the spring, King's sermons at black churches dealt increasingly with poverty and class exploitation. Only by reallocating power, King preached, could we "wipe out the triple interlocking evils of racism, exploitation, and militarism." He called for a "human rights revolution" that placed economic justice at the center. He talked of moving from a reform movement into a "new era, which must be an era of revolution." The time had come to raise new questions, to change the rules. America must be born again. "The whole structure of American life must be changed."

"For years," King told journalist David Halberstam in April 1967, "I labored with the idea of reforming the existing institutions of the society, a little change here, a little change there. Now I feel quite differently. I think you've got to have a reconstruction of the entire society, a revolution of values." By this he meant "the possible nationalization of certain industries, a guaranteed annual income, a vast review of foreign investments, an attempt to bring new life into the cities." Only these might stem the exhortations from those such as H. Rap Brown, who had succeeded Stokely Carmichael as head of SNCC, for African-Americans to "get your guns" and "kill the honkies."

On ABC's *Issues and Answers* that summer, King again called for a radical reconstruction of society. "Many of the allies who were with us during the first phase of the Movement," he said, "will not be with us now because it does mean dispersing the ghetto; it does mean living next door to them; and it does mean the government pouring billions of dollars into programs to get rid of slums and poverty and deprivation." Giving no quarter to former allies who now thought him misguided, King emphasized that "this is why the civil rights movement has to restructure itself, in a sense to gear itself for an altogether new phase of struggle."

Speaking to the tenth-anniversary convention of SCLC in Atlanta in mid-August, King made no effort to sugar-coat his militancy. He began by quoting Victor Hugo's *Les Misérables*: "*If the soul is left in darkness, sins will be committed. The guilty one is not he who commits the sin, but he who causes the darkness.*" Whites, he exclaimed, caused the darkness. "*They created discrimination. They created slums. They perpetuate unemployment, ignorance, and poverty.*" To combat those, he called for the creative extremism of civil disobedience. It was time to disrupt business as usual in "*earthquake proportions,*" until "*the tragic walls that separate the outer city of wealth and comfort and the inner city of poverty and despair shall be crushed by the battering rams of the forces of justice.*"

King then asked, "*Why are there 40 million poor people in America?*"

> *When you begin to ask that question, you are raising questions about the economic system, about a broader distribution of wealth. When you ask that question, you begin to question the capitalistic economy . . . But one day we must come to see that an edifice which produces beggars needs restructuring . . . You see, my friends, when you deal with this, you begin to ask the*

question, "Who owns the oil?" You begin to ask the question, "Who owns the iron ore?"

He quoted Jefferson—"I tremble for my country when I reflect that God is just"—and concluded that for America to be born again, there must be Christian democratic socialism.

That meant strategies that did not depend on the goodwill and political support of the federal government, and tactics that would compel "unwilling authorities to yield to the mandates of justice." King was intrigued by the idea of Marian Wright, a lawyer for the NAACP's Legal Defense Fund, to bring the destitute to Washington to stage sit-ins. The first black woman to pass the Mississippi bar, Wright discussed her proposal with SCLC's senior staff at a retreat in West Virginia in mid-September 1967. She persuaded King to mobilize indigent people to march to Washington to demand economic justice. To redeem the soul of America, King envisioned a Rainbow Coalition of the poor, an interracial alliance embracing Hispanics, Native Americans, Appalachian whites, and African-Americans trained in nonviolence, engaging in massive civil disobedience. He contemplated building a shantytown along the Reflecting Pool so that the politicians would have to see and smell the poverty so widespread in America. "This is it," he told Coretta. "This is really it."

In late October, King informed the press that since the government refused to take the necessary steps to provide jobs and decent incomes for those in need, the SCLC would "lead waves of the nation's poor and disinherited to Washington, D.C., next spring to demand redress of their grievances by the United States government." An army of the nation's outcast and disregarded would converge on the nation's capital, erect a tent city encampment, like the Bonus Army of 1932, and persist in staging protests in the capitol until the federal government dealt with the problems of poverty. A Poor People's Campaign (PPC) would confront the federal government itself and exert enough pressure so that it "can no longer elude our demands." Whether this led to repression, scorn, ridicule, or jail, "we accept it willingly, for the millions of poor are already imprisoned by exploitation and discrimination."

King devoted himself to drumming up support. He sprinkled terms like "aggressive nonviolence" and "nonviolent sabotage" into his speeches, maintaining that nonviolence now needed "disruptive dimensions." He wanted protesters engaging in civil disobedience in Washington to tie up traffic, shut down business in government buildings, and lay siege to the chambers of power. Concurrently, there would be sympathy boycotts and demonstrations throughout the nation. "Before, we mobilized one city at a time," King averred. "Now we are mobilizing a nation." If necessary, the PPC would engage in major dislocations to "cripple the operations of an oppressive society" until it responded to the pleas of its needy.

King clearly saw the need for nonviolence to "adapt to urban conditions and urban moods" and to reflect "heightened black impatience and stiffened white resistance." As Andy Young, one of the few in SCLC to support King's plans for the PPC, understood, "people don't respond until their own self-interest is threatened. People don't give up power and money voluntarily."

"Our nation is at a crossroads," King claimed in December. "It is impossible to underestimate the crisis we face in America." Accordingly, the PPC would provoke confrontations until Congress passed an Economic Bill of Rights. It would engage in "lying on highways, blocking doors at government offices, and mass school boycotts." King wanted to tie Washington into knots with "nonviolent but militant tactics as dramatic, as dislocative, as disruptive, as attention-getting as the riots without destroying property." This would be a "last, desperate demand for the nation to respond to nonviolence" and to prevent "the worst chaos, hatred and violence any nation has ever encountered." He told his colleagues, "We've got to go for broke this time . . . If necessary I'm going to stay in jail six months—they aren't going to run me out of Washington."

King capped the year with "A Christmas Sermon on Peace" for the Canadian Broadcasting Corporation. He acknowledged that the dream he had articulated at the Lincoln Memorial had become a nightmare. He described the punishing poverty he saw in the ghettos as the antithesis of his dream "that one day the idle industries of Appalachia will be revitalized, and the empty stomachs of Mississippi will be filled, and brotherhood will be more than a few words at the end of prayer, but rather the first order of business on every legislative agenda." He promised to turn his "bolder dream, a dream of revolution rather than one of reform," into reality.

Yet the strident opposition to the PPC within SCLC continued into the new year. Few board members agreed with King that the PPC should demand a comprehensive series of proposals, including $30 billion in anti-poverty spending; a binding federal commitment to full employment; enactment of a guaranteed annual income bill; and funds to construct at least five hundred thousand low-income housing units each year. Few on the staff thought it made sense to threaten the occupation of government buildings or the blocking of traffic on bridges and highways.

Bevel yearned for the SCLC to devote everything to bringing the Vietnam War to an end; Jackson wanted its resources to go to spreading Operation Breadbasket nationwide. Williams thought the SCLC should assist southern blacks to run for elective office; Young feared that its plan for massive civil disobedience would degenerate into aimless disorder and provoke more white repression. Others thought the PPC would only exacerbate the backlash and enrage the best civil rights president in history. Most hurtful of all to King, longtime adviser Bayard Rustin went public with his insistence that many of the "people who marched on Washington in 1963 for Negro dignity are not prepared to have their taxes raised to make economic dignity possible." He called upon King to cancel the Poor People's Campaign, which he termed a betrayal of racial justice in pursuit of a pipe dream of radicalism.

King pulled back—a little. He spoke more often of creating public sympathy rather than of closing down the capital. "We have, through massive nonviolent action, an opportunity to avoid a national disaster and create a new spirit of class and racial harmony. We can write another luminous moral chapter in American history." But that still failed to subdue what Attorney General Ramsey Clark remembered as "a paranoia, literally," in government circles that the PPC would ignite violent rioting.

More than ever, Hoover's FBI viewed King and the SCLC as a threat to national security. Its machinery of intimidation, disinformation, and disruption went into high gear. Going well beyond the powers given it by Congress and the courts, the agency hampered King's fund-raising efforts; fed the press anti-SCLC editorials and embarrassing questions to ask King; and spread rumors that the Poor People's Campaign was disorganized and broke, that its adherents would come to bodily harm in Washington, and that demonstrators would have their "welfare checks from the Government discontinued." Young realized, "We had become the enemy."

The opposition from within and without, the attacks from the left and the right, brought King unceasing misery. His head ached, his eyes burned, his mind strayed. Unable to sleep, he would talk all night long to one or another aide, frequently referring to an apocalyptic vision of a race war ending in a fascist state. They will "treat us like they did our Japanese brothers and sisters in World War Two. They'll throw us into concentration camps."

All the failures of the movement, all the poverty in Mississippi, all the burned babies in Vietnam tortured King. The greater his guilt, the more reckless his partying and extramarital affairs. Thinking only martyrdom might redeem him, King fixated on his own death. He "knew they were out to get him" and often contended "that his time was up." When aides thought him too morbid, he responded, "I'm just being realistic." By then the FBI had recorded some fifty assassination plots against the preacher. King himself knew of many, including a recent offer of a $100,000 reward, by two St. Louis supporters of George Wallace's American Independent Party, to the killer of Martin Luther King, Jr.

In early February he told his Ebenezer congregation, "*I think about my own death, and I think about my own funeral.*" He explained that he did not want a long, elaborate funeral. "*Tell them not to mention that I have a Nobel Peace Prize, that isn't important.*" What he would want said was "*that Martin Luther King tried to give his life serving others.*" In thunderclap rhythm, he drummed:

"*. . . that I tried to be right on the war question.*"

"*. . . that I did try to feed the hungry.*"

"*. . . that I did try, in my life, to clothe those who were naked.*"

"*. . . that I tried to love and serve humanity.*"

"*. . . that I was a drum major for justice . . . For peace . . . For righteousness. And all of the other shallow things will not matter.*"

"*. . . then my living will not be in vain.*"

A month later, King preached a sermon about shattered dreams. He spoke of his dream of the Beloved Community turning into a nightmare of civil war, and of the schizophrenia in all our lives. *"There is a Mr. Hyde and a Dr. Jekyll in us. I want you to know this morning that I'm a sinner like all of God's children. But I want to be a good man."* Sex was sacred, he reflected. *"It's beautiful. It's holy. But"*—he paused—*"if one becomes a slave to sex, you can never satisfy it! And then the long road of promiscuity comes along. And then you discover what hell is.*

"There is much good in the worst of us, and so much bad in the rest of us," he continued. But *"God does not judge us by the separate incidents or the separate mistakes that we make, but by the total bent of our lives. In the final analysis, God knows that his children are weak and they are frail. In the final analysis, what God requires is that your heart is right."* His voice cracked. *"You don't need to go out saying that Martin Luther King is a saint. Oh, no. I want you to know this morning that I'm a sinner like all of God's children. But I want to be a good man."* What counted was trying, repenting, being on the right road.

For America, King claimed, this meant coming home from racism, war, and poverty amid plenty. *"There's a famine in this country, a moral and spiritual famine, because somewhere America strayed away from home. I can hear the voice of God saying, 'America, it isn't too late if you will only come to yourself.' "* Like America, King implied, he had to rise from the dark places and follow the road to salvation.

But first he needed to place "the problems of the poor at the seat of government of the wealthiest nation in the history of mankind." Despite the long hot summers of violence, King knew that "not a single basic cause of the riots had been corrected. All of the misery that stoked the flames of rage and rebellion remains undiminished." He redoubled his efforts to enlist volunteers from different races and ethnicities into his army of the poor, and to gain support from liberal religious groups and labor unions.

Just as he began to gain momentum, James Lawson, now a minister of a church in Memphis, pleaded with him to assist in a strike by the city's black sanitation workers over the mayor's refusal to recognize their union. His aides objected to King volunteering—as he had done in Albany in 1961—to come into a situation at the last moment that others had planned and controlled. "We felt like you couldn't take on everything, and if we went into Memphis, we'd get bogged down there and never get back to Washington," said Andy Young. "But Martin said he couldn't turn his back on those garbage workers." Picturing the mainly poor black displaced rural migrants "carrying the man's garbage," King claimed, "it is criminal to have people working on a full-time basis and a full-time job getting part-time income."

Late in January, when heavy rains made sewer work impossible in Memphis, twenty-one black workers had been sent home with only two hours of wages while their white coworkers remained "on the clock" and received a full day's pay. On top of that, two black workers had been crushed to death sitting in their compactor because they were not allowed to sit out the rain in the cab like white workers. To make matters worse, the dead men's status as unclassified workers meant that their families received no death benefits. To protest the unjust treatment by the city, a "wildcat strike" by the mostly black sanitation workers began on February 12.

Memphis's newly elected segregationist mayor, Henry Loeb, eager to crush black assertiveness and stay any black gains, resolved to break the strike. He issued an ultimatum: Return to work or be fired. The next day he began hiring nonunion workers to replace the strikers. Loeb's blue-helmeted riot police then brutally maced and clubbed African-Americans peacefully walking in a protest march that had been organized by black ministers and union leaders. This galvanized the black community, stimulating almost daily marches and a boycott of the downtown stores. A local labor dispute had become a racial struggle with national implications.

King thought the conflict was a good way to dramatize race-based poverty and to highlight the interplay of class and racial oppression—the very reason for a PPC. He would speak in Memphis the next day, March 18. As Ralph Abernathy told Coretta, "We're going to Washington by way of Memphis."

Facing some thirteen hundred striking sanitation workers, members of the American Federation of State, County and Municipal Employees, and about fourteen thousand of their supporters in the cavernous Mason Temple—the largest indoor crowd he had ever addressed in the South—King whipped them into an emotional frenzy.

He credited Memphis blacks for *"highlighting the economic issue . . . going beyond purely civil rights to questions of human rights."* [YES!] Nothing was gained without pressure, he exhorted, urging them to *"escalate pressure"* and force Loeb to say yes when he wanted to say no. [YES, YES, YES.] *"If we are going to get equality, if we are going to get adequate wages, we are going to have to struggle for it."*

Close the city down with a mighty daylong general strike, he shouted to thunderous applause and cries of "Yeah!" "Yeah! "Yeah!" As King described what would happen—*"not a Negro in this city will go to any job downtown,"* and *"no Negro in domestic service will go to anybody's house or anybody's kitchen,"* and *"black students will not go to anybody's school"*—the assemblage rocked the rafters with whoops of approval and foot-stomping bedlam. *"America is going to hell,"* he said in closing, if it *"does not use her vast resources of wealth to end poverty and make it possible for all of God's children to have the basic necessities of life."*

Moved by the spirit in the hall, Lawson suggested that King join their protest. He agreed to return on March 22 to lead a march that would turn Loeb around. The fight in Memphis would mark the start of the Poor People's Campaign.

On March 22 an unseasonable sixteen inches of snow fell on Memphis, closing the city. Lawson postponed the march until March 28. That unseasonably hot day, a late plane sidetracked King, and the march, scheduled to begin at ten A.M., had to wait and wait. A group of black militants who called themselves the Invaders, eager to embarrass Lawson and the "Uncle Tom" preachers, began haranguing the crowd to forget nonviolence and have a "good race riot." Holding crudely lettered signs proclaiming GARBAGE STINKS. SO DOES LOEB and LOEB EATS SHIT, rather than the professionally printed I AM A MAN placards, they chanted, "Black Power! Black Power! Black Power!"

When King finally arrived, the Invaders taunted him as "Uncle Chicken Wing!" "You have a dream, King," one yelled derisively. "Tell us about your dream?" By then the milling crowd of six thousand had become chaotic. As soon as the front rows of dignitaries stepped off to march, the sound of smashed glass coming from the rear interrupted the familiar strains of "We Shall Overcome." As store

windows shattered, looting along Beale Street ensued. Dozens of ma-
rauders, some armed with pipes, bricks, and poles, grabbed armfuls of
clothes, TVs, stereo sets. "Kids were throwing things and running,"
one minister reported. The police "waded into the crowd and started
beating people . . . started shooting tear gas." They clubbed and
maced looters, peaceful marchers, and innocent bystanders alike. By
nightfall, sixty-two people had been wounded, a sixteen-year-old boy
had been shot dead, more than two hundred had been arrested, and
thirty-eight hundred National Guardsmen patrolled the streets, en-
forcing a dusk-to-dawn curfew.

As the march dissolved into mayhem, colleagues pushed King into
a car and whisked him away from the salvos of tear gas. With a police
motorcycle leading them, they rushed to Memphis's finest new hotel,
the Hilton Rivermont, rather than to the Lorraine Motel, in the black
neighborhood where King usually stayed. Fully dressed, King lay in
bed, unmoving, the covers pulled over his head. For the first time, a
march he had proposed and led had turned violent, and an innocent
young man had been killed. He was "in a kind of despair," Young remembered, "that I had never seen before." Abernathy thought him almost catatonic.

More deeply depressed than ever, King could not sleep at all that
night. He was sure "we live in a sick nation." Perhaps "we just have to
admit that the day of violence is here." He wondered if he "should just
step back and let the violent forces run their course," Abernathy recalled. He had no idea what to do next. He called Coretta to commis-
erate, but she could not raise his spirits. He walked the room, "so
upset and so troubled." Eventually, King telephoned Levison, expressing his fear that opponents like Adam Clayton Powell, Jr., who had
just told the press that the day of "Martin Loser King" had "come to
an end," would use the incident to belittle him further and depict it as
a harbinger of what the PPC would do to Washington. King knew
they would say, "Martin Luther King is dead, he's finished. His nonviolence is nothing, no one is listening to it . . . Martin Luther King is at
the end of his rope."

They said just that. The next day the Memphis *Commercial Appeal* printed a cartoon of the fleeing Martin Luther King, captioned
"Chicken à la King." Its editorial claimed that the march had shat-

tered King's "pose as a leader of a non-violent movement." The whole
nation now questioned his credibility, it continued, and doubted that
the PPC could be peaceful. "Furthermore, he wrecked his reputation
as a leader as he took off at high speed when violence occurred, instead of trying to use his persuasive prestige to stop it." *The St.
Louis Globe-Democrat*, following an FBI handout almost verbatim, depicted
King as "a man who stoops to using anti-Democratic and dictatorial
means to try to force his will on the highest legislative body in the
United States, a man who hides behind a façade of 'non-violence' as
he provokes violence." The conservative newspaper insisted that what
had happened in Memphis would "be only the prelude to civil strife
in our Nation's Capitol." Its cartoon showed a haloed, thick-lipped
King shooting up "trouble," "violence," and "looting" with a pistol
while declaring, "I'm not firing it, I'm only pulling the trigger."

Other "cooperative media sources" of the FBI saddled King with
responsibility for the riot and depicted him as a hypocritical coward
who had fled the scene he provoked to seek safety in a plush hotel—
"white owned, operated, and almost exclusively white patronized."
Even *The New York Times* declared the march a "powerful embarrassment to Dr. King" and urged him to call off the PPC: SCLC's protest
in Washington, it went on, was likely to "prove counterproductive"
and lead to "another eruption of the kind that rocked Memphis."
Congress chimed in with a chorus of variations on West Virginia Democratic senator Robert C. Byrd's characterization of King as a "self-
seeking rabble-rouser" who had encouraged the riot, and his demand
that the administration block any march led by King.

A downcast King met with leaders of the Invaders the next morning. He heard their complaints about Lawson and their protestations
of innocence. He knew the local movement was riven by class, gener-
ational, and ideological tensions, and exacerbated by covert FBI operations to disrupt black protests, yet he asked, "What must be done to
have a peaceful march, because you know I have got to lead one.
There is no other way." He had to prove nonviolence's viability, that
the violent march was a singular occurrence. The Invaders responded
with promises to work with the SCLC on a second march if they received financial help for their community-organizing plans. Minutes
later, King told the press that SCLC would organize a second march

in Memphis. "Nonviolence as a concept" was now on trial, he said, adding, "We are fully determined to go to Washington. We feel it is an absolute necessity."

In Atlanta, a forlorn King spent the night alone. On Saturday, March 30, he summoned his executive staff to plan for his return to Memphis. Few favored it, and some used the meeting to renew their opposition to the PPC. Besieged from all sides and angered that his lieutenants chose not to support him when he needed them most, King lashed out at their selfish scrabbling. He assailed them as he never had before, accusing Young—who questioned the viability of a movement of polyglot poor people—of giving in to doubt; attacking James Bevel for not supporting "anything that isn't your own idea" and thinking the PPC "a bunch of bullshit"; and denouncing Jesse Jackson for belittling Memphis as too unimportant and the PPC as too unformed. King, according to Young, "said we had all let him down . . . said, 'I can't take all this on myself, I need you to take your share of the load.' " He demanded they return "to Memphis to help me" and stop trying to drag him into their pet projects.

"Ralph, give me my car keys. I'm getting out of here," King blurted. When Jackson tried to follow him out of the room, King whirled on him. "Jesse, don't bother me. If you're so interested in doing your own thing, that you can't do what this organization is structured to do, go ahead. If you want to carve out your own niche in society, go ahead. But for God's sake, don't bother me!" Chastened, the staff began the necessary planning for Memphis.

On Wednesday, April 3, King returned to Memphis, checking in to the black-owned Lorraine Motel, where his room, 306, faced a parking lot below and the back windows of a cheap, run-down rooming house across the street. He learned that afternoon that a U.S. district court judge in Memphis had issued a restraining order against the march. King said he would march anyway. "We are not going to be stopped by Mace or injunctions," he informed reporters. "It is a matter of conscience. We have a moral right and responsibility to march."

A heavy rainstorm buffeted the city that night. Sensing that few people would venture out in the storm to hear him speak at Mason Temple, King sent Abernathy in his place. His phone soon rang. Aber-

nathy pleaded, "They want to hear you, not me. This is your crowd."
They had braved tornado warnings, he went on; don't let them down.
Wearily, King gave in, despite his exhaustion.

King mounted the podium to the accompaniment of blasts of
thunder. He began in sorrow, his voice filled with self-pity, his theme
one of death. He spoke of his stabbing, of the present being a time of
nonviolence or nonexistence. *"But only when it's dark enough can you
see the stars,"* he said. King saw God in the masses of people rising up
[YESSIR! YESSIR!], and whether they were in Johannesburg, South
Africa; Nairobi, Kenya; Accra, Ghana; New York City; Atlanta, Georgia; Jackson, Mississippi; or Memphis, Tennessee [TELL IT,
DOCTOR!], *"the cry is always the same: 'We want to be free.' "* [OH YES!]
The applause shook the stained-glass windows. The rain rattled windows and hammered the roof. King warned that *"if something isn't
done, and in a hurry* [YES, DOCTOR!], *to bring the colored peoples of
the world out of their long years of poverty, their long years of hurt and
neglect, the whole world is doomed."*

He spoke of the many threats on his life *"from some of our sick
white brothers"* just as the storm crested. *"But it doesn't matter with me
now."* He paused. *"Because I've been to the mountaintop."*

The sounds of sobs alternated with thunderclaps. What happened
to him, he said, *"doesn't matter with me now, because I've been to the
mountaintop.* [GO AHEAD.] *And I don't mind. Like anybody, I would
like to live a long life—longevity has its place."* The thousands seated
before him hushed. His voice trembled. *"But I'm not concerned about
that now."* He had delivered this peroration before, but never with
such fervor. As lightning flashed, King exclaimed, *"I just want to do
God's will. And He's allowed me to go up to the mountain. And I've
looked over, and I've s-e-e-e-e-e-n the promised land.* [YES, YES, YES.] *I
may not get there with you. But I want you to know tonight* [OH YEAH.]
that we, as a people, will get to the promised land. [YES! GO AHEAD.]
*And I'm happy tonight. I'm not worried about anything. I'm not fearing
any man. Mine eyes have seen the glory of the coming of the Lord . . ."*
He did not finish. As the audience cheered wildly, King stumbled into
Abernathy's embrace.

The assembly's enthusiastic reception elated King. He went off
happily for a late dinner and the companionship of one of his special

female friends. Many hours later, he returned to the Lorraine Motel, where he joked with his brother and then left with another longtime mistress for her room. Abernathy would not awaken him until noon.

Later that day Young returned from court with the announcement that the judge would allow a restricted march on the following Monday. Although they were set to march anyway, Young's positive news led to a pillow fight and much horseplay between King and his colleagues. He then got ready for dinner, relishing the prospect of his favorite soul-food meal at a preacher friend's home.

Having a moment to spare, King stepped out on his room's balcony, looked down at the parking lot, and joshed with his driver and jazz musician Ben Branch. "Ben," he said, smiling, "I want you to sing 'Precious Lord' for me tonight like you never sung it before." He added, "I want you to sing it real pretty."

A ringing noise pierced the air. Some thought it a car backfire or a firecracker. Others took cover near the rented limousine. The bullet—shot out of a high-velocity rifle from the rooming house opposite the motel—smashed through King's neck, exploded his right cheek and jaw, and severed his spinal cord.

King flew backward. His body slammed up against the wall, then fell to the balcony floor. Abernathy rushed to his friend and leader. He took him in his arms. Blood gushed from the gaping wounds. "Martin, Martin, this is Ralph. Do you hear me? This is Ralph." No answer. The bullet, fired by one man but aimed by many, stilled King's voice forever—yet his words would never die.

BIBLIOGRAPHICAL ESSAY

All scholarly endeavors are essentially collaborative—this one perhaps more than most. It is the result of teaching Martin Luther King, Jr., for some forty years and reading about him for longer than that. Part of what I have learned from, and been inspired by, is listed in this bibliographical essay. Like anyone writing about Martin Luther King, Jr., I am foremost indebted to Clayborne Carson, the director and editor in chief of the massive Martin Luther King, Jr., Papers Project at Stanford University and the King Center in Atlanta. To date, six volumes of *The Papers of Martin Luther King, Jr.* have been published, and eight more are projected. Carson has also edited *The Autobiography of Martin Luther King, Jr.* (New York: Warner Books, 1998), based on the words of King, and coedited the equally indispensable *A Knock at Midnight: Inspiration from the Great Sermons of Reverend Martin Luther King, Jr.* (New York: Warner Books, 1998) and *A Call to Conscience: The Landmark Speeches of Dr. Martin Luther King, Jr.* (New York: Warner Books, 2001). These works can be supplemented with James M. Washington, ed., *A Testament of Hope: The Essential Writings and Speeches of Martin Luther King, Jr.* (New York: HarperCollins, 1986), and *I Have a Dream: Writings and Speeches That Changed the World* (New York: HarperCollins, 1992).

There is no way I can adequately state my indebtedness to David J. Garrow for the books on King he has written and the collections of articles and sources he has edited, and to Taylor Branch for his towering epic trilogy on the life and times of King. By far, the most masterly researched biography of King is the work by Pulitzer Prize–winning David J. Garrow, *Bearing the Cross: Martin Luther King, Jr., and the Southern Christian Leadership Conference* (New York: William Morrow, 1986). In a class by itself is Taylor Branch, *Parting the Waters: America in the King Years, 1954–63*; *Pillar of Fire: America in the King Years, 1963–65*, and *At Canaan's Edge, America in the King Years, 1965–68* (New York: Simon & Schuster, 1988, 1998, and 2006). No less sterling, for its analysis of King's leadership of the SCLC, is Adam Fairclough, *To Redeem the Soul of America: The Southern Christian Leadership Confer-*

ence and Martin Luther King, Jr. (Athens: University of Georgia Press, 1987). Although written before many of the papers of King and the SCLC were available to scholars, David L. Lewis, *King: A Biography* (New York: Praeger, 1970), is daringly insightful. Equally so are Michael Eric Dyson, *I May Not Get There with You: The True Martin Luther King, Jr.* (New York: Free Press, 2000), and Vincent Harding, *Martin Luther King: The Inconvenient Hero* (Maryknoll, N.Y.: Orbis Books, 1996).

Stewart Burns, *To the Mountaintop, Martin Luther King Jr.'s Sacred Mission to Save America 1955–1968* (San Francisco: HarperCollins, 2004); James A. Colaiaco, *Martin Luther King Jr.: Apostle of Militant Nonviolence* (Basingstoke, England: Macmillan, 1993); Drederick L. Downing, *To See the Promised Land: The Faith Pilgrimage of Martin Luther King, Jr.* (Macon, Ga.: Mercer University Press, 1986); Peter J. Ling, *Martin Luther King, Jr.* (London: Routledge, 2002); and Stephen B. Oates, *Let the Trumpet Sound: The Life of Martin Luther King, Jr.* (New York: Harper & Row, 1982), offer vital insights. Good brief biographies include Adam Fairclough, *Martin Luther King, Jr.* (Athens: University of Georgia Press, 1990); Marshall Frady, *Martin Luther King, Jr.* (New York: Viking, 2002); and John A. Kirk, *Martin Luther King, Jr.* (London: Pearson Longman, 2005).

King's own books add much yet must be used with caution. They are purportedly as King saw it, and as much the work of ghostwriters as of King: *Stride Toward Freedom: The Montgomery Story* (New York: Harper & Brothers, 1958); *Strength to Love* (New York: Harper & Row, 1963); *Why We Can't Wait* (New York: Mentor, 1964); *Where Do We Go from Here?: Chaos or Community?* (Boston: Beacon, 1968); and *Trumpet of Conscience* (New York: Harper & Row, 1968). Except where otherwise noted, the quotations from King used in this book come from the sources in the above three paragraphs.

For a comprehensive collection of articles about King, see David J. Garrow, ed., *Martin Luther King, Jr.: Civil Rights Leader, Theologian, Orator*, 3 vols. (Brooklyn, N.Y.: Carlson Publishing, 1989). Other useful collections include Peter J. Albert and Ronald Hoffman, eds., *We Shall Overcome: Martin Luther King, Jr., and the Black Freedom Struggle* (New York: Pantheon, 1990); C. Eric Lincoln, ed., *Martin Luther King, Jr.: A Profile* (New York: Noonday Press, 1984); and Brian Ward and Tony Badger, eds., *The Making of Martin Luther King, Jr., and the Civil Rights Movement* (New York: New York University Press, 1996).

For views of King from others in the movement and SCLC, see Ralph D. Abernathy, *And the Walls Came Tumbling Down* (New York: Harper & Row, 1989); Septima Clark, *Echo in My Soul* (New York: Dutton, 1962); Dennis C. Dickerson, *Militant Mediator: Whitney M. Young, Jr.* (Lexington: University of Kentucky Press, 1998); James Farmer, *Lay Bare the Heart: An Autobiography of the Civil Rights Movement* (New York: Arbor House, 1985); James Forman, *The Making of Black Revolutionaries: A Personal Account* (New York: Macmillan, 1972); John Lewis with Michael D'Orso, *Walking with the Wind: A Memoir of the Movement* (New York: Simon & Schuster, 1988); Mary King, *Freedom Song: A Personal Story of the 1960s Civil Rights Movement* (New York: Morrow, 1987); Floyd McKissick, *Three-Fifths of a Man* (New York: Macmillan, 1969); Cleveland Sellers, *The River of No Return: The Autobiogra-*

phy of a Black Militant and the Life and Death of SNCC (New York: Morrow, 1973); Roger Wilkins, *A Man's Life* (New York: Simon & Schuster, 1982); Roy Wilkins with Tom Matthews, *Standing Fast: The Autobiography of Roy Wilkins* (New York: Viking, 1982); and Andrew Young, *An Easy Burden: The Civil Rights Movement and the Transformation of America* (New York: HarperCollins, 1996).

It is necessary and vital to consider Martin Luther King, Jr., in the larger context of the overall struggle for black freedom and equality. Good starting points are the following collections of scholarly articles: Raymond D'Angelo, *The American Civil Rights Movement, Readings and Interpretations* (New York: McGraw-Hill/Dushkin, 2001); Jack E. Davis, ed., *The Civil Rights Movement* (Malden, Mass.: Blackwell, 2001); Charles W. Eagles, ed., *The Civil Rights Movement in America* (Jackson: University Press of Mississippi, 1986); Jeffrey Ogbar, ed., *Problems in American Civilization: The Civil Rights Movement* (Boston: Houghton Mifflin, 2003); and Armstead L. Robinson and Patricia Sullivan, eds., *New Directions in Civil Rights Studies* (Charlottesville: University Press of Virginia, 1991). Also see the following surveys of the movement: Adam Fairclough, *Better Day Coming: Blacks and Equality, 1890–2000* (New York: Penguin Books, 2001); Steven F. Lawson, *Running for Freedom: Civil Rights and Black Politics in America Since 1941*, rev. ed. (New York: McGraw-Hill, 1997); Manning Marable, *Race, Reform, and Rebellion: The Second Reconstruction in Black America, 1945–1982* (Jackson: University Press of Mississippi, 1984); Mark Newman, *The Civil Rights Movement* (Westport, Conn.: Praeger, 2004); Harvard Sitkoff, *The Struggle for Black Equality, 1954–1993*, rev. ed. (New York: Hill & Wang, 1993); and Robert Weisbrot, *Freedom Bound: A History of America's Civil Rights Movement* (New York: Plume, 1990). A particularly outstanding analysis is Robert J. Norrell, *The House I Live In: Race in the American Century* (New York: Oxford University Press, 2005). Also see Sara Bullard, *Free at Last: A History of the Civil Rights Movement and Those Who Died in the Struggle* (New York: Oxford University Press, 1993), and Ted Ownby, ed., *The Role of Ideas in the Civil Rights South* (Jackson: University Press of Mississippi, 2002).

The major historiographies of the movement include Charles W. Eagles, "Toward New Histories of the Civil Rights Era," *Journal of Southern History* 66 (November 2000), 815–48, and "The Civil Rights Movement," in John B. Boles, ed., *A Companion to the American South* (Malden, Mass.: Blackwell, 2002); Adam Fairclough, "State of the Art: Historians and the Civil Rights Movement," *Journal of American Studies* 24 (December 1990), 387–98; and Steven F. Lawson, "Freedom Then, Freedom Now: The Historiography of the Civil Rights Movement," *American Historical Review* 96 (April 1991), 456–71. Three indispensable analyses of the movement's origins are Aldon D. Morris, *The Origins of the Civil Rights Movement: Black Communities Organizing for Change* (New York: Free Press, 1984); Doug McAdam, *Political Process and the Development of Black Insurgency, 1930–1970* (Chicago: University of Chicago Press, 1982); and J. Mills Thornton, *Dividing Lines: Municipal Politics and the Struggle for Civil Rights in Montgomery, Birmingham, and Selma* (Tuscaloosa: University of Alabama Press, 2002). The significance of local activism versus national leaders and organizations is discussed in Steven F. Lawson and

Charles Payne, *Debating the Civil Rights Movement, 1945–1968* (Lanham, MD: Rowman and Littlefield, 1998). Highly recommended is Kim Lacy Rogers, "Oral History and the History of the Civil Rights Movement," *Journal of American History* 75 (1988), 567–76.

For the era after Reconstruction, see John Egerton, *Speak Now Against the Day: The Generation Before the Civil Rights Movement in the South* (Chapel Hill: University of North Carolina Press, 1994); Adam Fairclough, *Race and Democracy: The Civil Rights Struggle in Louisiana, 1915–1972* (Athens: University of Georgia Press, 1995); Grace Elizabeth Hale, *Making Whiteness: The Culture of Segregation in the South, 1890–1940* (New York: Pantheon, 1998); Robin D. G. Kelley, " 'We Are Not What We Seem': Rethinking Black Working-Class Opposition in the Jim Crow South," *Journal of American History* 80 (June 1993), 75–112, and *Race Rebels: Culture, Politics, and the Black Working Class* (New York: Free Press, 1994); Robert Korstad and Nelson Lichtenstein, "Opportunities Found and Lost: Labor, Radicals, and the Early Civil Rights Movement," *Journal of American History* 75 (December 1988), 786–811; David Levering Lewis, *W.E.B. DuBois: The Fight for Equality and the American Century, 1919–1963* (New York: Henry Holt, 2000), 132–42; Howard N. Rabinowitz, *Race Relations in the Urban South, 1865–1890* (Urbana: University of Illinois Press, 1978); Harvard Sitkoff, *A New Deal for Blacks: The Emergence of Civil Rights as a National Issue* (New York: Oxford University Press, 1978); Patricia Sullivan, *Days of Hope: Race and Democracy in the New Deal Era* (Chapel Hill: University of North Carolina Press, 1996); and the classic C. Vann Woodward, *The Strange Career of Jim Crow*, 3rd ed. (New York: Oxford University Press, 1974).

On Atlanta and Georgia, see Leroy Davis, *A Clashing of the Soul: John Hope and the Dilemma of African American Leadership and Black Higher Education in the Early Twentieth Century* (Athens: University of Georgia Press, 1998); John Dittmer, *Black Georgia in the Progressive Era, 1900–1920* (Urbana: University of Illinois Press, 1977); Clifford M. Kuhn, et al., *Living Atlanta: An Oral History of the City, 1914–1948* (Athens: University of Georgia Press, 1990); and Stephen G. N. Tuck, *Beyond Atlanta: The Struggle for Racial Equality in Georgia, 1940–1980* (Athens: University of Georgia Press, 1999).

The importance of World War II is underscored in Richard M. Dalfiume, "The 'Forgotten Years' of the Negro Revolution," *Journal of American History* 55 (June 1968), 90–106; Pete Daniel, "Going Among Strangers: Southern Reactions to World War II," *Journal of American History* 77 (December 1990), 886–911; Daniel Kryder, *Divided Arsenal: Race and the American State during World War II* (New York: Cambridge University Press, 2000); Neil R. McMillen, ed., *Remaking Dixie: The Impact of World War II on the American South* (Jackson: University Press of Mississippi, 1997); Robert J. Norrell, *Dixie's War: The South and World War II* (Tuscaloosa: University of Alabama Press, 1992); Harvard Sitkoff, "Racial Militancy and Interracial Violence in the Second World War," *Journal of American History* 58 (December 1971), 661–81; and Neil A. Wynn, *The Afro-American and the Second World War*, rev. ed. (New York: Holmes and Meier, 1993).

The increasing significance of American race relations in U.S. foreign policy and the place of the movement within the larger context of international relations is the subject of Carol Anderson, *Eyes Off the Prize: The United Nations and the African American Struggle for Human Rights, 1944–1955* (New York: Cambridge University Press, 2003); Thomas Borstelmann, *The Cold War and the Color Line: American Race Relations in the Global Arena* (Cambridge, Mass.: Harvard University Press, 2001); Mary L. Dudziak, *Cold War Civil Rights: Race and the Image of American Democracy* (Princeton, N.J.: Princeton University Press, 2000); Michael L. Krenn, ed., *Race and U.S. Foreign Policy During the Cold War* (New York: Garland, 1998), and *The African American Voice in U.S. Foreign Policy Since World War II* (New York: Garland, 1998); Brenda Gayle Plummer, *Rising Wind: Black Americans and U.S. Foreign Affairs, 1935–1960* (Chapel Hill: University of North Carolina Press, 1996); Azza Salama Layton, *International Politics and Civil Rights Policies in the United States, 1941–1960* (Cambridge, U.K.: Cambridge University Press, 2000); and Penny M. Von Eschen, *Race Against Empire: Black Americans and Anticolonialism, 1937–1957* (Ithaca, N.Y.: Cornell University Press, 1997).

Other key postwar developments bearing on King's career are analyzed in Numan V. Bartley, *The Rise of Massive Resistance: Race and Politics in the South During the 1950's* (Baton Rouge: Louisiana State University Press, 1969); Glenn Feldman, ed., *Before Brown: Civil Rights and White Backlash in the Modern South* (Tuscaloosa: University of Alabama Press, 2004); Michael J. Klarman, "How *Brown* Changed Race Relations: The Backlash Thesis," *Journal of American History* 81 (June 1994), 81–118; George Lewis, "*With Bated Breath*": Segregationists, Anti-Communism and Massive Resistance in the South of the United States, 1945–1965* (Gainesville: University of Florida Press, 2004); Michael S. Mayer, "With Much Deliberation and Some Speed: Eisenhower and the *Brown* Decision," *Journal of Southern History* 52 (February 1986), 43–76; Neil R. McMillen, *The Citizens' Council: Organized Resistance to the Second Reconstruction, 1954–1964* (Urbana: University of Illinois Press, 1971); Harvard Sitkoff, "Harry Truman and the Election of 1948: The Coming of Age of Civil Rights in American Politics," *Journal of Southern History* 37 (November 1971), 597–616; Clive Webb, ed., *Massive Resistance: Southern Opposition to the Second Reconstruction* (New York: Oxford University Press, 2005); and Jeff Woods, *Black Struggle, Red Scare: Segregation and Anti-Communism in the South, 1948–1968* (Baton Rouge: Louisiana State University Press, 2004).

The King family history and Martin's upbringing is nowhere better described than in Taylor Branch, *Parting the Waters*. For further insight, I consulted Coretta Scott King, *My Life with Martin Luther King, Jr.* (New York: Holt, Rinehart and Winston, 1969); Christine Farris King, *My Brother Martin: A Sister Remembers Growing Up with Rev. Dr. Martin Luther King, Jr.* (San Francisco: HarperCollins, 1992); Dexter Scott King, *Growing Up King: An Intimate Memoir* (New York: Warner Books, 2003); Martin Luther King, Sr., with Clayton Riley, *Daddy King: An Autobiography* (New York: Morrow, 1980); and Gary M. Pomerantz, *Where Peachtree Meets Sweet Auburn: A Saga of Race and Family* (New York: Penguin Books, 1997). On the black church, see C. Eric Lincoln and Lawrence Mamiya, *The Black Church in the African-American Experience* (Durham, N.C.: Duke University Press, 1990), and Gayraud S.

Wilmore, *Black Religion and Black Radicalism* (Garden City, N.Y.: Doubleday, 1973). On King's education, see John J. Ansbro, *Martin Luther King, Jr.: The Making of a Mind* (Maryknoll, N.Y.: Orbis Books, 1982); Lerone Bennett, Jr., *What Manner of Man: A Biography of Martin Luther King, Jr.* (Chicago: Johnson, 1964); Noel L. Erskine, *King Among the Theologians* (Cleveland: Pilgrim Press, 1994); William R. Miller, *Martin Luther King, Jr.* (New York: Avon, 1969); and for King's Morehouse days, Benjamin E. Mays, *Born to Rebel: An Autobiography* (Athens: University of Georgia Press, 1987).

King's plagiarism is discussed in detail in "Becoming Martin Luther King, Jr.— Plagiarism and Originality: A Round Table," *Journal of American History* 78 (1991), 11–123. Criticism of King from the far right appears in Theodore Pappas, *Plagiarism and the Culture War: The Writings of Martin Luther King, Jr., and Other Prominent Americans* (New York: Hallberg, 1998). Also highly critical of King is Eugene D. Genovese, *The Southern Front: History and Politics in the Cultural Cold War* (Columbia: University of Missouri Press, 1995). A defense of King, placing his "voice-merging" in a distinct black oral tradition, is Keith D. Miller, *Voice of Deliverance: The Language of Martin Luther King, Jr., and Its Sources* (New York: Free Press, 1992). Other defenses come from Dyson, *I May Not Get There with You*, and Richard Lischer, *The Preacher King: Martin Luther King, Jr., and the Word That Moved America* (New York: Oxford University Press, 1995). Their views are challenged by Richard King, *Civil Rights and the Idea of Freedom* (New York: Oxford University Press, 1992). Georgia Davis Powers, *I Shared the Dream: The Pride, Passion, and Politics of the First Black Woman Senator from Kentucky* (Far Hills, N.J.: New Horizon Press, 1995) is the memoir of one of King's lovers.

My starting places for King's beliefs are Lewis V. Baldwin, *There Is a Balm in Gilead: The Cultural Roots of Martin Luther King, Jr.* (Minneapolis: Augsburg Fortress, 1991), and *To Make the Wounded Whole: The Cultural Legacy of Martin Luther King, Jr.* (Minneapolis: Augsburg Fortress, 1991); James H. Cone, *Martin & Malcolm & America: A Dream or Nightmare* (Maryknoll, N.Y.: Orbis Books, 1991); James P. Hanigan, *Martin Luther King, Jr., and the Foundations of Militant Nonviolence* (Lanham, Md: University Press of America, 1984); Kenneth L. Smith and Ira G. Zepp, Jr., *Search for the Beloved Community: The Thinking of Martin Luther King Jr.* (Valley Forge, Pa.: Judson Press, 1974, 1988); and Ira G. Zepp, Jr., *The Social Vision of Martin Luther King, Jr.* (Brooklyn, N.Y.: Carlson, 1989). Also see Luther D. Ivory, *Toward a Theology of Radical Involvement: The Theological Legacy of Martin Luther King Jr.* (Nashville: Abingdon Press, 1997); Greg Moses, *Revolution of Conscience: Martin Luther King Jr., and the Philosophy of Nonviolence* (New York: Guilford Press, 1997); Hanes Walton, *The Political Philosophy of Martin Luther King, Jr.* (Westport, Conn.: Greenwood, 1971); William D. Watley, *Roots of Resistance: The Nonviolent Ethic of Martin Luther King Jr.* (Valley Forge, Pa.: Judson Press, 1985); and Charles R. Wilson, *Judgement & Grace in Dixie: Southern Faiths from Faulkner to Elvis* (Athens: University of Georgia Press, 1995). On Gandhi's influence, see George Frederickson, *Black Liberation: A Comparative History of Black Ideologies in the United States and South Africa* (New York: Oxford University Press, 1995); and Sudarshan

Kapur, *Raising Up a Prophet: The African-American Encounter with Gandhi* (Boston: Beacon Press, 1992).

King's preaching is analyzed by a dozen experts in Carolyn Calloway-Thomas and John Louis Lucaites, eds., *Martin Luther King, Jr., and the Sermonic Power of Public Discourse* (Tuscaloosa: University of Alabama Press, 1993). Also see Lischer, *The Preacher King*, and Hortense J. Spillers, "Martin Luther King and the Style of the Black Sermon," *Black Scholar* 3 (September 1971), 14–27. King's Personalism is explained in Rufus Burrow, Jr., *Personalism: A Critical Introduction* (St. Louis: Chalice Press, 1999). Of special interest are Stewart Burns, "From the Mountaintop: The Changing Political Vision of Martin Luther King, Jr.," *History Teacher* 27 (November 1993), 7–18; David L. Chappell, *A Stone of Hope: Prophetic Religion and the Death of Jim Crow* (Chapel Hill: University of North Carolina Press, 2004); and Charles Marsh, *God's Long Summer: Stories of Faith and Civil Rights* (Princeton, N.J.: Princeton University Press, 1997).

For analyses and accounts relevant to Chapter 2, I am most indebted to Clayborne Carson, "Martin Luther King, Jr.: Charismatic Leadership in a Mass Struggle," *Journal of American History* 74 (September 1987), 448–454; Frye Gaillard, *Cradle of Freedom: Alabama and the Movement That Changed America* (Tuscaloosa: University of Alabama Press, 2004); J. Mills Thornton, *Dividing Lines*; and Lamont H. Yeakey, "The Montgomery, Alabama, Bus Boycott, 1955–56" (Ph.D. diss., Columbia University, 1979). Invaluable are the collections of primary sources assembled in Stewart Burns, ed., *Daybreak of Freedom: The Montgomery Bus Boycott* (Chapel Hill: University of North Carolina Press, 1997), and the articles in David Garrow, ed., *The Walking City: The Montgomery Bus Boycott, 1955–56* (Brooklyn, N.Y.: Carlson, 1989). The historical context is supplied by Catherine Barnes, *Journey from Jim Crow: The Desegregation of Southern Transit* (New York: Columbia University Press, 1983).

Several firsthand accounts are still quite useful, including Robert Graetz, *A White Preacher's Memoir: The Montgomery Bus Boycott* (Montgomery, Ala.: Black Belt Press, 1999); Fred Gray, *Bus Ride to Justice: Changing the System by the System: The Life and Works of Fred D. Gray, Preacher, Attorney, Politician: Lawyer for Rosa Parks* (Montgomery, Ala.: Black Belt Press, 1999); Rosa Parks with Jim Haskins, *Rosa Parks, My Story* (New York: Dial Books, 1992); Lawrence D. Reddick, *Crusader Without Violence: A Biography of Martin Luther King, Jr.* (Chicago: Johnson, 1964); Jo Ann Gibson Robinson, *The Montgomery Bus Boycott and the Women Who Started It: The Memoir of Jo Ann Gibson Robinson*, David Garrow, ed. (Knoxville: University of Tennessee Press, 1987); and Solomon S. Seay, *I Was There by the Grace of God* (Montgomery, Ala.: New South Books, 1990). Also see Bayard Rustin, "Reminiscences," Oral History Research Office, Columbia University; Glenn Smiley, *Nonviolence: The Gentle Persuader* (Nyack, N.Y.: Fellowship Publications, 1991); and Mary Stanton, *Journey Toward Justice: Juliette Hampton Morgan and the Montgomery Bus Boycott* (Athens: University of Georgia Press, 1966). Also see John White, " 'Nixon Was the One': Edgar Daniel Nixon, the MIA, and the Montgomery Bus Boycott," in Brian Ward and Tony Badger, eds., *The Making of Martin Luther King, Jr., and the Civil Rights Movement* (New York: New York University Press, 1996), 45–63.

Chapter 3, King's fallow period, 1957–1962, is best approached by Carson, "Martin Luther King, Jr.: Charismatic Leadership in a Mass Struggle"; Fairclough, *To Redeem the Soul of America*; Garrow, *Bearing the Cross*; and August Meier, "On the Role of Martin Luther King," *New Politics* 4 (Winter 1965), 52–59. Vital background appears in Bartley, *The Rise of Massive Resistance*.

The background on King's three advisers comes from Jervis Anderson, *Bayard Rustin: Troubles I've Seen* (New York: HarperCollins, 1997); Martha Biondi, *To Stand and Fight, The Struggle for Civil Rights in Postwar New York City* (Cambridge, Mass.: Harvard University Press, 2001); John D'Emilio, *Lost Prophet: The Life and Times of Bayard Rustin* (New York: Free Press, 2003); Joanne Grant, *Ella Baker: Freedom Bound* (New York: Wiley, 1998); Daniel Levine, *Bayard Rustin and the Civil Rights Movement* (New Brunswick, N.J.: Rutgers University Press, 2000); Charles Payne, "Ella Baker and Models of Social Change," *Signs* 14 (1989), 885–99; and Barbara Ransby, *Ella Baker and the Black Freedom Movement: A Radical Democratic Vision* (Chapel Hill: University of North Carolina Press, 2003). Also see Paula F. Pfeffer, *A. Philip Randolph: Pioneer of the Civil Rights Movement* (Baton Rouge: Louisiana State University Press, 1990). Ella Baker's complaints are corroborated in Cynthia Stokes Brown, ed., *Ready from Within: Septima Clark and the Civil Rights Movement* (Trenton, N.J.: Africa World Press, 1990).

Recent analyses of the role of women in the movement include Bettye Collier-Thomas and V. P. Franklin, eds., *Sisters in the Struggle: African American Women in the Civil Rights–Black Power Movement* (New York: New York University Press, 2001); Lynne Olson, *Freedom's Daughters: The Unsung Heroines of the Civil Rights Movement from 1830 to 1970* (New York: Scribner, 2001); Belinda Robnett, *How Long? How Long? African-American Women in the Struggle for Civil Rights* (New York: Oxford University Press, 1997); and Deborah G. White, *Too Heavy a Load: Black Women in Defense of Themselves, 1894–1994* (New York: Norton, 1999).

On SNCC, the best and most detailed account is Clayborne Carson, *In Struggle: SNCC and the Black Awakening of the 1960s* (Cambridge, Mass.: Harvard University Press, 1981). William H. Chafe, *Civilities and Civil Rights: Greensboro, North Carolina, and the Black Struggle for Freedom* (New York: Oxford University Press, 1980) places the sit-in in Greensboro, North Carolina, in its necessary historical context; and David Halberstam, *The Children* (New York: Random House, 1998) narrates a collective biography of the Nashville SNCC students. On the Atlanta sit-ins, see Ronald H. Bayor, *Race and the Shaping of Twentieth-Century Atlanta* (Chapel Hill: University of North Carolina Press, 1996); Cynthia Griggs Fleming, *Soon We Will Not Cry: The Liberation of Ruby Doris Smith Robinson* (Lanham, Md.: Rowman and Littlefield, 1998); the articles in David J. Garrow, ed., *Atlanta, Georgia, 1960–1961: Sit-ins and Student Activism* (Brooklyn, N.Y.: Carlson, 1988); and Winston A. Grady-Willis, *Challenging U.S. Apartheid: Atlanta and Black Struggles for Human Rights, 1960–1977* (Durham, N.C.: Duke University Press, 2006). Also see Clifford M. Kuhn, " 'There's a Footnote to History!': Memory and the History of Martin Luther King's October 1960 Arrest and Its Aftermath," *Journal of American History* 84 (September 1997), 583–95; Harris Wofford, *Of Kennedys and Kings: Making Sense of the*

Sixties (New York: Farrar, Straus & Giroux, 1980); Howard Zinn, *SNCC: The New Abolitionists* (Boston: Beacon Press, 1965); and the reminiscences by SNCC members in Cheryl Greenberg, ed., *A Circle of Trust: Remembering SNCC* (New Brunswick, N.J.: Rutgers University Press, 1998).

For King and President Kennedy, I relied on Carl Brauer, *John F. Kennedy and the Second Reconstruction* (New York: Columbia University Press, 1977); John Hart, "Kennedy, Congress and Civil Rights," *Journal of American Studies* 13 (August 1979), 165–78; and Mark Stern, *Calculating Visions: Kennedy, Johnson, and Civil Rights* (New Brunswick, N.J.: Rutgers University Press, 1992). Also see James C. Harvey, *Civil Rights During the Kennedy Administration* (Hattiesburg: University and College Press of Mississippi, 1971); Jonathan Rosenberg and Zachary Karabell, *Kennedy, Johnson, and the Quest for Justice: The Civil Rights Tapes* (New York: Norton, 2003); Steven A. Shull, *The President and Civil Rights Policy: Leadership and Change* (New York: Greenwood, 1989); and Allan Wolk, *The Presidency and Black Civil Rights: Eisenhower to Nixon* (Rutherford, N.J.: Fairleigh Dickinson University Press, 1971). The perspectives of the president and attorney general are presented in Arthur M. Schlesinger, Jr., *A Thousand Days: John F. Kennedy in the White House* (New York: Fawcett, 1965), and *Robert Kennedy and His Times* (New York: Ballantine, 1978).

On the Freedom Rides, Raymond Arsenault, *Freedom Riders: 1961 and the Struggle for Racial Justice* (New York: Oxford University Press, 2006), is superb. Although dated, still worth reading are Inge Powell Bell, *CORE and the Strategy of Nonviolence* (New York: Random House, 1968); August Meier and Elliot Rudwick, *CORE: A Study in the Civil Rights Movement* (New York: Oxford University Press, 1973); and James Peck, *Freedom Ride* (New York: Simon & Schuster, 1962). Memorable reminiscences of Freedom Riders appear in Howell Raines, ed., *My Soul Is Rested: Movement Days in the Deep South Remembered* (New York: G. P. Putnam's Sons, 1977). Also see Branch, *Parting the Waters*; Lewis, *Walking with the Wind*; and Phil Noble, *Beyond the Burning Bus: The Civil Rights Revolution in a Southern Town* (Montgomery, Ala.: New South Books, 2003).

We still lack a book-length account of the Albany movement. I have depended on Branch, *Parting the Waters*; Howard Zinn, *The Southern Mystique* (New York: Knopf, 1964); and Zinn, *SNCC*. Also see the essays in the special issue of the *Journal of South-West Georgia History* (Fall 1984); King's article, "The Time for Freedom Has Come," *New York Times* magazine, September 16, 1961; and journalist Pat Watters, *Down to Now: Reflections on the Southern Civil Rights Movement* (New York: Pantheon Books, 1971). The spirit of the movement comes alive in Guy and Candie Carawan, eds., *Freedom Is a Constant Struggle: Songs of the Freedom Movement with Documentary Photographs* (New York: Oak Publications, 1968); Jerry Silverman, *Songs of Protest and Civil Rights* (New York: Chelsea House, 1992); and Wyatt Walker, *Somebody's Calling My Name: Black Sacred Music and Social Change* (Valley Forge, Pa.: Judson, 1979).

For Chapter 4, the Birmingham struggle, I relied primarily on Glen T. Eskew, *But for Birmingham: The Local and National Movements in the Civil Rights Struggle* (Chapel Hill: University of North Carolina Press, 1997); Andrew Manis, *A Fire You*

Can't Put Out: The Civil Rights Life of Reverend Fred Shuttlesworth (Tuscaloosa: University of Alabama Press, 1999); and Thornton, *Dividing Lines*. David J. Garrow, ed., *Birmingham, Alabama, 1956–1963: The Black Struggle for Civil Rights* (Brooklyn, N.Y.: Carlson, 1989), is a highly useful collection of essays. The church bombing is the subject of Frank Sikora, *Until Justice Rolls Down: The Birmingham Church Bombing Case* (Tuscaloosa: University of Alabama Press, 2005).

On King's letter and the various denominational views on race, see Joel L. Alvis, *Religion and Race: Southern Presbyterians, 1946–1983* (Tuscaloosa: University of Alabama Press, 1994); Kenneth K. Bailey, *Southern White Protestantism in the Twentieth Century* (New York: Harper & Row, 1964); Jonathan S. Bass, *Blessed Are the Peacemakers: Martin Luther King, Jr., Eight White Religious Leaders, and the "Letter from Birmingham City Jail"* (Baton Rouge: Louisiana State University Press, 2001); Haig A. Bosmajian, "Rhetoric of Martin Luther King's 'Letter from Birmingham Jail,' " *Midwest Quarterly* 8 (1967), 126–43; James A. Colaiaco, "The American Dream Unfulfilled: Martin Luther King, Jr., and the 'Letter from Birmingham Jail,' " *Phylon* 45 (March 1984), 1–18; Donald E. Collins, *When the Church Bell Rang Racist: The Methodist Church and the Civil Rights Movement in Alabama* (Macon, Ga.: Mercer University Press, 1998); Samuel S. Hill, *Southern Churches in Crisis* (New York: Holt, Rinehart and Winston, 1966); Andrew Manis, " 'Dying from the Neck Up': Southern Baptist Resistance to the Civil Rights Movement," *Baptist History and Heritage* 34 (Winter 1999), 33–48; Mark Newman, *Getting Right with God: Southern Baptists and Desegregation, 1945–1995* (Tuscaloosa: University of Alabama Press, 2001); Malinda Snow, "Martin Luther King's 'Letter from Birmingham Jail' as Pauline Epistle," *Quarterly Journal of Speech* 71 (1985), reprinted in Garrow, *Birmingham, Alabama, 1956–1963*.

See also Earl Black, *Southern Governors and Civil Rights: Racial Segregation as a Campaign Issue in the Second Reconstruction* (Cambridge, Mass.: Harvard University Press, 1976); William Nunnelley, *Bull Connor* (Tuscaloosa: University of Alabama Press, 1991); Gail Williams O'Brien, *The Color of the Law: Race, Violence, and Justice in the Post–World War II South* (Chapel Hill: University of North Carolina Press, 1999); and the personal account of Diane McWhorter, *Carry Me Home: Birmingham, Alabama—The Climactic Battle of the Civil Rights Revolution* (New York: Simon & Schuster, 2001). Charles Morgan, Jr., *A Time to Speak* (New York: Holt, Rinehart and Winston, 1964), is the view of a southern white liberal in Birmingham.

The increasingly vital role of television news in aiding the movement is examined in Paul Burstein, "Public Opinion, Demonstrations, and the Passage of Antidiscrimination Legislation," *Public Opinion Quarterly* 43 (Summer 1979), 157–72, and Robert J. Donovan and Ray Scherer, *Unsilent Revolution: Television News and American Public Life* (New York: Cambridge University Press, 1992). The views of King by a mostly sympathetic white southern journalist are recounted in Barbara B. Clowse, *Ralph McGill: A Biography* (Macon, Ga.: Mercer University Press, 1998), and Harold H. Martin, *Ralph McGill, Reporter* (Boston: Little, Brown and Company, 1973). How the media perceived and presented King is the subject of Richard Lentz, *Symbols, the News Magazines, and Martin Luther King* (Baton Rouge: Louisiana State University

Press, 1990). Paul L. Fisher and Ralph Lowenstein, eds., *Race and the News Media* (New York: Praeger, 1967) is a good collection of contemporary viewpoints. Also see Jannette L. Dates and William Barlow, eds., *Split Image: African Americans in the Mass Media* (Washington, D.C.: Howard University Press, 1990).

For Chapter 5 and the March on Washington: Patrik Henry Bass, *Like a Mighty Stream* (Philadelphia: Running Press, 2002); Thomas Gentile, *March on Washington: August 28, 1963* (Washington, D.C.: New Day Publications, 1983); and Doris E. Saunders, *The Day They Marched* (Chicago: Johnson, 1963). More insightful are Branch's *Pillar of Fire* and Levine, *Bayard Rustin*. Also see Drew Hansen, *The Dream: Martin Luther King, Jr., and the Speech That Inspired a Nation* (New York: Ecco, 2003); J. Robert Cox, "The Fulfillment of Time: King's 'I Have a Dream' Speech," in Michael C. Leff and Fred Kauffeld, eds., *Texts in Context: Critical Dialogues on Significant Episodes in American Political Rhetoric* (Davis, Calif.: Hermagoras Press, 1989); Keith D. Miller and Emily M. Lewis, "Touchstones, Authorities and Marian Anderson: The Making of 'I Have A Dream,'" in Ward and Badger, eds., *The Making of Martin Luther King, Jr.*, 147–61; Nicolaus Mills, "Heard and Unheard: What Really Happened at the March on Washington," *Dissent* 35 (Summer 1988), 288–91; and Scott A. Sandage, "A Marble House Divided: The Lincoln Memorial, the Civil Rights Movement, and the Politics of Memory, 1939–1963," *Journal of American History* 80 (June 1993), 135–67.

The St. Augustine campaign is well described and analyzed in David Colburn, *Racial Change and Community Crisis: St. Augustine, Florida, 1877–1980* (New York: Columbia University Press, 1985); Frady, *Martin Luther King, Jr.*; Paul Good, *The Trouble I've Seen: White Journalist—Black Movement* (Washington, D.C.: Howard University Press, 1975); and Pat Watters, *Down to Now; Reflections on the Southern Civil Rights Movement* (New York: Random House, 1971). On Klan involvement, see Trevor Armbrister, "Portrait of an Extremist," *Saturday Evening Post* 231 (August 22, 1964); Michael R. Belknap, *Federal Law and Southern Order: Racial Violence and Constitutional Conflict in the Post-Brown South* (Athens: University of Georgia Press, 1987); David Chalmers, *Hooded Americanism: The First Century of the Ku Klux Klan* (Chicago: Quadrangle, 1968); and Wyn Craig Wade, *The Fiery Cross: The Ku Klux Klan in America* (New York: Simon & Schuster, 1987). David Garrow, ed., *St. Augustine, Florida, 1963–1964: Mass Protest and Racial Violence* (Brooklyn, N.Y.: Carlson, 1989), is a useful collection. The extent to which the business community accepted or rejected racial integration is debated in Elizabeth Jacoway and David Colburn, eds., *Southern Businessmen and Desegregation* (Baton Rouge: Louisiana State University Press, 1982). Also see the essay by Tony Badger, "Segregation and the Southern Business Elite," *Journal of American Studies* 18 (April 1984), 105–9.

On the 1964 civil rights legislation, see James F. Findlay, "Religion and Politics in the Sixties: The Churches and the Civil Rights Act of 1964," *Journal of American History* 77 (June 1990), 66–92; Hugh D. Graham, *The Civil Rights Era: Origins and Development of National Policy, 1960–1972* (New York: Oxford University Press, 1990); Robert D. Loevy, *To End All Segregation: The Politics of the Passage of the Civil Rights Act of 1964* (Lanham, Md.: University Press of America, 1990); and *The Civil Rights*

Act of 1964: The Passage of a Law That Ended Racial Segregation (Albany: State University of New York Press, 1997); and Charles W. Whalen and Barbara Whalen, *The Longest Debate: A Legislative History of the 1964 Civil Rights Act* (New York: New American Library, 1985). For the Civil Rights and the Voting Rights acts, see James C. Harvey, *Black Civil Rights During the Johnson Administration* (Jackson: University Press of Mississippi, 1973); Nick Kotz, *Judgment Days: Lyndon Baines Johnson, Martin Luther King, Jr., and the Laws That Changed America* (Boston: Houghton Mifflin, 2005); Benjamin Muse, *The American Negro Revolution: From Nonviolence to Black Power, 1963–1967* (Bloomington: Indiana University Press, 1968); Stern, *Calculating Vision*; and Denton Watson, *Lion in the Lobby: Clarence Mitchell, Jr.'s Struggle for the Passage of Civil Rights Laws* (New York: Morrow, 1990). President Johnson's thoughts and views are captured in Michael R. Beschloss, ed., *Taking Charge: The Johnson White House Tapes, 1936–1964* (New York: Simon & Schuster, 1997), *Reaching for Glory: Lyndon Johnson's Secret White House Tapes, 1964–1965* (New York: Simon & Schuster, 2002), and Rosenberg and Karabell, *Kennedy, Johnson, and the Quest for Justice*.

The struggles in Mississippi and at the 1964 Democratic convention are superbly conveyed in Eric R. Burner, *And Gently Shall He Lead Them: Robert Parris Moses and Civil Rights in Mississippi* (New York: New York University Press, 1994); John Dittmer, *Local People: The Struggle for Civil Rights in Mississippi* (Urbana: University of Illinois Press, 1994); Len Holt, *The Summer That Didn't End* (New York: Morrow, 1965); Chana Kai Lee, *For Freedom's Sake: The Life of Fannie Lou Hamer* (Urbana: University of Illinois Press, 1999); Marsh, *God's Long Summer*; Charles Payne, *I've Got the Light of Freedom: The Organizing Tradition and the Mississippi Freedom Struggle* (Berkeley: University of California Press, 1995); and Ransby, *Ella Baker and the Black Freedom Movement*.

My account of King's troubles with the FBI leans heavily on David J. Garrow, *The FBI and Martin Luther King, Jr.* (New York: Penguin Books, 1981); Kenneth O'Reilly, *Racial Matters: The FBI's Secret File on Black America, 1960–1972* (New York: Free Press, 1989); and Athan Theoharis, *Spying on Americans: Political Surveillance from Hoover to the Huston Plan* (Philadelphia: Temple University Press, 1978). Also see Michael Friendly and David Gallen, *MLK and the FBI File* (New York: Carroll & Graf, 1993). The head of the FBI is thoroughly scrutinized in Curt Gentry, *J. Edgar Hoover: The Man and the Secrets* (New York: Penguin Books, 1991); Richard Powers, *Secrecy and Power: The Life of J. Edgar Hoover* (New York: Free Press, 1987); Anthony Summers, *Official and Confidential: The Secret Life of J. Edgar Hoover* (New York: G. P. Putnam's Sons, 1993); and Athen G. Theoharis and John Stuart Cox, *The Boss: J. Edgar Hoover and the Great American Inquisition* (Philadelphia: Temple University Press, 1988). Also see William Keller, *The Liberals and J. Edgar Hoover: Rise and Fall of a Domestic Intelligence State* (Princeton, N.J.: Princeton University Press, 1989).

Chapter 6 and the Selma campaign must begin with Charles E. Fager, *Selma 1965: The March That Changed the South* (Boston: Beacon Press, 1974); David J. Garrow, *Protest at Selma: Martin Luther King, Jr., and the Voting Rights Act of 1965* (New Haven, Conn.: Yale University Press, 1978); and Thornton, *Dividing Lines*. Local memoirs include those by attorney J. L. Chestnut and Julia Cass, *Black in Selma: The Uncommon Life of J. L. Chestnut, Jr.* (New York: Farrar, Straus & Giroux, 1990); Amelia P. Boynton, *Bridge Across Jordan, The Story of the Civil Rights Struggle in Selma* (New York: Carlton Press, 1979); and schoolgirls Sheyann Webb and Rachel West Nelson, as told to Frank Sikora, *Selma, Lord Selma: Girlhood Memories of the Civil Rights Days* (Tuscaloosa: University of Alabama Press, 1980). Also see Renata Adler, "Letter from Selma," *The New Yorker* (April 10, 1965); Duncan Howlett, *No Greater Love: The James Reeb Story* (New York: Harper & Row, 1966); Stephen Longenecker, *Selma's Peacemaker: Ralph Smelzer and Civil Rights Mediation* (Philadelphia: Temple University Press, 1987); Gary May, *The Informant: The FBI, the Ku Klux Klan, and the Murder of Viola Liuzzo* (New Haven, Conn.: Yale University Press, 2005); and Mary Stanton, *From Selma to Sorrow: The Life and Death of Viola Liuzzo* (Athens: University of Georgia Press, 1998).

The overall quest for black voting rights is surveyed in Steven F. Lawson, *Black Ballots: Voting Rights in the South, 1944–1969* (New York: Columbia University Press, 1976). Its consequences are debated by Chandler Davidson and Bernard Grofman, eds., *Quiet Revolution in the South: The Impact of the Voting Rights Act, 1965–1990* (Princeton, N.J.: Princeton University Press, 1994); J. Morgan Kousser, *Colorblind Injustice: Minority Voting Rights and the Undoing of the Second Reconstruction* (Chapel Hill: University of North Carolina Press, 1999); and Steven F. Lawson, *In Pursuit of Power: Southern Blacks and Electoral Politics, 1965–1982* (New York: Columbia University Press, 1985). Also see Numan V. Bartley and Hugh D. Graham, *Southern Politics and the Second Reconstruction* (Baltimore: Johns Hopkins Press, 1975); James W. Button, *Blacks and Social Change: Impact of the Civil Rights Movement in Southern Communities* (Princeton, N.J.: Princeton University Press, 1989); and Pat Watters and Reese Cleghorn, *Climbing Jacob's Ladder: The Arrival of Negroes in Southern Politics* (New York: Harcourt, Brace and World, 1967).

On King and Malcolm X, see Lewis V. Baldwin, "A Reassessment of the Relationship Between Malcolm X and Martin Luther King Jr.," *Western Journal of Black Studies* 13 (Summer 1989), 103–13; Clayborne Carson, "A 'Common Solution': Martin and Malcolm's Gulf Was Closing, but the Debate Lives On," *Emerge* 9 (February 1998), 44–52; Kenneth B. Clark, *The Negro Protest: James Baldwin, Malcolm X and Martin Luther King Talk with Kenneth B. Clark* (Boston: Beacon Press, 1963); Cone, *Martin & Malcolm & America*; and Eugene Victor Wolfenstein, *The Victims of Democracy: Malcolm X and the Black Revolution* (Berkeley: University of California Press, 1981). Simon Wendt, *The Spirit and the Shotgun: Armed Resistance and the Struggle for Civil Rights* (Gainesville: University Press of Florida, 2007), is particularly perceptive.

My account of the Chicago campaign owes much to Alan B. Anderson and George W. Pickering, *Confronting the Color Line: The Broken Promise of the Civil Rights Movement in Chicago* (Athens: University of Georgia Press, 1986); Garrow, *Bearing the Cross*; David Halberstam, "The Second Coming of Martin Luther King," *Harper's* (August 1967), 39–51; Arnold R. Hirsch, "Massive Resistance in the Urban North: Trumbull Park, Chicago, 1953–1966," *Journal of American History* 88 (September 1995), 522–50; James J. Ralph, Jr., *Northern Protest: Martin Luther King, Jr., Chicago, and the Civil Rights Movement* (Cambridge, Mass.: Harvard University Press, 1993); and Kenneth L. Smith, "The Radicalization of Martin Luther King, Jr.: The Last Three Years," *Journal of Ecumenical Studies,* 26 (Spring 1986), 270–288. The collection of articles by David J. Garrow, ed., *Chicago 1966: Open Housing Marches, Summit Negotiations, and Operation Breadbasket* (Brooklyn, N.Y.: Carlson, 1989), is indispensable, as is the much broader collection by John Charles Boger and Judith Welch Wegner, eds., *Race, Poverty, and American Cities* (Chapel Hill: University of North Carolina Press, 1996).

For the issue of race and housing, see Brian J. L. Berry, *The Open Housing Question: Race and Housing in Chicago, 1966–1976* (Cambridge, U.K.: Ballinger, 1979); Lynn Eley and Thomas Casstevens, eds., *The Politics of Fair-Housing Legislation* (San Francisco: Chandler, 1968); Arnold R. Hirsch, *Making the Second Ghetto: Race and Housing in Chicago, 1940–1960* (New York: Cambridge University Press, 1983); Tamar Jacoby, *Someone Else's House: America's Unfinished Struggle for Integration* (New York: Free Press, 1998); Douglas S. Massey and Nancy A. Denton, *American Apartheid: Segregation and the Making of the Underclass* (Cambridge, Mass.: Harvard University Press, 1993); and Stephen Grant Meyer, *As Long as They Don't Move Next Door: Segregation and Racial Conflict in American Neighborhoods* (New York: Rowman & Littlefield, 2001). Background on educational inequality is in Michael W. Homel, *Down from Equality: Black Chicagoans and the Public Schools, 1920–1941* (Urbana: University of Illinois Press, 1984).

Starting points for understanding Black Power are Floyd B. Barbour, ed., *The Black Power Revolt* (Boston: P. Sargent, 1968); Stokely Carmichael and Charles V. Hamilton, *Black Power: The Politics of Liberation in America* (New York: Vintage, 1967); Stokely Carmichael with Ekwueme Michael Thelwell, *Ready for Revolution: The Life and Struggles of Stokely Carmichael (Kwame Ture)* (New York: Scribner, 2003); Julius Lester, *Look Out, Whitey! Black Power's Gon' Get Your Mama!* (New York: Grove Press, 1968); and Komozi Woodard, *A Nation Within a Nation: Amiri Baraka (LeRoi Jones) and Black Power Politics* (Chapel Hill: University of North Carolina Press, 1999). These should be supplemented with Rod Bush, *We Are Not What We Seem: Black Nationalism and Class Struggle in the American Century* (New York: New York University Press, 1999); Steve Estes, *I Am a Man!: Race, Manhood, and the Civil Rights Movement* (Chapel Hill: University of North Carolina Press, 2004); Timothy B. Tyson, *Radio Free Dixie: Robert F. Williams and the Roots of Black Power* (Chapel Hill: University of North Carolina Press, 1999); and William L. Van Deburg, *New Day in Babylon: The Black Power Movement and American Culture, 1965–1975* (Chicago: University of Chicago Press, 1992). King's thoughts on Black Power are spelled out in *Where Do We Go from Here?*

The effect of black radicalization on public attitudes is covered in William Brink and Louis Harris, *Black and White: A Study of U.S. Racial Attitudes Today* (New York: Simon & Schuster, 1967), and Howard Schuman, Charlotte Steeh, and Lawrence Bobo, *Racial Attitudes in America: Trends and Interpretations* (Cambridge, Mass.: Harvard University Press, 1985). Also see Hazel Erskine, "The Polls: Demonstrations and Race Riots," and "The Polls: Negro Housing," *Public Opinion Quarterly* 31 (Winter 1967–68), 663–75; (Fall 1967), 484–86. Other consequences are discussed by Herbert H. Haines, "Black Radicalization and the Funding of Civil Rights, 1957–1970," *Social Problems* 32 (October 1984), and *Black Radicals and the Civil Rights Mainstream, 1954–1970* (Knoxville: University of Tennessee Press, 1988). Also see Kevin L. Yuill, "The 1966 White House Conference on Civil Rights," *Historical Journal* 41 (March 1998).

The passions and significance of the urban racial riots can be grasped in Robert E. Conot, *Rivers of Blood, Years of Darkness* (New York: Bantam, 1967); Joe R. Feagin and Harlan Hahn, *Ghetto Revolts: The Politics of Violence in American Cities* (New York: Macmillan, 1973); Sidney Fine, *Violence in the Model City: The Cavanaugh Administration, Race Relations and the Detroit Riot of 1967* (Ann Arbor: University of Michigan Press, 1989); Tom Hayden, *Rebellion in Newark: Official Violence and the Ghetto Response* (New York: Vintage, 1967); and Gerald Horne, *Fire This Time: The Watts Uprising and the Meaning of the 1960s* (Charlottesville: University of Virginia Press, 1995). One must consult the Kerner Commission, *Report of the National Advisory Commission on Civil Disorders* (New York: Bantam Books, 1968). Also see Jack M. Bloom, *Class, Race, and the Civil Rights Movement* (Bloomington: Indiana University Press, 1987), and Raymond S. Franklin, *Shadows of Race and Class* (Minneapolis: University of Minnesota Press, 1991).

The literature on the "white backlash" is voluminous. Most helpful are Peter Applebome, *Dixie Rising: How the South Is Shaping American Values, Politics, and Culture* (New York: Harcourt Brace, 1996); Mary C. Brennan, *Turning Right in the Sixties: The Conservative Capture of the GOP* (Chapel Hill: University of North Carolina Press, 1995); Dan T. Carter, *From George Wallace to Newt Gingrich: Race in the Conservative Counterrevolution, 1963–1994* (Baton Rouge: Louisiana State University Press, 1996); Thomas Byrne Edsall with Mary Edsall, *Chain Reaction: The Impact of Race, Rights, and Taxes on American Politics* (New York: Norton, 1991); Jean Hardisty, *Mobilizing Resentment: Conservative Resurgence from the John Birch Society to the Promise Keepers* (Boston: Beacon Press, 1999); Gary Orfield, "Race and the Liberal Agenda: The Loss of the Integrationist Dream, 1965–1974," in Margaret Weir, et al., eds., *The Politics of Social Policy in the United States* (Princeton, N.J.: Princeton University Press, 1988); and Tom Wicker, *Tragic Failure: Racial Integration in America* (New York: William Morrow, 1996). The responses of whites to racial change in other cities, and the negative view of the more radical King, can be followed in Kenneth D. Durr, *Behind the Backlash: White Working-Class Politics in Baltimore, 1940–1980* (Chapel Hill: University of North Carolina Press, 2003); Ronald Formisano, *Boston Against Busing: Race, Class, and Ethnicity in the 1960s and 1970s* (Chapel Hill: University of North Carolina Press, 1991); Kevin Kruse, *White Flight: America and the Making of Modern Conservatism* (Princeton, N.J.: Princeton University Press, 2005); Matthew Lassiter, *The Silent Majority: Suburban Politics in the Sunbelt South* (Princeton, N.J.: Princeton University Press, 2005); J. Anthony Lukas, *Common Ground: A Turbulent Decade in the Lives of Three Boston Families* (New York: Knopf, 1985); Michael Novak, *The Rise of the Unmeltable Ethnics: Politics and*

Culture in the 1970s (New York: Transaction, 1972); Jonathan Rieder, *Canarsie: The Jews and Italians of Brooklyn Against Liberalism* (Cambridge, Mass.: Harvard University Press, 1985); Jim Sleeper, *The Closest of Strangers: Liberalism and the Politics of Race in New York* (New York: Viking, 1990); and Michael Wenk, S. M. Tomasi, and Geno Baroni, eds., *Pieces of a Dream: The Ethnic Worker's Crisis with America* (New York: Center for Migration Studies, 1972).

My interpretations in Chapter 8 of King's last year are indebted to Garrow, *Bearing the Cross*; Harding, *Martin Luther King: An Inconvenient Hero*; Manning Marable, "King's Last Years: 1966–1968—From Civil Rights to Social Transformation," in Howard Richards and Cassie Schwerner, eds., *Fulfill the Dream* (Richmond, Ind.: Earlham College, 1988), and "The Legacy of Martin Luther King, Jr.," in Manning Marable, *Crisis of Color and Democracy: Essays on Race, Class, and Power* (Monroe, Minn.: Common Courage Press, 1992); Smith, "Radicalization of Martin Luther King, Jr."; and Young, *An Easy Burden*. Also see James A. Colaiaco, "Martin Luther King, Jr., and the Paradox of Nonviolent Direct Action," *Phylon* 47 (1986), 16–28, and Garth Baker-Fletcher, *Somebodyness: Martin Luther King, Jr., and the Theory of Dignity* (Minneapolis: Fortress Press, 1993).

On King and Vietnam, see Adam Fairclough, "Martin Luther King, Jr., and the War in Vietnam," *Phylon* 45 (Spring 1984), 19–39. My account of King's antiwar activities is based on Henry Darby and Margaret Rowley, "King on Vietnam and Beyond," *Phylon* 47 (March 1986), 43–50; Simon Hall, *Peace and Freedom: The Civil Rights and Antiwar Movements in the 1960s* (Philadelphia: University of Pennsylvania Press, 2005); Benjamin Harrison, "Impact of the Vietnam War on the Civil Rights Movement in the Midsixties," *Studies in Conflict and Terrorism* 19 (1996); and Herbert Shapiro, "The Vietnam War and the American Civil Rights Movement," *Journal of Ethnic Studies* 16 (1989). See Bayard Rustin, "Dr. King's Painful Dilemma," *New York Amsterdam News*, March 3, 1967. Also useful are Rhodri Jeffreys-Jones, *Peace Now!: American Society and the Ending of the Vietnam War* (New Haven, Conn.: Yale University Press, 1999); Robert Mullen, *Blacks and Vietnam* (Washington, D.C.: University Press of America, 1981); Clyde Taylor, ed., *Vietnam and Black America: An Anthology of Protest and Resistance* (Garden City, N.Y.: Anchor/Doubleday, 1973); James E. Westheider, *Fighting on Two Fronts: African Americans and the Vietnam War* (New York: New York University Press, 1997); and Nancy Zaroulis and Gerald Sullivan, *Who Spoke Up?: American Protest Against the War in Vietnam, 1963–1975* (Garden City, N.Y.: Doubleday, 1984). For conflicting views on the impact and consequences of the antiwar movement, see Adam Garfinkel, *Telltale Hearts: The Origins and Impact of the Vietnam Antiwar Movement* (New York: St. Martin's Press, 1995), and Melvin Small, *Antiwarriors: The Vietnam War and the Battle for America's Hearts and Minds* (Wilmington, Del.: SR Books, 2002). King's views on foreign policy and war were not confined to Vietnam. See Lewis V. Baldwin, *Toward the Beloved Community: Martin Luther King, Jr., and South Africa* (Cleveland: Pilgrim Press, 1995); James H. Cone, "Martin Luther King, Jr., and the Third World," *Journal of American History* 74 (September 1987), 455–67; and Thomas Noer, "Martin Luther King, Jr., and the Cold War," *Peace & Change* 22 (April 1997), 111–31.

King's economic views are the subject of Marian Wright Edelman, *Lanterns: A Memoir of Mentors* (Boston: Beacon Press, 1999); Charles Fager, *Uncertain Resurrection: The Poor People's Washington Campaign* (Grand Rapids, Mich.: Eerdmans, 1969); Garrow, *Bearing the Cross*; the state-of-the-scholarship Thomas F. Jackson, *From Civil Rights to Human Rights: Martin Luther King, Jr., and the Struggle for Economic Justice* (Philadelphia: University of Pennsylvania Press, 2007); and Douglas Sturm, "Martin Luther King, Jr., as Democratic Socialist," *Journal of Religious Ethics* 18 (Fall 1990), 79–105. On the Poor People's Campaign, see Gerald McKnight, *The Last Crusade: Martin Luther King, Jr., the FBI, and the Poor People's Campaign* (Boulder, Colo.: Westview, 1998). The FBI's vendetta against King is further elaborated on in Nelson Blackstock, *COINTELPRO: The FBI's Secret War on Political Freedom* (New York: Vintage, 1975); Michael Friedly and David Gallen, *Martin Luther King, Jr.: The FBI File* (New York: Carroll & Graf, 1993); and Ward Churchill and Jim Vander Wall, *The COINTELPRO Papers: Documents from the FBI's War Against Dissent in the United States* (Boston: South End Press, 1990).

Michael K. Honey, *Going Down Jericho Road: The Memphis Strike, Martin Luther King's Last Campaign* (New York: Norton, 2007), is unparalleled in its depth of research and accuracy of analysis. Also see Joan Turner Beifuss, *At the River I Stand* (Memphis: B&W Press, 1985); Steve Estes, " 'I Am A Man!': Race, Masculinity, and the 1968 Memphis Sanitation Strike," *Labor History* 41 (Spring 2000), 153–70; Laurie Beth Green, "Race, Gender, and Labor in 1960s Memphis: 'I Am a Man' and the Meaning of Freedom," *Journal of Urban History* 30 (March 2004), 465–89; and David M. Tucker, "Rev. James M. Lawson, Jr., and the Garbage Strike," in *Black Pastors and Leaders: Memphis 1819–1972* (Memphis: Memphis State University Press, 1975).

James Earl Ray's attorney, William F. Pepper, *Orders to Kill: The Truth Behind the Murder of Martin Luther King, Jr.* (New York: Carroll & Graf, 1996), and *An Act of State: The Execution of Martin Luther King, Jr.* (London: Verso, 2003), makes the case for a conspiracy theory. He is refuted by Gerald Posner, *Killing the Dream: James Earl Ray and the Assassination of Martin Luther King, Jr.* (New York: Random House, 1998). On a conspiracy, see also William B. Huie, *He Slew the Dreamer: My Search, with James Earl Ray, for the Truth About the Murder of Martin Luther King, Jr.* (Montgomery, Ala.: Black Belt Press, 1997); Gerold Frank, *An American Death: The True Story of the Assassination of Martin Luther King, Jr., and the Greatest Manhunt in Our Time* (New York: Doubleday, 1972); and Mark Lane and Dick Gregory, *Murder in Memphis: The FBI and the Assassination of Martin Luther King* (New York: Thunder's Mouth Press, 1993). See also Lewis Baldwin, *The Legacy of Martin Luther King, Jr.: The Boundaries of Law, Politics, and Religion* (Notre Dame, Ind.: University of Notre Dame, 2002), and Jules Witcover, *The Year the Dream Died: Revisiting 1968 in America* (New York: Warner Books, 1997).

ACKNOWLEDGMENTS

I often think I was destined to write *King: Pilgrimage to the Mountain-top*. Certainly no other person has had a greater impact on my life, and there is none I admire more than King. I still remember the exhilaration I experienced as a youngster in New York City reading accounts of the Montgomery Bus Boycott in faraway Alabama. Yet more vividly, I recall meeting King and his shaking my hand at a civil rights demonstration in Virginia in 1962. Most of all, I'll never forget standing in the rain on an Atlanta street as his casket went by. I knew this was a book I wanted to write. It would take four decades of learning and teaching about King to do so. Many would help along the way.

Like all historians I am deeply indebted to all those who have preceded me in this endeavor. This book could not have been written without the previously mentioned multivolume *Martin Luther King, Jr., Papers*, skillfully edited by Clayborne Carson and his associates, and without the many fine biographies of King and monographs on particular aspects of his career that others have written. I hope my bibliography conveys at least a sense of my deep appreciation to these journalists and scholars. I am likewise indebted to the many individuals in the movement and in the historical profession, far too many to mention, who have helped me to understand King during the past four decades; to those who have made me a better historian by commenting on my previous articles and books; to those who have sharpened my perceptions on history in innumerable panels for the American Historical Association, the American Studies Association, the Association for the Study of Negro Life and History, the Organization of American Historians, and the Southern Historical Association; and to all my students, undergraduate and graduate, who have shared their insights and understandings with me. However, inadequately, I thank all the above. In addition, I owe thanks to June Kim of Hill and Wang for her cheerful assistance, and especially to my editor and publisher, Thomas LeBien, for his skill in helping me clarify the "arc" of King's life, for making sure I wrote what was in my heart, and for being there for me from start to finish.

A special debt is owed to two wonderful historians and friends who have read every word of *King: Pilgrimage to the Mountaintop*, and immeasurably improved it. Bill Chafe, best friend, collaborator, and chief critic, has, as always, been my sounding board and has taught me so much in the process of our many long conversations. And Bill Leuchtenburg, who from my very first attempt as a graduate student to write civil rights history has been my mentor, model, and inspiration, and who has made this book, like my previous ones, far better than it could possibly have been without him. Any errors or shortcomings are, of course, my own.

Last, but certainly not least, my heartfelt thanks to my wife, my partner, my love, Gloria, to whom I dedicate this book.

INDEX

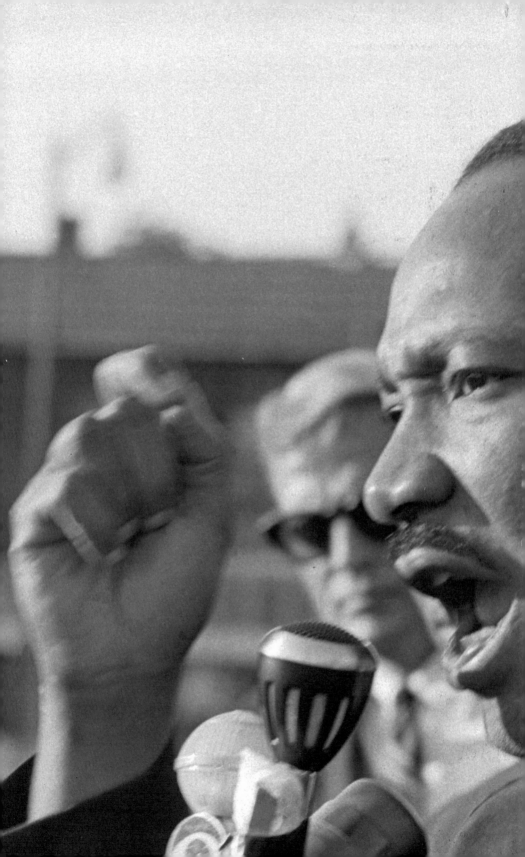